Genders and Sexualities in History

Series Editors: John Arnold, Joanna Bou

CU00494089

Palgrave Macmillan's series, Genders a
modate and foster new approaches to l
and sexualities. The series will promote world-class scholarship that concentrates
upon the interconnected themes of genders, sexualities, religions/religiosity, civil
society, class formations, politics and war.

Historical studies of gender and sexuality have often been treated as discon-
nected fields, while in recent years historical analyses in these two areas have
synthesised, creating new departures in historiography. By linking genders and
sexualities with questions of religion, civil society, politics and the contexts of
war and conflict, this series will reflect recent developments in scholarship, moving away from the previously dominant and narrow histories of science, scientific
thought, and legal processes.

The result brings together scholarship from contemporary, modern, early modern, medieval, classical and non-Western history to provide a diachronic forum
for scholarship that incorporates new approaches to genders and sexualities in
history.

Men of War: Masculinity and the First World War in Britain is an investigation of
the subtleties of gender and identity and their transformations in the challenge
of total war. The book examines how British servicemen used the mythology of
the First World War and their experience of military service to define themselves
as men. *Men of War* scrutinises men's sense of masculine identity in the period
both in relation to other men at the battlefront and also in relation to men and
women at home. Meyer's analysis of masculinities in the First World War is a
fascinating critical exploration of men and self-fashioning in the context of martial homosociality and prevailing concepts of the heroic. The book interrogates
the tensions between masculinity in war and men's evolving domestic identity.
In a thoroughly integrated study, which brings to its field a wealth of original
material, public and personal, Meyer explains how the First World War changed
men profoundly, both in their relations with spouses and children and also with
regard to their broader sense of citizenship and the self. In common with all volumes in the 'Genders and Sexualities in History' series, Jessica Meyer's *Men of
War* presents a multifaceted and meticulously researched scholarly study, and is
a sophisticated contribution to our understanding of the past.

Titles include:

Matthew Cook
QUEER DOMESTICITIES
Homosexuality and Home Life in Twentieth-Century London

Jennifer Evans
RECONSTRUCTION SITES
Spaces of Sexual Encounter in Cold War Berlin

Dagmar Herzog (*editor*)
BRUTALITY AND DESIRE
War and Sexuality in Europe's Twentieth Century

Jessica Meyer
MEN OF WAR
Masculinity and the First World War in Britain

Jennifer D. Thibodeaux (*editor*)
NEGOTIATING CLERICAL IDENTITIES
Priests, Monks and Masculinity in the Middle Ages

Genders and Sexualities in History Series
Series Standing Order 978–0–230–55185–5 Hardback
979–0–230–55186–2 Paperback
(*outside North America only*)

You can receive future titles in this series as they are published by placing a standing order. Please contact your bookseller or, in case of difficulty, write to us at the address below with your name and address, the title of the series and the ISBN quoted above.

Customer Services Department, Macmillan Distribution Ltd, Houndmills, Basingstoke, Hampshire RG21 6XS, England

Men of War

Masculinity and the First World War in Britain

Jessica Meyer
Independent scholar

© Jessica Meyer 2009

Softcover reprint of the hardcover 1st edition 2009 978-0-230-22201-4

All rights reserved. No reproduction, copy or transmission of this
publication may be made without written permission.

No portion of this publication may be reproduced, copied or transmitted
save with written permission or in accordance with the provisions of the
Copyright, Designs and Patents Act 1988, or under the terms of any licence
permitting limited copying issued by the Copyright Licensing Agency,
Saffron House, 6-10 Kirby Street, London EC1N 8TS.

Any person who does any unauthorized act in relation to this publication
may be liable to criminal prosecution and civil claims for damages.

The author has asserted her right to be identified
as the author of this work in accordance with the Copyright,
Designs and Patents Act 1988.

First published 2009 by
PALGRAVE MACMILLAN

Palgrave Macmillan in the UK is an imprint of Macmillan Publishers Limited,
registered in England, company number 785998, of Houndmills, Basingstoke,
Hampshire RG21 6XS.

Palgrave Macmillan in the US is a division of St Martin's Press LLC,
175 Fifth Avenue, New York, NY 10010.

Palgrave Macmillan is the global academic imprint of the above companies
and has companies and representatives throughout the world.

Palgrave® and Macmillan® are registered trademarks in the United States,
the United Kingdom, Europe and other countries.

ISBN 978-0-230-30232-7   ISBN 978-0-230-30542-7 (eBook)
DOI 10.1007/978-0-230-30542-7

A catalogue record for this book is available from the British Library.

Library of Congress Cataloging-in-Publication Data
Meyer, Jessica.
    Men of war : masculinity and the First World War in Britain / Jessica Meyer.
        p.   cm. — (Genders and sexualities in history)
    Revision of the author's thesis (Ph. D.)—Cambridge University, 2005.
    Includes bibliographical references and index.
    1. World War, 1914–1918—Social aspects—Great Britain.   2. World War,
    1914–1918—Psychological aspects.   3. Masculinity—Great Britain—
    History—20th century.   4. Men—Identity.   I. Title.
    D524.7.G7M49 2009
    940.3′1—dc22   2008030087

For Matthew,
with all my love

Contents

List of Figures

List of Abbreviations

ASC	Army Service Corps
DCMS	Deputy Commissioner Medical Services
HMSO	His Majesty's Stationary Office
IWM	Imperial War Museum
NA	The National Archives
NCO	Non-commissioned Officer
RAMC	Royal Army Medical Corps

Acknowledgements

This book began as a PhD thesis which was supervised in turn by Dr Max Jones and Dr Deborah Thom. Their insight and advice has been invaluable throughout. I am also extremely grateful to Professor Jay Winter, who not only helped me to formulate the initial question but, as an examiner of my dissertation, helped me to turn it from a thesis into a book.

At various points the Cambridge Overseas Trust, the University of Cambridge Faculty of History and Pembroke College, Cambridge have all provided me with funds which assisted me in undertaking research and for which I am very grateful. I would also like to thank Rosie and Eric Brown for their hospitality, including a room with a view over the best garden in London, while I was carrying out research at the Imperial War Museum.

Without the help of the staff of the National Archives, Kew and the Department of Documents at the Imperial War Museum, London the majority of research for this book would not have been possible. I am particularly grateful to Clare Sexton at the IWM for all her assistance in handling issues of copyright clearance. I would like to thank Greg Ashe, Lionel Baker, Mrs Ruth J. Bannan, Frank Calcraft, Michael Foot, John Fordham, Mr R. Forward, Mrs Lyn Frangleton, Doug Goodman, Hilary Hamilton, Susan Johnson, Mrs N. Kent, Hilary Layton, Mrs Rachel Littlewood, Diana Macgregor, Pamela Miller, John Munden, Stewart Murray, J. Nicholson, A. Jane Pearce, Ann and Daniel Potts, Mrs C. Robertson, Gloria Siggins, Mr H. Sturdy, Harry Wilkinson, Miss Daphne Harman Young and the copyright holders of the papers of A. M. McGrigor and H. J. Hayward for their kindness in allowing me to quote so often and so extensively from the collections for which they hold the copyright, Tony Stiff for his permission to use excerpts from *The Mudhook Machine Gunner*, and Greta Plowman for permission to use excerpts from *A Subaltern on the Somme*. Every effort has been made to trace copyright holders of all materials quoted and the author, the publisher and the Imperial War Museum would be grateful for any information which might help to trace those whose identities or addresses are not currently known.

I am extremely grateful to Anthony Fletcher and his mother, Delle, for allowing me to read and quote from the papers of Reggie

Chenevix Trench and to use Reggie's photograph to illustrate Chapter 3. In addition, I would like to thank Anthony for his kindness, wisdom and the many interesting discussions in Oxford and elsewhere that helped shape my ideas, particularly as regards Chapter 3. Many other colleagues have also offered insight, raised points of interest and asked awkward questions during the writing of this book. The Gender and History reading group at the University of Cambridge, the Gender and History Workshop at the University of Oxford and the International Society for First World War Studies have given me opportunities to present aspects of the work in progress and offered insightful feedback. Mike Roper, Ana Carden-Coyne and Wendy Gagen have all provided advice and encouragement at various points. Heather Ellis, Stella Moss, Dan Todman, Stacy Gillis, Jenny Macleod and Pierre Purseigle have, in addition to giving me much sound advice, been the staunchest of friends throughout, while Frank Piotrkowski has done more than anyone to help me keep faith with myself.

My deepest debt of gratitude is to my family who have supported me unstintingly and who have never ceased to believe in me. Above all, I thank my husband, Matthew Daws, without whose support and computer skills this book would never have been completed. His love and patience have seen me through so many crises, both large and small, that it is only right that it should be dedicated to him, with all my love.

Introduction

> But the dead men had their revenge after all. As the war fell
> back into the past, my particular generation, those who had
> been 'just too young', became conscious of the vastness of the
> experience they had missed. You felt yourself a little less than a
> man, because you had missed it.[1]

Written in the early years of a new world war, Orwell's essay on wartime
patriotism evokes the image of an earlier conflict specifically in terms of
gender. For Orwell, and other writers of his generation, the First World
War was an important point of reference for the construction of their
identity as men who had not fought. For them, the First World War
was an arena in which the masculinity of those who had participated
in it was defined, an experience that set them apart as a generation.[2]
War experience was something that five million British men had gained
which Orwell and his contemporaries, because of their age, had not,
and which separated those who had it from the rest of British society
because of what they had seen, heard, smelt, tasted and, above all, felt
in the course of four years of warfare.

The identities that men gained through war experience were implic-
itly gendered. War was, and to a great extent remains, a sphere of
masculine attainment and suffering. Stefan Dudink, Karen Hagemann
and John Tosh have identified war as one of the 'seemingly "natural"
homelands of masculinity',[3] while Samuel Hynes has argued that the
soldiers' tale of war is that of the *men* who were there. Even in the era of
total war, when the recruitment of women, along with rest of the state
and society, became imperative to a successful war effort, the narrative
of warfare continued to be dominated by those who fought as soldiers,
a group that was, and still is, predominantly male. War experience, as

1

a unique aspect of a man's life, remains a potentially defining incident in the formation of male identity.[4] It has the power not only to isolate those who participate from 'other men – cut[ting] off men who fought from older and younger men who did not share that shaping experience, and intensif[ying] the feeling every modern generation has anyway, that it is separate, a kind of secret society in a world of others',[5] but also to reinforce their gender difference as individuals whose sex had, in part, dictated that they must fight.[6]

This book explores the question of how British servicemen who fought in the First World War used their experience to define them-selves as men, both in relation to other men and to women. It looks in particular at the written narratives within which they constructed mas-culine identities including letters written home from the fighting front, wartime diaries, letters of condolence to the families of the fallen, letters from disabled ex-servicemen to the Ministry of Pensions and memoirs written in the years after the war. Two identities emerge most clearly from these documents as ideals to be emulated and striven towards. The first is the heroic, associated primarily with the battlefront and the homosocial society of the military sphere, and only secondarily with the home front that men sought to defend. The second, equally important, identity that men sought to establish was the domestic, located much more clearly in relation to women with its emphasis on men's roles as good sons, husbands and fathers, as both protector and provider. These identities were central to social definitions of appropriate masculinity during the war years, even as the demands they placed on men created tensions in how individual identity was constructed.[7] By exploring the ways in which men used the written word to negotiate these individual identities, this book demonstrates how the war affected social and cul-tural understandings of what it was to be a man in the era of the First World War.

*   *   *

In the literature of the First World War, the authority of the man who was there has often been asserted at the expense of alternative per-spectives of age and gender.[8] Indeed, some soldier writers constructed their sense of difference through portrayals of those who were *not* there, particularly women, as 'fictive inhabitants of world that had effec-tively insulated itself from the trenches' city of dreadful night'.[9] The social construction of those who fought as a separate gender group did not, however, emerge solely from the narratives of combatants such as Siegfried Sassoon and Richard Aldington.[10] Even before hostilities had broken out, the First World War was constructed by British social and cultural discourses as both gendered and gendering through the role it would play in 'making men'. For many social commentators of the Edwardian era, the often-predicted great European conflict would help to cure British society of the physical degeneracy of the working classes, exposed in Britain by the defeats suffered during the Boer War, and the moral degeneracy of the middle classes, evident in the continuing influence of Decadence as an artistic aesthetic.[11] War, it was argued, would turn these physical weaklings and moral degenerates into 'men' by exposing them to masculinizing experiences or eliminating them through violence. The men who survived, far from being isolated from the society that had sent them into battle, would instead reinvigorate it with their newly acquired physical health and moral strength. These narratives dominated the early years of the war when gendered propaganda was used to encourage men to enlist, evoking the associations made between participation in warfare and physically and morally virtuous masculinity.[12]

As the war progressed, however, the exigencies of total warfare meant that women increasingly adopted roles that challenged social and political assumptions about the gendered nature of citizenship and relations between the genders.[13] At the same time, the physical and psychological damage wrought on men by trench warfare was demonstrating that war could destroy as well as make men. Both these developments threw the question of the war as a sphere of masculine development and attainment open to debate. As Joan Scott has noted, war has the power both to make 'women visible as historical actors' and 'destabilise the stereotypes of masculinity.'[14] It 'is the ultimate disorder, the disruption of all previously established relationships'.[15]

Considerable attention has been paid to how women's place and status in British society as citizens, workers, wives and mothers was affected by the First World War. Such studies have firmly placed women in the history of the war as gendered actors. The pressures that total warfare placed on society provided opportunities for women, particularly in terms of employment, that gave them greater freedom and, in turn, the ability to press for consideration as full citizens by the state based on their war service.[16] At the same time, as the wives and mothers of soldiers, both actual and potential, women came under increased scrutiny from the state, even as war placed greater burdens on them as household providers.[17] Such competing pressures had huge implications for the definition of femininity in British wartime society, changing the lives of women in a variety of ways.[18]

These discussions of the changing roles of women have raised questions as to how and to what extent the war destabilize stereotypical masculinities. Sandra Gilbert, for instance, has argued that while women's power as workers and writers increased during the war, men 'had been transformed into dead-alive beings whose fates could no longer be determined according to the rules that had governed Western history from time immemorial'.[19] Any gains that women made were, however, only temporary, with 'many women return[ing] into embittered unemployment or guilt-stricken domesticity after World War I.'[20] Men, despite their emasculating experiences of the trenches were thus able to regain social dominance in the war's aftermath. Similar arguments have been made about the political status of women after the war.[21]

While this reading of gender relations during the First World War has been criticized for ignoring the extent to which women understood their own experiences of war as dehumanizing,[22] the understanding of war as simply an emasculating force for all who fought in it has, until recently, rarely been challenged. Eric Leed's 1979 study of combat and identity in wartime, which argues that men's experience of warfare was dehumanizing because it took place within the context of the uncanny and alien world of no man's land, has been particularly influential. Men's wartime identities were, according to Leed, 'formed beyond the margins of normal social experience.' This, he argues 'was precisely what made them so lasting, so immune to erosion by the routines of postwar social and economic life, and so difficult to grasp with the traditional tools of sociological and psychological analysis.'[23] Experiences of war created identities that were discontinuous with those constructed in peace time, permanently alienating men from the society that they were supposed to be defending. This was particularly true for men disabled by the war. Often associated with disabled children, the war disabled were, according to several studies, alienated from both their mature masculine identities and the society they had sacrificed their lives to defend.[24]

Yet a number of more recent studies of both wartime morale and the war disabled have pointed to the fact that British soldiers in the First World War were civilian volunteers and conscripts. Many retained strong ties with their civilian and domestic identities throughout the war through home leave, articles in local papers and letters to their families.[25] Such contacts allowed men to construct their wartime identities within a socially familiar context, limiting the isolation that they felt as soldiers. It also made reintegration into civil society somewhat easier for the war disabled. According to Deborah Cohen, the charity that many disabled found themselves reliant on 'had a symbolic value. Each benevolent institution testified to a promise redeemed; each served to reconcile the disabled with their fellow citizens.'[26] At the same time, the cheerful stoicism expected of the disabled became 'a sign that they had the strength to overcome their injuries. Despite their pain, they had not lost control of their demeanor.... the British disabled measured their manhood by fortitude in the face of adversity. The most manly veteran was the one who suffered without complaint.'[27]

Even with continuing contact with home, however, men's identities in wartime could still be constructed in terms of absence or alienation from the familiar.[28] The male victim, whether of the violence of warfare or of the dominant social expectation that the appropriate role for men in time of war was that of soldier, was undoubtedly one of the most culturally powerful identities to emerge from the war. The large number of psychological casualties, whose responses to warfare were not necessarily accepted as legitimate reactions, leading to brutal treatment by the military authorities, have become symbolic of all men who fought in the war.[29] Nicoletta Gullace has noted the social power of the narrative of victimhood: 'As women used the uniform to identify the soldierly spirit and manly will inherent in every British Tommy, soldiers, military rejects, and conscientious objectors all began instead to assert personal suffering as the locus of true manhood.'[30]

*   *   *

Samuel Hynes has argued that 'Once the soldier was seen as a victim, the idea of the hero became unimaginable.'[31] Yet the idea of the soldier hero was not destroyed by the war. In the 19th century, the figure of the imperial soldier hero, alongside that of the imperial adventurer, was one of the most potent and widespread images of idealised masculinity in cultural circulation. In history, fiction, children's literature, on the lecture circuit and in newspapers, the soldier was celebrated as the epitome of both the imperial ideal and appropriate masculinity.[32] The continuing potency of this ideal in the early years of the First World War can be seen in the use of the image of the soldier hero in recruiting posters, particularly in the famous image of Kitchener, already heroic through his military exploits in Khartoum.[33] This image was to remain iconic long after the war was over, not simply as an ironic symbol of military bluster, but as an icon of the purpose with which individuals in Britain had gone to war. This sense of heroic purpose found expression in the writings of authors such as Ian Hay, Percy Westerman and 'Sapper', who continued to portray warfare in much the same way as Victorian writers such as G.A. Henty had done, as an arena in which boys could, through their independent actions, achieve the status of men.[34] Writing for more adult audiences, popular middlebrow novelists such as Warwick Deeping, Gilbert Frankau and Ernest Raymond depicted their fictional ex-servicemen as transformed by war experience into individuals with the moral power to uphold the social order they had defended while in uniform.[35] The figure of soldier hero, defined by qualities of endurance, adaptability, courage and duty, was ultimately able to maintain its status in British culture as 'one of the most durable and powerful forms of idealized masculinity in the Western cultural tradition',[36] alongside that of the more avant-garde figure of the soldier victim.

The soldier hero was not, however, the sole form of idealized masculinity to influence British culture in the years preceding the First World War or be affected by the experiences of total warfare. Despite the influence of the public schools and institutions such as the Boy Scouts in defining war and adventure as the ultimate spheres of masculine attainment, ideals of a more domestic form of masculinity also existed in British culture at this time. These ideals were, in many ways, less elite than those of the soldier hero, which dominated middle-class institutions.[37] As John Tosh notes, 'In most societies that we know of, setting up a new household is the essential qualification for manhood. The man who speaks for familial dependants and who can transmit his name and his assets to future generations is fully masculine.'[38] This understanding of appropriate male identity was influential in the 19th century among the working and lower-middle classes,[39] as well as the professional middle classes for whom 'The home was central to masculinity, as the place both where the boy was disciplined by dependence, and where the man attained full adult status as householder.'[40] Although by the turn of the 20th century domesticity was losing its appeal among the middle classes in favour of masculinities defined by adventure,[41] the power of the domestic role of men as providers and protectors remained strong, as was made apparent by use of domestic imagery in recruiting posters.[42] The figure of the domestic male as independent householder, able to support dependants through his own work, maintained its position throughout the war, finding expression in the postwar years in an increase in masculine domesticity.[43]

*   *   *

How then, did the war alter perceptions and expectations of appropriate masculinities in Britain? If experience of war could not destroy the image of the soldier hero as a masculine ideal, how could the experiences of the trenches be understood as heroic? If such experiences were alienating, defined primarily through separation and absence from the familiarity of family life, how did domesticity retain, and indeed increase, its importance to the definition of the socially acceptable male? How did these two understandings of appropriate masculinities interact with each other to shape the identities of men who, as civilian volunteers and conscripts, took on the role of soldier having already established, or been in the process of establishing, their mature domestic identities as independent men? It is by exploring these questions in greater depth that we can begin to understand how the war's impact on the gender identities of the men who served shaped understandings and memories of the war as a whole.

To begin to address these questions of identity, we must look first to the ordinary soldier's war, made up as it was of 'small details and large emotions.'[44] It is, as Dan Todman notes, difficult to study how people thought in the past, but historians can examine how they wrote about war and, through personal narratives, begin to approach soldiers' subjective interpretations of what they experienced.[45] Such personal narratives have increasingly taken centre stage in the remembering and recounting of the war in both academic and popular histories.[46] These narratives have formed the source material of a number of histories of the war which examine the war 'from the bottom up',[47] thereby illuminating a variety of previously unexamined perspectives on the experience of war.

Gender history is one perspective that has been particularly well served by this approach. How women wrote about their experiences of war has been the subject of a number of studies, many of them arguing that the war was pivotal in the development of feminine literary voices. This goes beyond Sandra Gilbert's assertion of the increased social power of female author during the war years. As Sharon Ouditt has shown, women's narratives of the war are multifarious, narrating a variety of experiences that can be aligned with a variety of political and social positions.[48] Where Ouditt has examined a huge variety of narratives, from personal memoirs through women's magazines to political essays, Jane Potter and Alison Light have demonstrated how fiction written by and for women during the war could serve to reassert conservative values as much as they provided spaces for women to demonstrate social power.[49]

Potter also examines the ways in which women's wartime and post-war memoirs were used to justify the war and the patriotism it inspired, as well as express disillusionment. Such personal narratives, be they memoirs, letters or diaries, have been vital to the project of locating women's experiences in the history of the war. As Angela Smith points out:

> The First World War gave many women the opportunity to travel and work in a way that no one could have imagined in the first years of the twentieth century. Many of them wrote about their unusual experiences, providing vital evidence to aid the writing of women's histories... The result is an exploration of a personal consciousness at a time of crisis, which can lead to a fuller picture of the development of women's literature in the long term – not just one narrative, but many.[50]

It also has the potential to uncover shifts in public culture at a moment of crisis. As Carol Acton has argued in relation to grief, 'While... individuals are governed by or subject to the larger discourses that surround them and press upon them, at the same time, in engaging with these discourses, individuals necessarily participate in the the the construction of that wartime government to which they are subject.'[51] Thus women's personal narratives of grieving open up to investigation the ways in which the state attempted to manage wartime bereavement, even as it was forced to respond to individual's private attempts to come to terms with their loss.

Smith argues that women's writing about the war is unique because:

> they are not combatant, but they are not non-combatant either; they have the best and the worst of both worlds; allied with soldiers rather than civilians, yet subordinate to them in the eyes of society, and in their own consciousness. This perspective creates for them a subject position that provides a unique basis for written records; perhaps a kind of bridge between the opposing worlds of the home and the battle front.[52]

Yet it is not only women's writing that explores and exposes the relationship between men and women, battle front and home front, the individual and the state. As Margaret Millman has noted, 'men's stories afforded insights into the way war confirmed, challenged or disrupted a form of hegemonic masculinity represented by the figure of the soldier.'[53] This figure, itself constructed through narratives of soldiers' lives, both real and fictional, created by journalists and novelists as much as by soldiers themselves,[54] provided the public with an image of what a soldier hero should be. With the dramatic rise in civilian enlistment and eventual conscription into the British armed forces, an increasing number of literate men were in a position to construct their own narratives of warfare. Through letters, diaries, poems, trench journals, cartoons, memoirs and oral histories, men who fought in the First World War recalled, recounted and reconstructed their experiences of war. While many of these narratives use the cultural ideal of the soldier hero as a framework within which to narrate their own experience, ironically or otherwise, the majority are, first and foremost, accounts of subjective experiences through their status as personal, self-reflexive texts.[55]

Although few comment directly on masculinity as a specific aspect of identity, because combat was so firmly gendered as a male activity soldier's narratives of warfare inevitably reflect on how they understood themselves to be men, both physically and emotionally.[56] Joanna Bourke has shown how changing understandings of gendered subjectivities were expressed through discussions of the body. From mutilation through comradeship to the memorialization and memory of the dead, men, she argues, physically embodied their experience of war which was, in turn, reflected in the way they wrote about it.[57] Such physicality is, of course, central to the experience of war and to its narratives. As Santanu Das has shown, 'The writings of the First World War are obsessed with tactile experiences', with touch becoming more important than sight to writers attempting to convey their perceptions of this unprecedented experience.[58] Bodily functions were also central to the ways in which they constructed their war experience. Food, and its consumption,[59] cleanliness, exhaustion and physical endurance were all subjects of fascination in men's narratives, written about endlessly and in detail.

Yet while the physical was central to men's experience of war, and for the disabled their experience of the world after war,[60] war narratives could also transcend the body. In trying not only to describe but also explain their experiences, whether to their families, their descendants, the state, or even themselves, men sought to link the physical realities of day-to-day life with the abstractions that had been central to pre-war definitions of masculinity. Concepts of courage, chivalry, honour, protection of the home and provision for dependants were negotiated by men, often through descriptions of the physical, but also through the use of cultural references and discussions of abstract emotions and ideas. It is in these negotiations that men's subjective masculinities can be found and where we can begin to uncover how war changed understandings of masculinity for the men who fought in it as well as for wider British society.

There are, however, difficulties with the use of personal narratives in the study of war. One of these is the question of representativeness. Samuel Hynes titled his book on the subject of men's narratives of war *The Soldiers' Tale*, arguing that 'if all the personal recollections of all the soldiers of the world's wars were gathered together, they would tell a huge story of men at war – changing, as armies and weapons and battlefields changed, but still a whole coherent story.'[61] Yet, despite a tendency on the part of historians to treat battlefront narratives as conveying a message of universal wartime masculinity, not all men experienced the same war in the same way.[62] Five million men served in the British armed forces during four years of the war. They came from different backgrounds, had different levels of education, served in different theatres for different lengths of time and in different roles. Some were wounded, others were not; many were killed, most were not. Class has commonly been seen as a key divider of men who fought. Janet Watson, for example, has argued that the attitudes of middle-class men to war experience were defined by an ethos of service, while those of working-class men were shaped by a view of warfare as a form of work.[63] Regional backgrounds were also powerful forces in shaping men's experiences of war, as demonstrated by Helen McCartney and Keith Grieves.[64] Many of these differences in experience are reflected in the forms of narrative examined in this book, exposed in the variety of attitudes men expressed towards both warfare and what it meant to be a man at war.

As Dennis Winter has noted, however:

When all allowance is made for the diversity of men and the changing nature of their war, there remains a strong impression that there was much more during the Great War to unite men than to divide them. When old soldiers of the war meet, they talk with unexpected warmth of their common experience so long ago.[65]

Danger, discomfort, grief, excitement, even pleasure were all experiences of warfare that had the power to transcend differences of class, region and role. War brought men of disparate backgrounds together, creating shared experiences and sites of memory[66] that, in their turn, shaped men's identities in warfare. We do, however, need to be cautious in our analysis of soldiers' recollections. As Dan Todman notes, 'We cannot assume that because a man was there at the time he is giving us a version of the war which is reliable, accurate or useful.'[67] Such narratives may be shaped by variables including the time, context and form in which it is being told. Within this diversity, however, can be seen common threads of cultural understanding, both of warfare and of masculinity, which men drew on to define their individual identities as soldiers and as men.

Todman and Watson have both looked extensively at the effects of time, particularly retrospection, on the way in which tales of war came to be dominated by narratives of disillusion. Rather than tracing the alterations in narrative that occurred over the course of the entire 20th century, as experience became memory, this study focuses the form that men's narratives took over a briefer space of time, between 1914 and 1977. This allows for some discussion of the ways in which understandings of masculinity changed as the war years grew more distant, while retaining a focus on the narrative of those who experienced it directly. By concentrating on the form which the narratives of the men who were there took, from letters home, diaries and letters of condolence written during the war years to the postwar narratives of letters to the Ministry of Pensions and war memoirs, this book explores how the telling of the tale itself shaped the tale told.

Watson and Todman are by no means alone in examining retrospective narratives as a source for exploring how the war came to be understood in British culture. Samuel Hynes' study of the soldiers' tale is dominated by memoirs and autobiographical fictions.[68] Others have analysed oral histories collected from the 1970s onwards.[69] All these forms of narrative have yielded important information about men's experiences and understanding of war. But if we are to look at soldiers' narratives critically, we must bear in mind the fact that memoirs, even those that remained unpublished for decades, are often written with a specific audience in mind.[70] An interviewer may shape the construction of an oral history.[71] Fictions may aim for dramatic effect as much as an absolute 'truth'.[72] Contemporaneous narratives are even more likely to be influenced by the context in which they are written. As Michael Roper points out, 'personal accounts of the past are never produced in isolation from these public narratives, but must operate within their terms. Remembering always entails the working of past experience into available cultural scripts.'[73] Questions of audience and context must, therefore, be investigated if we are to fully understand the ways in which any given narrative reflects the subjective experience of warfare of the man who wrote it. By focussing on the different genres of narrative that men used to write about their experiences, this study uncovers the ways in which the construction of identity was shaped by these external cultural forces as much as by the experiences themselves.

Such influences can be clearly seen in the narrative forms examined in this book, and it is in the differences of subject, tone and inflection created by such influences that men's constructions of masculine identities can be read. Letters that soldiers wrote home from the front, discussed in Chapter 1, form the most direct interface between men's experiences of war and the civilian identities they inhabited before the war. The narratives contained in these letters are clearly shaped by the expectations of their intended recipients, those who knew the authors in terms of domesticity rather than in terms of their newly acquired martial identities. The personal diaries examined in Chapter 2, by comparison, while recounting many similar experiences of war, are more concerned with the martial identity of the author, giving descriptions of experiences a different inflection. There is more scope for grumbling about life as a soldier, and the soldier himself is constructed as a far more physical being in descriptions of daily life.

The potential for conflict between these two identities, the domestic and the martial, are highlighted in the letters of condolence examined in Chapter 3. In these narratives, the masculinity of the dead man is constructed by others seeking to define him in terms of their own recollection of him, be that as a civilian or a soldier. The effects of retrospection are also an element of Chapters 4 and 5, examining the letters of disabled ex-servicemen to the Ministry of Pensions and veteran's postwar memoirs respectively. In both these forms of expression, ex-servicemen attempt to construct a narrative of recalled masculinity that will impress or gain the sympathy of a contemporary audience. Again, the question of intended audience is vital to both these discussions, particularly in understanding how disabled men constructed their narratives in response to the expectation of the Ministry of their role in postwar society as independent wage earners. Memoirs, meanwhile, expose not only the ways in which postwar domesticity influenced men's memory of the war but also the ways in which men's martial identities inflected on their postwar domesticity.

What a close examination of these five forms of narrative demonstrates is how soldiers and ex-servicemen constructed their individual identities as men in face of the experience of warfare, both immediately and retrospectively. The influence of lived experience and social expectations of appropriate masculinity are explored, examining both the ways in which individual men negotiated the social discourses of the soldier hero and the independent householder to construct personal masculine identities, and the ways in which different narrative forms shaped the expression of these identities. In doing so, this book demonstrates not only the effect of war experience on understandings of masculinity but also the effect of social ideals of masculinity on understandings of the war. Thus we can begin to unravel the complexities of what it meant for British soldiers and ex-servicemen of the First World War to be men at war.

1
Writing Home: Men's Letters from the Front

On 8 September 1917, Cyril Newman, a lance corporal with the 9th Battalion The London Regiment wrote to his fiancée, Winnie, of his emotions on receiving two letters from her. 'I feel a different person,' he wrote, 'ten years younger – a hundred times lighter at heart. We all feel like this. The arrival of mail is vital to our happiness....."No post" gives us a kind of malaise.'[1] Newman was expressing the feelings of the majority of British soldiers who, throughout the First World War, were delighted to receive mail from home. As an on-going source of contact with the home front, letters served as a reminder of what men were fighting for, a conduit for news from home and an important emotional outlet for soldiers.

The mobilization of the postal service during the First World War was one of the most successful aspects of the British war effort. The Army Post Office, a Special Reserve unit of the Royal Engineers, dispatched servicemen within days of the outbreak of war to set up an Advanced Base Post Office and an Army Base Post Office in the Harve. By 18 August 1914, the Army B.P.O. had dispatched and received its first mail.[2] The scale of postal work was far greater than the Corps had been called upon to deal with in previous conflicts. In one week in October, the army received 2,087 bags of mail and by 1917 the Army was sending home 8,926,831 letters a week.[3] Over the course of the war, '12.5 million letters were sent weekly and... "for practically every letter sent out to the front a letter came home".'[4]

The importance of this service to morale was acknowledged by the army which specified the postal service as 'one of the army departments "without which the fighting troops cannot be maintained in a state of efficiency."'[5] Packages containing food, clothing, reading material and other goods were often sent to the front, providing both practical

14

comfort and concrete evidence for many men of the home front's appreciation of their efforts and sacrifices. It was, however, letters from home that men valued most highly, containing as they did both assurances that men at the front had not been forgotten by their loved ones and reminders of the familiar home life that they had left behind.[6] In reply, men's letters offered reassurances as to their health and well-being, and news on the war from the perspective of the trench and the route march.

Men's letters home have been read by many historians as illustrative of the distances, both geographic and psychic, between men and their correspondents on the home front. 'Letters home,' Michael Roper argues, 'were always conditioned by the tension between being at the front and writing to those who had no direct experience of it.'[7] Others, however, have argued that strong connections continued to exist between men's wartime and civilian lives, connections that were maintained through the regular exchange of letters.[8] However, letters home not only acted as conduits of news that kept the home front connected and informed. They also served as spaces in which men could continue to enact their domestic roles even as they attempted to inhabit the martial role of the soldier.

The civilian mobilization that the First World War entailed meant that, prior to 1914, the majority of men who eventually served had little expectation of assuming the identity of 'soldier'. By 1918 the British army had grown to over 5 million, some 22.11% of the British male population.[9] Before the war, these soldiers were students, businessmen, labourers, artisans, sons, husbands, nephews, fathers. While cultural norms of the time valourized the soldier and his skills as the epitome of masculinity,[10] and some men did attempt to fulfil their martial fantasies or sense of duty through joining the Territorial Army, many of the British civilians who eventually served had identities that focussed on other masculine norms, those of the dutiful son and provident husband, norms that, in the 19th and early 20th centuries, were as important to discourses of masculinity as that of the soldier hero.[11] These were the identities that, during the war, found expression in letters home through numerous references to life at home, domestic worries, celebrations of domestic success and dreams and assurances of future domestic happiness. In creating a space in which men wrote both as soldiers and domestic figures, letters home offered an important connection for men between their lives as soldiers and the civilian lives and expectations that they had put on hold for the duration.

Despite military regulations concerning the censoring of letters, the practicalities of warfare made strict adherence to these regulations difficult.[12] Officers were trusted to self-censor their letters, while the letters of Other Ranks were censored by their officers.[13] Other Ranks also had the luxury of a monthly 'green envelope' which would be uncensored. These were intended to provide men with the opportunity to communicate personal matters without the knowledge of officers, although the irregularity of their provision, particularly as the war proceeded, meant that many officers became extremely familiar with the details of their men's marital and monetary concerns. Even when men wrote directly of their experiences of warfare, censorship was generally more concerned with practical details, such as names and places which could be of use to the enemy, than the effect of explicit descriptions of experiences on the morale of the home front. Indeed, a number of men wrote highly descriptive letters to their families which were explicitly intended for publication in local papers.

Even with this relative freedom of expression, however, men felt limited in what they could write. R. Macgregor marked one letters to his father, which described the explosion of a mine that killed 20 men, with the words 'NOT TO BE PUBLISHED'.[14] D. Manning felt so constrained that he complained, 'Its quite a job to know how to write a letter over here for there are so many things we are forbidden to say that there seems nothing left but the weather one can talk about and so far that's been glorious.'[15] Newman, who made full use of his green envelopes to write love letters to his fiancée, got a fit of caution before the Somme, telling her, 'A testing time is coming shortly dear, to both of us. I must not say more.'[16]

Reassurance

Despite restrictions, both official and self-imposed, most men wrote regular letters to their families, informing those at home about their lives as soldiers. In the first instance, letters allowed men to reassure their family as to their safety. At its most basic, such reassurance took the form of the Field Service Postcard, a pre-printed card which allowed servicemen to cross out options, ranging from 'I am quite well' to 'I am injured and being sent down to base', as appropriate. Nothing else, however, was to be written on the cards, so letters were a necessary adjunct, providing space for men to illustrate their claims with specific anecdotes.

The most common form of reassurance that men offered in their letters was, in effect, the same as that provided by the Field Service Postcard, that they remained in good health despite bad weather, poor food and lack of sleep. E. F. Chapman complained in one letter, 'The weather is very cold' but immediately went on to reassure his mother that:

> with your leather jerkin under my tunic, and the thick gray cardigan Father used to wear as well, in addition to the Army jerkin worn outside the tunic, I keep perfectly warm, and really enjoy this cold spell. With all these clothes on, I am probably warmer in the trenches than you are at home![17]

Men also offered their families reassurance about their safety in relation to their distance from the battlefield. For those in support roles, this could be relatively easy. G. R. Barlow, serving behind the lines as a telegraphist in the 31st Division Signal Company, Royal Engineers, pointed out to his aunt that, despite the fact that 'our infantry in hottest of fighting' during the 1918 spring offensive, 'I have not been in any great danger since the affair began and am now in a very safe place.'[18] T. Watkins similarly assured his mother, 'I am quite safe as we ASC do not go near the firing line so we are all right and we get plenty of food.'[19] Rest periods could be used to offer similar reassurance. 'Do not let your thoughts picture your Boy dashing over bloodstained battlefields or sitting in a trench under shellfire,' Newman wrote to Winnie at the height of the battle of the Somme, 'That Boy of yours is having a change of air in a quiet – mysteriously quiet – little hamlet.'[20]

For men who were actually in the front line, offering reassurance could be more difficult. Chapman used a comparative approach, telling his mother that 'Life in the front line was distinctly to be preferred [to being in support]. The working parties were very hard, often lasting all night, and when you have not had your full amount of sleep for some time, it is hard to keep going.'[21] A more common tactic, however, was to emphasize the safety of the trenches. 'It sounds silly I know but it is a fact that out here I am as safe as you are at home,' claimed B. A. Reader. 'You couldn't have a safer place than a trench, provided you keep your head down.'[22] B. Britland similarly reassured his mother that, despite there being 'a great deal of shelling... just here... there is not much danger so long as we keep in our dugouts.'[23]

Discomfort and danger

Reassurance, however, was not the only reason men had for writing home. They tried to maintain contact with those at home through descriptions of what they were experiencing. As a result, men often described their lives in a level of detail that could be far from reassuring. W. B. P. Spencer, for example, complained about how 'In some places the mud came over my knees. This is not exaggerated. In most places over one's ankles. The first night it was horrid, raining all night. No room to move.'[24] Living conditions were equally uncomfortable for C. E. Foster in Gallipoli, where he found that 'Life in a funk-hole is just about as uncomfortable as you can imagine. Everything is full of dust, flies swarm and the heat is oppressive.'[25] Route marches were another source of complaint, as was the quality of food. Reader wrote of 'a brute of a march today and when we got here I found my feet were bleeding in one or two places. Consequently I had trouble in getting my socks off,'[26] while O. Lyle noted that, although bully beef 'seemed, as it most certainly is, most excellent corned beef, ... it soon palls & becomes ultimately most repugnant.'[27]

Men not only wrote of the discomforts but also the dangers they faced as soldiers. Reader bluntly told his brother, 'Of course, we all have to do dangerous work. I had to carry boxes of live bombs up to the firing line with shrapnel shrapping all round.'[28] Spencer noted, 'I never realised before I came out here how dreadful steel fire is. Very few people did.'[29] He thought that being shelled was 'the most awful part of war. Bullets are nasty, but gun fire is horrid.'[30] Chapman disagreed. 'I have tasted most forms of "frightfulness" – shells, bullets and gas in a mild form. I can stand shell fire well, but I hate bullets! There is the consciousness that they are aimed, and they make such a horrid crack. I would rather have a shell any day.'[31]

While men were able to write about the fears and dangers of being under fire, they found it much harder to write about the more active experience of battle. Macgregor, for one, found the experience of battle to be dreamlike and distanced:

> We soon saw a target, a body of some 100 Huns, and gave them 5 rounds rapid. They seemed to be walking towards us in quite the ordinary way. None of the glory of a charge, or bugles, or singing or anything. In fact the whole battle seemed extraordinarily silent. I fired twice, and the range was such that I couldn't miss. Moreover I was absolutely steady in my aim, and knew it was good. Then they stopped walking forward and my men started curling up on the

ground, or rolling on their backs, kicking up their legs, again quite
the natural thing to do. Had anyone spoken to me, I should have told
him, 'Oh yes, there's casualties, that's all.' It all seemed so natural, and
commonplace.[32]

Macgregor's letter is unusual in its description of the perpetration of
an act of violence against the enemy. Those who did write about firing
on the enemy often qualified the act with excuses of ignorance, such
as Newman's comment that 'One seldom sees the result of one's firing and I am glad. I do not want to <u>know</u> that I have killed a man.'[33]
Men may, as Joanna Bourke has argued, have been able to validate their
experiences of killing in ways that protected their sense of identity as
moral men.[34] Their letters to their families, however, appear not to have
been considered the appropriate space in which to attempt such expla-
nation. Instead, the figure of the soldier constructed in these letters is
one who does not participate in the primary act associated with soldiering. Instead, by describing their experiences through the narrow
focus of vision and action that marks both Macgregor and Newman's
descriptions, the association between action and effect is strictly limited.

This is not to say that men were necessarily inhibited about writing
of the effects of battle where they observed them. Concerns other than
self-censorship, however, influenced men's ability to describe their experiences. Newman, for instance, appears to have been willing to describe
his experiences of the Battle of the Somme to his fiancée but found himself unable to articulate them fully. Following a period that he described
as both 'a time of great peril' and a 'period of trial', he wrote to Winnie
that 'Some time I may be able to give you an account of what we have
been through' but refused to go into further detail.[35] Men found their
experiences of battle were beyond the power of language to convey to
those who had not shared them.[36] As J. E. Hind commented, 'What am
I doing? – I am having the greatest experience of my life. Altogether too
wonderful to give you anything but the slightest idea.'[37]

Where men did attempt to describe battle their descriptions often possessed the dreamlike quality noted in Macgregor's letter through their
disassociation of death from the action of battle. C. M. Tames's description of the aftermath of First Ypres was of 'men and horses all mixed
up in death. It was as I have said just like a dream, I could not believe
my own eyesight, and could not realise what I saw to be reality, only a
dream, or I might say a nightmare.'[38] R. P. Harker described one trench
he occupied as having 'All round about . . . at the back and in the fields at
the sides . . . lots of dead Frenchmen lying about who had been unburied

for weeks.... I don't think people at home realise this side of the war as apart from fighting in fierce attacks and counter-attacks.'[39]

One reason for this sense of dislocation between action and effect was the increasing number of men killed during bombardments rather than in battle. As S. G. Wright wrote of one bombardment, 'I could only see five of our chaps unhurt, and dead and wounded were lying around in heaps. It was awful, and I wonder we didn't all go mad.'[40] Not all experiences of the violence of bombardment were so entirely de-personalized. Macgregor wrote of encountering a:

> forward Observing Officer going up, just as the firing line was being reoccupied. He said 'Pretty good shooting that, Eh!' I damned him heartily, and still pray that he may burn in hell, for as he was speaking they led passed six men blind and vilely wounded by one of our own shells that dropped short. We lost more by our own guns that morning than from the Huns.[41]

The fact of injury was, in this case, clearly visible and describable, even if the source was not.

Thus, despite the distance between action and effect in their descriptions of violence, men could be explicit about the effects of violence in their letters home. J. W. McPherson wrote to his family about the injuries he observed at Gallipoli: 'Men had lost arms and legs, brains oozed out of shattered skulls, and lungs protruded from riven chests; and worst of all, many had lost their faces and were, I should think, unrecognisable to their nearest friends.'[42] He commented in another letter on 'the horrible smell of dead men and beasts unburied and only half buried!! It was more than a smell, it clung to the lips and flavoured the food and drink and woke me repeatedly in the night.'[43] Tames also wrote of the smell, commenting that 'it does seem indeed very strange to me to be in such a position as to see dead men and horses, and to smell them all day and night, everywhere, and at all times, it is really an awful life and an unnatural one.'[44] It was this sense of strangeness that men found themselves struggling to convey.[45] While some of their attempts to do so could be banal and bathetic, ultimately failing to convey what had been seen and experienced, the need to explain what they were living through to those at home remained a powerful motivating force for many men writing letters home throughout the war.

Reaction

This need to describe the life they were leading included not only the general experiences associated with warfare but also men's individual reactions to such experiences. Foremost among these reactions was the desire to run away that most men had when faced with shellfire. B. A. Reader described how one night he was:

> carrying rations up to the line when shells started bursting about 5 minutes walk in front of us. We knew that if they didn't stop by the time we got up there we should all be 'goners', and it needed all my will power to keep on walking. I felt like dumping my load and running.[46]

Two months later he wrote to his mother,

> An army order has been issued to the effect that 'Men between 18 & 19 are to [be] sent back, but any who choose can volunteer to stay with their Batt.' The temptation to get out of this ghastly business is far greater than you can possibly conceive, but of course there's only one decent thing for me to do, that is to stay here, but oh! it's going to be very hard.[47]

Letters to his family provided the intimate space for this 18-year-old to express his feelings of fear, which he felt otherwise unable to do in his role of a soldier.

The fear of showing fear might condition men's behaviour amongst fellow soldiers.[48] In their letters home, however, men were able to expose their fear to those who knew and cared for them as something other than soldiers. Newman certainly viewed his identity as a soldier under shellfire as very different from that of the man writing letters to his fiancée:

> The fierce overwhelmingly cruel onrush of a high-explosive shell, the ear-splitting and sickening crash as it bursts forces to the surface of man's nature reserves of stern endurance, and a hardness of heart so that for the time being one becomes Spartan without thought for the sweet ways of life. One 'plays the man' keeping under all sensitive, tender-hearted feelings that, if indulged in, might render one a coward. But, after the trial has passed, or the fierceness subsided for time, the real nature of man as nurtured in the heart ... craves for a woman's love.[49]

Letters could thus provide appropriate spaces in which men could speak of fear so that, in the heat of battle and before their comrades, they were better able to 'play the man'. G. Donaldson felt able to admit to his mother that 'in th[e] 1/2 hour before [a] gas attack started, I came nearer to "having the wind up" or in other words, losing my nerve than has been the case before.'[50] He also noted, however, that 'I have fortunately got the knack of disguising any effect the business has on my nerves'[51] which enabled him to gain the confidence of his company by acting the role of the soldier in an appropriately stoical manner. O. Lyle, on the other hand, was not able to overcome his fear in this manner. After the Battle of Loos during which two of his men were killed, he wrote to his brother about how he:

> lost my nerve for three days. It was just hell – especially at night. I couldn't sleep at all. Every time a shot was fired I had to get up and see if everything was alright. I also had a damnable feeling that if I had made the superfluous volunteers go back the Bosch might not have spotted us & those two poor blighters might have been all right. It is a most awful feeling to think that you've caused a loss of life. One can imagine what a murderer must feel like. Luckily we were relieved soon after and I recovered, but at one time I thought I was going to break down. I had always rather scoffed at fellows I had met at home suffering from nerves, as, to outward apperances [*sic*], they always seemed quite fit. But I now know that one seems quite fit but feels perfectly bloody.[52]

Through experiences such as these, men expressed a more complicated understanding of what it meant for a man to be brave in wartime, an understanding that they communicated to their families in letters home.[53] Subtly, the idea of what defined the heroic soldier was beginning to change for both the home and fighting fronts.

The extent of such changes can also be seen in the ways in which men wrote home of their disillusionment with the experience of war. G. R. Barlow compared his feeling on enlistment with those he felt a year later: 'Twelve months ago I believed that the new armies were representative of democracy and honour . . . .That we had volunteered because of our love of honour and peace . . . . I am [now] absolutely "fed-up". This Army life is the most idle and useless existence conceivable.'[54] This sense of pointlessness persisted. Two years later, he was still complaining of 'the weary drudgery of the Army.'[55] Reader explained to his parents that:

> I have undergone the various emotions caused by war, have seen most things that happen in war and don't think much of it. I have seen mines (3) go up, have been knocked down by the explosion

of an aerial torpedo ... have seen men killed and wounded and have had to carry a mortally wounded man to a dressing station on a stretcher ... It was awful .... War is a rotten game.[56]

As an under-age enlistee, Reader was, in 1916, entitled to take up the Army's offer to release him from service. Although he ultimately decided not to do so, he explained to his mother that he was 'very glad that Dad has asked for me, as I am horribly fed up with this game.'[57] In expressing his desire to leave the army, Reader was rejecting the cultural ideal of war as an arena of masculine fulfilment and the image of the soldier as hero. As with his feelings of fear, letters to his family provided space in which he could expose his sense of disillusionment and vulnerability, emotions that he was unable to express in other areas of his life.

Change

Not all men became as disillusioned as Reader, however. Indeed, while danger and discomfort were acknowledged by men writing home, for many the war was also an arena of adventure in which men's characters were able to develop.[58] Men used their letters home to describe how, through their experience of soldiering, they were changing, physically, mentally and spiritually, becoming hardened to danger and learning how to endure. These were seen not merely as necessary but praiseworthy development to masculine identity that gave an important sense of meaning to men's experiences of war, a sense that they, in turn, attempted to express in their letters home.

The most tangible way in which men described war as affecting them was in terms of their physical health and development. Despite the dangers inherent in warfare, the outdoor life and and physical exercise which soldiering involved were seen as conducive to good health. Barlow, for one, believed that:

The infantry have a life that makes for good health. They have good, wholesome, plain food, manual tasks, and live about twelve hours of every day in the open. Who wouldn't be well? I do not think that the trenches and dugouts are very healthy. The men don't have enough exercise or sleep but the rest in the villages more than counteracts those drawback.[59]

Barlow does not mention here the shell and rifle fire that made the trenches distinctly unhealthy places to be, but, even so, the paradox that J. M. Winter has noted of improved life expectancy among the British civilian population during the war does, to some extent, apply to those on military service.[60] The exercise and relatively regular diet were an improvement for many of the increasingly urban and often undernourished population who found themselves in the ranks.[61]

Men themselves certainly believed that war experience was improving them physically. C. E. Foster commented:

> In spite of this graveyard existence and the atmosphere made so insalubrious by bullets as well as corpses we seem to thrive. The weak-lings go of course. But those who have been here since the first look splendid. I have no doubt that the exacting discipline has a most favourable effect upon the body.[62]

For B. Britland, evidence of his improved health was to be found in the fact that he was 'living in conditions which 12 months ago would have killed me & I never felt better in my life.'[63] M. Holroyd boasted, 'I can only just get into the coat now, with no waistcoat on, so even if it hasn't shrunk a little, my chest has greatly expanded.'[64]

It was not only physical development, however, that men presented as evidence to their families of the positive effects of war experience. They also described their experiences as a process of moral and psychological maturation. Barlow, for instance, told his aunt that 'I don't think that the life has brutalised me, perhaps contact with coarse and rough people has made me a little coarse and rough but that only makes me realise the value of refinement.'[65] Newman, a Baptist Sunday school teacher, was even more positive in his interpretation of his changing attitude to vice. In one letter he explained, 'I used to look upon smoking, drinking and swearing from a narrow viewpoint but my outlook has broadened considerably – not unwisely I think. When I joined the army the language disgusted and shamed me but unless it is merely vulgar or uttered in anger I do not now protest.'[66] Nor was it only in relation to questions of morality that Newman expressed a sense of psychic development. He felt that 'I am a better man, with a tested Faith a more earnest hope and a truer love. I have faced death and have not flinched from it, have learnt to be content in whatever state I am placed and to endure suffering and hardship cheerfully.'[67] J. E. Hind similarly felt that 'A few years ago I should not have possessed assurance enough to do a quarter of that which comes natural now. The life, here has done worlds for me.'[68]

Even horror, danger and discomfort could be transmuted into positive learning experiences in the narratives of letters. Barlow reassured his aunt, 'I am getting more and more accustomed to these discomforts. The discomforts of army life seem to be rather frightful when regarded as a whole but really they are few.'[69] During the 1918 offensive he became 'quite hardened to [marching] and suffer[ed] very little discomfort.'[70] Macgregor used his familiarity with the discomforts of war to cast himself as more experienced and, by implication, a better soldier, than his companions. Having served overseas since September 1914, he wrote to his father in 1915, 'the trenches aren't really very bad though these Kitcheners like to think they are. Only a "Contemptible" like I am, knows what a really wet trench is.'[71] Familiarity with the conditions of war allowed Macgregor to present himself as an experienced soldier with its attendant implications of enhanced masculinity.

Holroyd's appraisal of his first time in the front line at Ypres also cast the war as a masculinizing process. During this visit:

> just 10 [were] killed and wounded out of 26 officers in the battalion, and about 15 or 20 per cent of the men, mostly by shell fire. Very interesting, not to say exciting, experience. It's making men of us, I believe. I know I've got quite a new robust feeling after it.[72]

For E. F. Chapman, his return to France following a period of convalescence made him:

> about the happiest man in the whole B.E.F. The first few weeks out here nearly broke me. Instead of breaking me it broke me in. Since then I have been able to bear any strain that has been put on me.... I believe the worst is over, for me at all events, for I have been broken in and can stick things pretty well now.[73]

Chapman here echoes the language of masculine maturation that appeared in much 19th-century juvenile literature about war, in which the trial of battle was portrayed as a source of moral improvement.[74]

Adventure

In keeping with the narrative of war as a sphere of masculine maturation, many men constructed their ability to endure discomfort as praiseworthy stoicism and thus a positive aspect of their masculine identity as soldiers. F. E. Packe, for instance, was proud of the fact that, although 'one feels the strain after a bit,' by trying very hard, 'I think

I succeeded in not fussing.'[75] This ability to endure was a great source of pride to men such as Chapman who wrote:

> I have a feeling of pride that I have stuck it all right for over 9 months, and have never been sick, or been away with a soft job. The soft jobs always go to the men who can't stick it in the line, or who are useless there. I hope I shall be able to stick it to the end, whatever the end is. I would not have missed the experience of the last 9 months for anything.[76]

Newman cast pride in his ability to endure in specifically masculine terms, telling Winnie, 'Above all, I have been given courage and strength to play the man.'[77]

Conversely, the inability to endure could be a source of shame. C. E. Foster explained of one trip to hospital:

> I'm torn between feeling I ought to stay here as long as I'm fit to crawl about, and a common sense prompting to go away, and seek conditions most suitable for recovery, strength and health, and the latter has triumphed.... But jaundice! To think of me being put out of business by jaundice, after having dodged shells and bullets and dysentery all these months! Well it makes one feel sore.[78]

His ability to endure the dangers of shells and bullets was undermined by his inability to endure illness. Reader also found his endurance tested, although by his age rather than by bodily strength. Aged 16 when he enlisted, he was serving on the Western Front by March 1916. In July of that year, he wrote, in relation to the Army's offer that he could leave service on account of his age, that 'The temptation to get out of this ghastly business is far greater than you can possibly conceive, but of course there's only one decent thing for me to do, that is to stay here, but oh! it's going to be very hard.'[79] He reinforced his decision a week later with the comment, 'I have decided to stick out here until I get knocked out as that is, in my opinion, the only decent thing to do.'[80] Masculine pride thus directly overrode his desire to protect himself from harm and his family from the grief that such harm might cause.

For Reader, the war became a test of his ability to endure. Newman saw it as a:

> Divine Plan for producing men – real men – to take the raw material and to thrust it into the hot furnace of temptation and to temper

it under constant blows of difficulty, hardship and disappointment. And even when it has come forth apparently true steel the process of testing never stops. Yet I thank God it is so – that man is always up against something. It appeals somehow to the heroic in one.[81]

For many men, however, warfare was not a test of their heroic abilities but simply a once-in-a-lifetime experience. J. W. McPherson, for example, explained his decision to put himself in harms way by remaining on the beach in an attack at Gallipoli: 'Risk and responsibility be damned, I thought. Here was the chance of a lifetime to see a real engagement at close quarters on the actual battlefield, a sight I have longed to see all my life, and was told was very difficult of realisation.'[82] J. E. Hind reflected that 'one day, if it pleases God ultimately to bring me Home, I shall look back upon these times – and especially these through which I am passing – with feelings of deepest affection, as being some of the finest of my life the equal to which will never come again.'[83]

This sense that the war was an extraordinary experience could serve as a source of consolation for men, as it did for G. Donaldson:

If you make up your mind that there are unpleasant things to face, & can see the light side of things as far as possible, & have a sense of humour (for there is humour even in being shelled, you know) & realise that after all this is one of the experiences of a lifetime, what is there to bother about.[84]

Such consolation could be found even in the most difficult moments. Writing from the Somme in 1916, Chapman told his mother:

We are scarcely ever in the same place for more than a few days. And as for one's friends, they change more rapidly than anything. Some get killed, and others get sent home to England, and you never hear of them again. But it is a grand life for all that, and good for a man to have lived.[85]

Enthusiasm

The sense of encouragement that the uniqueness which war experience offered meant that men's letters home remained full of enthusiasm throughout the war.[86] Having described his home-sickness at watching a sunset to his mother, Donaldson hastened to reassure her, 'don't think I am unhappy or pining!! because I'm not, & this is a great experience.

There have been some moments of excitement, too, I wouldn't have missed for anything.'[87] Newman similarly told his fiancée that 'I would not miss these present experiences – my flesh fails me at times but the spirit is somehow uplifted by the sheer magnitude of the forces opposed to it. There is some feeling of exhilaration in being equal to the occasion.'[88]

The enthusiasm expressed by men writing in the early years of the war is explicable by the initial khaki fever that gripped the nation, although this phenomenon was by no means simple or universal.[89] However, men continued to express enthusiasm for war experience throughout, as Newman's letter, written in 1918, shows. Men's need to reiterate their enthusiasm for war may, in part, indicate a need to camouflage mixed emotions and motivations that men may have felt as they embarked on their great adventure. What is interesting, however, is the persistence of enthusiasm, particularly for action, in men's letters home. Many men found the actual waging of war extremely dull, involving as it did a lot of hard work maintaining and repairing trenches, supporting the day-to-day business of trench life and marching to often undisclosed locations. As Spencer told his aunt, 'We...hope for some real fighting soon. One gets so tired of just being sniped at all day and sitting day after day with wet feet.'[90] Reader found surprising 'what a difference it makes when you can feel that you are getting a bit of your own back. Far better than sitting in a trench waiting for something to hit you',[91] while M. Holroyd assured an unnamed correspondent that 'I enjoyed hugely the day of the German attack. Good after being shelled with nothing to do.'[92]

If men in the front line looked forward to battle because they found life tedious and frightening, men in support positions often found life simply tedious. G. R. Barlow, serving as a telegraph operator, could even write enviously of aunt's 'experience of Zeppelin tremors while I'm veg-etating here and seeing no fun at all.'[93] C. W. Dawson, serving with the Indian Army on the North West Frontier envied his brother Harry who had been wounded serving on the Western Front. '[T]ell him when you see him next...,' he instructed his mother, 'that I am glad he's a jolly old hero. He always was a lucky dog – compared with me.'[94] Enthusiasm thus turned physical danger and pain of wounds into an experience that was to be envied because it was an integral part of the exceptional life experience of war service. Even death could be read as part of this experience: 'if we are meant to come back we shall and if not one can wish for nothing better'.[95] F. E. Packe told his mother. R. Watkins simi-larly assured his parents, 'if I don't [come back] I will die like a British soldier.'[96] War remained an arena in which men felt they could define themselves, even in death.

Domestic masculinity

Although men used their letters home as spaces in which to explore their emotions about war, from enthusiasm and exhilaration through horror and disillusion, they were, to some degree, constrained in the extent to which whey were able to fully articulate these emotions. As we have seen, censorship and inarticulateness could affect men's abilities to express themselves. Of all things that constrained men in describing their experiences, however, the most prominent was one that derived from their domestic rather than martial identities, the desire to protect their correspondents from worry or distress.[97] Newman, for example, mentioned to Winnie that 'half the camp is down with illness,' hastily adding, '(Keep it from my mother.)'[98] He also noted that his friend Reg, 'does not tell Nellie of the dangers here because, did he so, she would worry.'[99] Macgregor also sought to protect his parents through silence, writing to his father that 'I am sorry I haven't written sooner, but we have had a awful...time, and I didn't like to tell you I was quite well, lest a whizz-bang should cut me off in the middle of telling it.'[100] He also pointed out that 'Yes, I am keeping a lot of my news back. There are some things I can't even tell you.'[101]

What is most interesting about this desire to protect is who men sought to protect. The protection of mothers, wives and fiancées, while reasonably common, was not universal. Newman had no problems with telling his fiancée 'a little of events as I experience them.'[102] He appears, however, to have had greater concern for 'his Boys', the young men who had formed his Sunday school class and to whom he also wrote regularly, although none of these letters survive. G. R. Barlow did write to a child about the realities of warfare, in his case his young sister Nora, although he sought to cushion her from the full horror by having his aunt, to whom his explicit, descriptive letters were addressed, mediate the information Nora received. 'With regards to Nora,' he wrote, 'I am sure you are the best judge of what she should learn. I think that the truth is far more preferable than any charming fairy tale.'[103] R. P. Harker, on the other hand, was more protective of his young son Freddy. He noted in a detailed letter to his sister, 'I have written Freddy a long letter for his birthday but painted everything in rosy colours and not said anything about the rough or gruesome side of it so please don't let him see this letter.'[104] A. Butling took a similar stance. In his letters to his eldest sons, aged 12 and 14, he makes little mention of the discomforts or danger he was undergoing. His most explicit comment, in a letter to Eric, the younger boy, was that war was 'far different from home life. And I don't think you or George would like it a bit.'[105] Butling thus tried to protect his sons both from the knowledge of the realities of war and from any temptation to romanticize the experience.

Men's decisions over the regulation of the material of their letters to protect their correspondents indicates the extent to which these letters were rooted in men's pre-war lives and identities. The very fact that men wrote home as much as they did, once a day in Donaldson's case, and looked forward eagerly to news and gifts from home, indicates the on-going importance of home life to soldiers serving in the First World War. Men were unable to forget or ignore the identities they had left behind when they had enlisted, although they might, like Newman:

> thrust ruthlessly away emotional thoughts, tender feeling and... summon stern cold qualities of manhood to my aid. Had I thought of you... not seeing your face again, I might have flinched before the horror and terror that accompany Death out here. My courage might have weakened – but in the memorable lines of Lovelace – 'I should not love thee dear, so much Loved I not honour more' – so Duty, the doing of God's will became my supreme love.[106]

In this construction, the identity of the soldier is one that is enacted – 'Grace was given me to *play the man*' [My emphasis][107] – consciously assumed over that of the less manly identity of lover. The identity of lover, or son, or father could not, however, be ignored as it was central to the need to write letters. In their letters, men's martial and domestic identities converged both in the language used to describe their lives as soldiers and in their on-going involvement with the home front, both in terms of the hope and comfort it offered and the concern it engendered.

One of the clearest indications of the importance of the domestic to men at war was the use they made in their letters of similes and metaphors that compared war experiences with more familiar things. The comparison of a bombardment with a thunderstorm, for instance, was fairly common. C. M. Tames reported that 'the worst bombard-ment took place during the nights and reminded one of a thunderstorm, only stones and shot took the place of rain, and bursting shells that of lightening.'[108] G. R. Barlow described one bombardment as 'more awe-inspiring than the worst thunderstorm; terrible because each flash, each crash spelt destruction and ruin. Somehow it seemed to me to resemble magnificent music.'[109] G. Donaldson described the noise of an artillery attack on a German position as 'a sort of Belle Vue firework display,' noting that 'I am glad to say I thoroughly enjoyed the thing',[110] while M. Holroyd described his experience of the front line as 'a protracted and very enjoyable picnic, punctuated by the already unnoticed percussion of powerful pop-guns.'[111] He found shelling to be 'Splendid. Never knew there was such a good game, just like putting up toy soldiers on a toy castle and knocking em all over, only real.'[112] While such comparisons gave men a language with which to describe what they were experiencing, it also served to disguise the true nature of those experiences by diminishing the sense of fear and horror, as well as the dangers of death and mutilation that artillery shelling entailed.

The letters that were most effective in conveying experience through metaphor, however, were those that turned to specific domestic metaphors. A. T. Pile's description of offices where he worked as a clerk with the Royal Army Medical Corps (R.A.M.C.) as reminding 'me much of the office that I worked in London'[113] provided both a reference point for his correspondents and an evocation of an earlier identity as an office worker in peace. J. W. McPherson's description of ration biscuits as being 'the size and shape of the little pearl biscuits we used to buy from old Mother Allen to play shop with',[114] evoked an even earlier civilian identity, that of the child.

Home at the front

Nor can evidence of men's domestic mindset be seen only in their metaphors. It is also evident in the detailed descriptions of living arrangements that appear in most letters. E. E. F. Baker, for instance, described a diminutive pillbox he found himself living in some detail:

> The luxury of the place almost stinks. Along two adjoining sides, opposite the blanket-covered hole called 'door' we have constructed two couches of ammunition boxes. On the other two sides is seating accommodation for two. In the centre of the space is filled by a table 3ft by 1ft. Under the table a small 'Beatrice' oil stove.[115]

For B. Britland, home was a tent made of bivouac sheets:

> about 10 ft long by 7 ft broad & we have worked hard & made it fairly cosy.... It would amuse you to come & just have a peep at us when we are asleep. We simply take our boots & puttees off & pull an

empty sandbag on our feet. We put our overcoats on & our sleeping helmets. For a pillow we use the valise off our equipment & I don't think we should sleep much sounder on a feather bed.[116]

Some men's domestic arrangements were extremely elaborate, despite being cobbled together out of scraps and ingenuity. Newman's home, dubbed 'Sunnyside', was constructed out of:

sheets of tin [scrounged] from an R.E. dump for the roof and built up walls from debris.... We formed a window span and doorway, made a chimney and round part of a cooking stove.... We have installed our table and chair and made a shelf, on which our 'china' is set out including a cut-glass decanter rescued from rubbish inside a blown up house.... On the table earthenware jar – a one time container of Devonshire Cream, in which are two sunflowers. So you see how cosy we are.[117]

Such accommodations were sources of great pride, as G. R. Barlow noted of his billet: 'this place, I nearly wrote palace in my eagerness, is a bally cabine de luxe and we are durned proud of it.'[118]

Men used these descriptions of decoration to anchor their new experiences in the familiarity of home life. As Barlow pointed out, 'however one moves, the new hut or tent becomes a sort of representation of home.'[119] These descriptions not only helped to reassure those at home of the comforting familiarity of at least some of the activities their loved ones were engaged in but also served to maintain a topic of interest between men and the home front. Having replied with pleasure to his mother's news of the success of her roses, J. G. Taylor wrote of 'a smart little bed of geraniums and dahlias outside our office', noting that, 'Had we come here a month earlier we would have set a few seeds, but I think it is too late now.'[120]

Food was another familiar topic that was of shared interest to both men and their families, the more so as food shortages began to affect diet on the home front. Food sent out to men in parcels was the source of many expressions of gratitude in subsequent letters. Cakes, jams and even sweets served to remind men of home, particularly if they were home made.[121] The food men ate at the front also came in for a good deal of discussion, often in complaint at its limited nature, but also as a source of pleasure. O. Lyle noted that:

When we were in the trenches we existed for the most part on tinned stuff. Until you try, you can't think what wonderful tinned food can be got. Asparagas, steak & kidney pudding, squashed hat, lamb cutlets & pease,[*sic*] etc. etc. & they taste when heated in boiling water like dishes straight from a good cuisine.[122]

However, even the bare minimum of some foodstuffs could provide men with the comfort of familiarity. R. P. Harker found that 'We get tea twice a day but without milk or sugar and seem to thrive on it.'[123]

Food was not only a source of comfort. It also proved to be a considerable source of pride for men who, forced by the almost exclusively male society in which they found themselves, were learning to cook. Barlow, for instance, crowed over his discovery of 'the best way of extracting the maximum flavour out of café-au-lait....[M]y coffee has become renowned.'[124] J. E. Hind was equally proud of his ability to cook bacon: 'So that is another item to add to my list of achievements .... I mastered the art of dealing with eggs years ago – Oh! I intend to do all I can to become domesticated.'[125] Indeed, he discovered a liking for cooking and included a number of descriptions of meals he had cooked in his letters, including a long description of how he had managed to reheat a Christmas pudding sent from home using a mug and a mess tin to create a double boiler.[126] C. T. Newman also described his ingenuity in the cooking of a bread pudding inspired by an issue of currants: 'I soaked some dry biscuits in water, added a little bread, put in washed currants and condensed milk, put all in a pudding cloth and am watching over the boiling as carefully as a mother over her child.'[127]

Like Hind, Newman associated his developing skills as a cook with a development in his domestic identity as much as his identity as a soldier. As he told his fiancée, 'to bring an early cup of tea or breakfast to you will not be something strange and unknown. The art will have been learnt in the billets and trenches of France.'[128] The domestic skill of cookery was not the only one that men found the war cultivated in them. The care of clothes was equally important. Newman boasted of having 'washed a pair of socks and a towel this afternoon. A handy man am I not?'[129] Macgregor requested that a scrubbing brush be sent from home to make his domestic chores easier.[130] As Britland noted, 'You will see from what I have written that I am learning how to take care of myself.'[131]

In detailing their new-found domestic capabilities, men were portraying a quality associated with soldiering, that of adaptability to circumstances.[132] However, their mode of portrayal was primarily in domestic terms. Newman's numerous references to his new-found skills as a husband after the war indicate the strength of this association during the war itself.[133] By casting their ability to adapt and develop their skills in terms of domestic concerns, men were, in part, seeking to explain the experiences they were having in terms that would be familiar to their correspondents. But, in describing their experiences of war in terms of domesticity, these letters also indicate the extent to which men were unable to divorce their identities as soldiers from their domestic identities. Indeed, the two identities were not only interlinked but also served to reinforce each other as can be seen in the reasons that men gave for enlisting, the most common of which was defence of the home.[134]

Reasons for fighting

The concept of home for the soldier could encompass the general, as in the case of C. T. Newman's mention of the nation when asking his fiancée:

> Do you wonder, a little perhaps, why I with others are so anxious to go abroad? It is not that we forget our loved ones at home – far from that – it is their love that sustains us; we hunger to see them, to be near them, but honour and especially your country's honour comes before personal love.[135]

Others drew on ideas of the war as a purge that would cleanse England of its decadence and restore a familiar and desirable world order.[136] J. W. McPherson, for instance, hoped that 'this war puts us back to simpler conditions and relieves men of the burden of the objects which wealth and luxury and decadence have loaded them; and restores to the world some of its poetry and beauty, then all this bloodshed will not be in vain.'[137]

More common than general ideals, however, were men's mention of specific individuals as their motivation for fighting. G. R. Barlow, for example, felt that his aunt was 'worth fighting and dying for. I hope you will not mind me telling you that I volunteered so as to help protect you.'[138] Newman found inspiration in his fiancée as well as in his country. 'I am going forth cheerfully, willing to fight for her',[139] he wrote, and it is not entirely clear from his letter whether the pronoun refers to Winnie or England. Not all reasons for fighting were cast in such terms of pure idealism, however. John Townshend's motivations were apparently mercenary, although still with domestic concerns in mind.

'His parents are in straightened circumstances through the war and John enlisted to help them,' Winnie explained to Newman. 'He wrote to his Mother and said that there will now be no food or clothes to buy for him and he will send them money.'[140] Thus Townshend, when he enlisted, adopted the masculine role of provider for the home as much as that of protector.

Letters explaining why men chose to enlist and fight were often written as attempts to justify the separation from loved ones that war enforced. As their service continued, men increasingly expressed their connection with the home front less in terms of motivation that it gave them to be soldiers than its vital role in supporting their morale. As J. E. Hind wrote to his father:

> It would require a far more clever head than mine to explain in words let alone writing just the feeling in which we regard home out here and I am sure it is not until one is placed in the position of virtually being homeless, that it becomes possible to appreciate the one great home, over the water, where the welcome is ever warm and whose memory grows dearer every day. Had I never come out here I should never have known the full extent of the blessings of the home which has been mine these many years.[141]

Barlow similarly felt grateful to 'you who inspire us in our determination.'[142]

It was this sense of home as a source of both inspiration and comfort that made letters from home such an important boost to morale. Men often asked for more letters from home, as Macgregor did when he wrote to his mother:

> Please write a bit oftener. It seems a weary long time since I last had a letter. Please tell everyone to do this, for one sentence you can bet on seeing in every letter is 'Write soon, soon, soon,' and you know I value a letter from you more than from anyone.[143]

J. G. Taylor asked his father for 'another letter from you any time, telling me of your latest schemes with regard to the house, garden etc, and also of how business is progressing',[144] while C. W. Dawson told his mother, 'your letters are always interesting even when you've got nothing frightfully exciting to say.'[145] The news of the health of family members, meeting with friends, the possibility of home improvements, problems with rationing, the success, or otherwise, of children at school were topics that provided men with a touchstone of domestic normality that was of vital importance to their sense of identity in the strange and disturbing world of warfare that they had entered. The importance of this touchstone can be seen in men's appeals to it in moments of extremity. When Newman found 'conditions…worse than ever' in 1915, he wrote to his fiancée, 'I need a letter from you to lift my heart.'[146] Dawson wrote to his mother, while suffering from pneumonia, 'I have wanted you the past fortnight badly, mother, I have never been ill before & seem to miss you very much.'[147] In such moments, men rejected the endurance of danger and suffering that was so central to the definitions of martial masculinity in favour of identities as lovers and sons in need of comfort.

Continuing domesticity

Nor was it only comfort and pleasant news that men sought from their correspondents at home. Macgregor wanted to know the full details of his father's experience of being caught in a Zeppelin raid.[148] As Barlow told his aunt, 'I am quite as interested in your worries as in your pleasures.'[149] Such an interest in all aspects of domestic life meant that men continued to be involved in family concerns. When, shortly after his letter about the Zeppelins, Macgregor's mother fell ill, he wrote to his father:

> Please let me know the minute [illegible] be possible for me to [illegible] home and I'll plunk my name for leave, but not before you ask me. I quite agree that it might be dangerous to Mother, so don't hurry, but as soon as I get word from you that my presence will be beneficial and necessary up I go to the C.O. with urgent private affairs requiring immediate attention.[150]

His hesitation about returning home was expressed in terms of his domestic concerns for his mother's health rather than any worry about his duty as a soldier to remain at the front. D. Manning was similarly willing to place domestic concerns before military duty, writing to his wife, 'If the youngsters are bad at any time please don't hide if from me. I shall only be more worried and fancy they are worse than they really are and should they or you are [sic] seriously ill just try and get me a wire I'll do the rest.'[151]

The priorities of Macgregor and Manning indicate the importance men placed on their identities as husbands, sons and fathers throughout the war. For officers, such feelings of domestic responsibility probably had some influence on paternal attitudes towards the unit.[152] This connection can be seen in the behaviour of R. C. Trench, an officer in the Sherwood Foresters. Having waited to marry until he had completed his training as a chartered accountant and entered into business with his uncle, plans that the outbreak of war forestalled, Trench showed a similar sense of responsibility towards his men during the war, writing at length to both his wife and mother about his concerns for their welfare. His domestic and martial concerns merged in his discussions of food with his wife, Clare. In one letter he told her, 'I love hearing everything – especially that you are having good meals.' He then went on to suggest that she send him some dry kippers, noting, 'If successful we could get them for the men regularly.'[153] His concern for his wife's well-being, a facet of his domestic identity, thus merged with his concern for his men, a facet of his military role.

For others, paternalism meant caring for men's domestic concerns, even to the extent of providing financial assistance.[154] Macgregor sent his sister a cheque:

> to cash, if it is not too much trouble, and buy a suitable present for my God-daughter, Mary Duff [the daughter of his batman] .... It would ... be wise to buy something that can be sold on again easily, as I fear the Duffs are far from well off, my servant being at present under sentence, and Mrs Duff in hospital with an operation.[155]

He similarly wrote to his father that he had:

> given one [cheque] for £2:- to Drummer Larkum, who wishes to send it to his wife. You see she must live on 12/6 per week, and as he had 50fr. he wished to send it to her, but suffered from a morbid fear that the bank would try and do her, so he asked me to do the job, knowing I was in a bank.[156]

Not only did Macgregor see his paternalistic role extending to his men's home lives, his pre-war profession as an accountant assisted him in his paternalistic endeavours, thus fully merging his wartime and peacetime identities.

This merging of domestic and martial identities is also evident in both officers' and Other Ranks' attitudes towards their own domestic economy, over which a number of men expressed concern. Manning, a father of three, worried that 'the kiddies [*sic*] boots might get bad just now. I know what it is to have wet freezing feet and I couldn't bear to think you or they had to put up with it'.[157] Others expressed concern over household expenses related specifically to the war. T. Watkins, for example, told his mother not to 'worrie [*sic*] about sending me any parcels because I know its hard to get stuff if you do send me any just send me a few fags.'[158] Trench treated his mess bill as part of his domestic economy, writing, 'I hope [the packages Clare was sending him] are not costing too much but I have not spent anything here nor have I drawn a cheque except the two last month for 200 frs. altogether ... and have paid my mess bill to date.'[159] Earlier he had explained that he considered the packages 'really part of my Mess Bill as we all contribute anything we get to the mess.'[160] His household economy, as controlled by his wife, thus had a direct impact upon his experiences as a soldier, while the requirements of his life as a soldier made demands both on his finances and on his wife in regulating them.

After the war

For Macgregor, this burden was reversed, as he felt that it was his duty as the eldest son to support his family, sending his sister £5 for 'my Lodging and Ration allowance for 5 weeks' when on leave.[161] Less formally, Newman called the eight shillings he sent to Winnie in 1916 'a gift of love, of devotion.'[162] Such financial contacts allowed men to retain the domestic identity of provider even if that provision was derived from their earnings in their martial role as soldiers.

Closely allied to this desire to identify themselves as economic provider was men's desire to identify themselves as independent workers.[163] This identity was difficult to construct in the context of total war, where military necessity often overrode men's ability to act as sole provider, forcing the state to step into the breach.[164] Men sought to assert this aspect of their domestic masculinity, therefore, in their description of dreams about the future. Newman, for instance, wrote to his fiancée of his hopes that:

There ... will be a general increase in salaries after the war. ... But you must see, Dear One, that these three years of War have been wasted years. In place of study and effort to acquire knowledge and a higher position they have been spent in helping to keep back the might of Germany. The Future is uncertain. It will mean starting again – the regaining of lost knowledge, much study and effort – and much faith. To work and prosper for you will be a joy. No hardship will be too great for your dear sake. But it will take time – maybe two years before I shall be able to provide a home and make you my Wife.[165]

Newman was expressing the fears of many other young men who wrote of the future after the war in terms of their ability to fill a civilian masculine role as independent provider. Dawson, for instance, was pleased to hear that his brother, Harry, who had been invalided out of the Army in 1916, had received a degree and a position in the Colonial Office which allowed him 'to get settled & be able to look forward to a career.' By comparison, Dawson felt that his own future 'seems very vague at present. I shall be too old for the Varsity soon & shall have to start afresh I suppose – sticking on stamps or something.'[166] J. G. Taylor also worried about his lack of preparation for a civilian future, writing in May 1918:

> I do wish the whole business would soon be concluded, for the years seem to be slipping by, and as a 'Surveyor & Civil Engineer' I am practically speaking unborn. It has troubled me a good deal to think that when it is over, how useless I shall feel for a time, until I can 'get going' so to speak, for a dependent son of over 21 is not a desirable asset to any parent.... I am in a position which I have never thought I should be, on a/c of my youth, and therefore must do my utmost to establish my worth.[167]

He was pleased, therefore, when, shortly after the Armistice, his parents 'lost no time in asking the Surveyor to apply for my return to Civil employment' although he could 'see nothing very brilliant ahead. You see, my employment since leaving England has not had the slightest bearing on Surveying and Civil Engineering, so that is no assistance.'[168]

For young men such as Dawson and Taylor, their identities as soldier were less important for their future than their identities as civilian workers which had not had time to form prior to their enlistment. By becoming soldiers, they had undermined their civilian identities, leaving them dependent and without a defined career path at an age when such a situation could only be an embarrassment to both themselves and their parents. As G. R. Barlow put it, 'I suppose I am still in a period of transition from youth to manhood. I seem to have nothing stable on which to stand and no definite accomplishments for which to strive.'[169] Like Taylor, Barlow rejected the option of further service in the armed forces following the Armistice, opting instead for a guaranteed return to his pre-war job with the Post Office, thereby reinforcing the power of the identity of the civilian worker over that of the soldier.

The role of war in shaping men for the future was not, however, perceived as being entirely negative. Barlow, for one, viewed war as an experience that had shaped men into more active, involved members of society. 'I don't think that men will come back merely to look on,'[170] he told his aunt, although in a later letter he expressed a more pessimistic view, wondering if:

> we [have] learnt, as People, the great lessons for War? Do we now regard service and sacrifice as the ideal things of Life instead of personal benefits and profit? It seems too optimistic to hope that four or five years of War will teach us the truths which could not be impressed on our collective conscious by two thousand years of Peace.[171]

E. F. Chapman was more optimistic, arguing that:

> life can never be the same again as it was before August 4th 1914. But I think it will be better after the war than it ever was before. We must have learned a wisdom that nothing else could have taught us. And when we get home again we shall have the happiness of men who have seen terrible things, who have been to hell, and have come back to a blessed haven of peace. Different from the old careless happiness, but more permanent.[172]

The war was for Chapman, and many others, a force that, for all its horror, danger and uncertainty, had shaped both the society and individual men who had experienced it in positive ways.

C. S. Rawlins

One man who was undoubtedly changed by the war was Lt C. S. Rawlins (Figure 1). Having initially enlisted with the Staffordshire Territorials, with whom he served as a dispatch rider, he was sent to France in June 1915 with the 1st Battalion Welsh Regiment as a transport officer where he served at the Battle of Loos. In October of that year his regiment was transferred to Salonika but during the journey Rawlins fractured his skull by hitting a bridge while travelling on the top of a train. The injury caused him to be discharged as unfit and was to affect him all his life, although he 'bravely carried on an active and interesting life.'[173]

During his five months of active service, Rawlins wrote home to his parents on a weekly basis, alternating between his father and mother as addressees, with occasional letters to the family as a whole. The letters were long, containing a wealth of detailed observations about his experiences, as well as reflections on the nature and meaning of the war. Through them, Rawlins traced his development from an enthusiastic

Figure 1   C. S. Rawlins

patriot to an experienced soldier more willing to question the purpose of the war, although never his own reason for fighting, namely, the defence of his family.

Rawlins's enthusiasm for the experience of war is evident from his earliest letters. Even before embarking for France he wrote to his mother,

'It is a great & glorious thing to be going to fight for England in her hour
of desperate need', going on to specify, 'remember I am going to fight
for you, to keep you safe'.[174] A month and a half later, after arriving
in France, he wrote, 'I wouldn't miss this war for much gold: it is the
essence of adventure besides which all adventures either heard or read
about, pale into insignificance.'[175]

Such enthusiasm did not, however, prevent him from writing, often
in great detail, of the discomforts and dangers that he encountered. He
described a route march, for instance, where:

> the sun beats down pitilessly, the men have discarded their tunics
> and tucked their handkerchiefs under their hatbrims behind:...no
> one speaks, it is too hot: the sweat is dripping off my eyelashes, my
> clothes are drenched, my feet burn: the white dusty glaring road.[176]

On another occasion he noted, 'We had a violent thunder storm today &
everything is awash. I am writing with my feet in inches of water.'[177] As
with so many others, his letter provided a space for him to express his
fear of shellfire that he felt he could not expose before others:

> The road just there is rather bare of cover, but a little way along on
> the night was a large barn, shell holed: I would have given quids &
> quids just to run to that barn; but I am in front of my column, so
> I merely glance up in a casual way (what an effort!) as if I'd been
> weaned on shrapnel, whereas it's my baptism.[178]

Three days later, however, he was able to reassure his father that,
although:

> The big guns are roaring & thundering away up the line...it all comes
> natural now: my man told me this morning that there was a big duel
> during the night but I slept peacefully through it, even tho' my bed
> consists of six biscuit cases side by side & no padding on them.[179]

A month later, however, he commented to his mother, 'I have too vivid
an imagination for a soldier...it's so hard to keep one's mind off the
"feel" of bullets entering various parts of one's anatomy & things like
that',[180] and in September he admitted:

> I must be a bit of a coward myself after all, because I would give
> anything to be able to run or hurry along, anything but that slow

crawling walk: or I would like to get down in a ditch whenever the glaring star shell rises: I want to stop & hang my head & get down as low as possible. But one must stride along as nonchalantly as if out for a moonlight stroll at home![181]

Rawlins' fear of shellfire can thus seen to be regulated by the specific circumstances he found himself in. What remains consistent throughout the letters is both his need and ability to discuss these feelings of fear with his family, particularly his mother.

Shellfire, and the fear that is caused, were not the only potentially distressing elements in these letters. Death appeared, as in the bald statement, 'A few nights ago the enemy blew in a Sap and buried 17 men. 6 dead. My Company too.'[182] A letter to his mother during the Battle of Loos attempted to describe the experience:

I cannot write much: everything is chaos: riding, riding, all day, all night: for five days I have had no rest & snatched sleep where & when I could, anywhere: I am grimy & unshaven, plastered with mud.... All that has gone before is like a dream or a previous existence.[183]

It was in the wake of this experience that Rawlins appears to have reached his lowest ebb. 'I was sick at heart and broken in spirit after battle and could not think,' he wrote to his mother. 'I saw the faces and forms of my fallen comrades: how they looked: their jokes and last words only a few short hours before: I almost wished myself with them, out of it all...there was no good in the world: a world of death, and blood and filth unspeakable'. However, in the same letter he reaffirmed his willingness to carry on fighting 'only for your sake...England, and home, and you, and all things peaceful and beautiful, a dim remembrance of a long past existence.'[184]

As this final comment indicates, Rawlins's on-going relationship with home was of vital importance to the development of his identity as a soldier. Despite assuring his father, 'One does not often think about [home]; one is too busy & warfare hardens a man',[185] home clearly remained as vital to his morale as that of the men he observed who 'rip open the envelopes [from home] and gloat over the contents, puzzling out the words, then you hear them telling their mates – "Little Joe's started school", "Our Jinny got married last week to that chap...".'[186] This is clear from his use of metaphors in his description of shellfire. The sound of a Howitzer, for instance, was described as so familiar 'that one takes no more notice than you would of a train passing at home.'[187]

Less reassuring was his description of being shelled by Germans: 'about a dozen have dropped in the next field, about as far from me as Paradise Row is from our dining room window.' He went on to note, however, 'I think no more of it than I would a load of coal being tipped in the back lane!'[188] These details would have both aided his family, familiar with Paradise Row and the sound of coal being tipped, in understanding his experience and also indicate Rawlins's continued mental attachment to life at home.

Rawlins's on-going association with his domestic identity can also be seen in the more direct references he made to home life, both that of the past and of the present. The music of a band playing at a York-shire Light Infantry camp 'carries my thoughts (as a band always does) away back to the Golden Age of peace, garden parties, fetes and yeomanry sports day last year at Patshull. Dear little mother, won't we have a good time when I get home?'[189] He retained an interest in domestic affairs, commenting on the reported departure of a maid, 'I...was so sorry to hear of our Nellie having to leave...I shall miss her: I have a great affection for Nellie, I think she is the nicest and best girl we have ever had, or ever will have.'[190] He also kept abreast with his father's business interests, commenting, 'Your letters are very interesting and I am so pleased that everything at the works is going well.'[191] This interest was understandable as Rawlins clearly intended to return to working in the family business after the war, promising to 'return again to take a load off your shoulders.'[192] His role as a soldier was presented in his letters as a temporary one to be set aside in favour of his civilian identity at the war's end.

What is also clear from these letters, however, is that the two identities, the martial and the domestic, were in no way mutually exclusive. Just as R. C. Trench's letters combined his concerns as a husband and an officer, so Rawlins's letters also combined domestic concerns with military ones. 'We shall have to make tremendous money sacrifices soon,' he noted, going on to suggest that his father 'utilise my little bit of money in Lloyd's on the business, perhaps this will enable you to invest in the War Loan which it is everybody's duty to do as amply as possible.'[193] Concerns about domestic financial stability thus merged with those over the financial situation of the nation at war. A similar merging can be seen in Rawlins's concerns over war losses:

> Our best and fittest men are daily being killed & wounded: all our best blood is going to waste, & our race is bound to suffer terrible

depreciation in consequence & we ought to do all in our power to lessen this for the sake of our country's future . . . . every single man will have to marry 'after the war'.[194]

It is unclear how much Rawlins applied this prescription to his own case, but his casting of the problem of manpower in terms of marriage and fatherhood exposes the extent to which the domestic and the military were merged in his view of the world.

This merging of domestic and military concerns in his letters to his family goes some way to explaining Rawlins's continued willingness to fight, even at the bleakest moments of his service when he wrote that the war was 'God's judgement upon the world for our complex and vicious civilisation, and yet it is hard to see how to kill the best men in Europe is going to mend matters: all the degenerates, all the criminals are left.'[195] In the same letter he told his mother, 'I do not care for myself so much, only for your sake: we all have our work to do, & we will do it, & I must run the same risks as my comrades.'[196] His gratitude to his parents for 'the good life I have had; all thanks to you and Goss',[197] his identification with the work of the family firm, his concerns over the details of his family's domestic life, all clearly give a sense of purpose to his experience of war. By the time of his injury, Rawlins's understanding of war was more complex than seeing it as a great adventure, as he had initially, but his role as a soldier retained its meaning. If anything, his reasons for fighting, namely, the defence of a specific and personal home, had been reaffirmed. As he wrote to his mother in his final letter, 'I almost wished myself out of it all: only for your sake . . . you, and all things peaceful and beautiful, a dim remembrance of a long past existence.'[198] For Rawlins, being a soldier meant being a domestic man first.

Conclusion

Letters to and from the home front were a vital aspect of British servicemen's war experience. For an army recruited from the civilian population, letters home provided not only a boost to morale but also a crucial link to the identities they had left behind upon enlistment. In such letters, men found spaces in which they could present themselves to their families not only as soldiers, through their descriptions of war experiences, but also as domestic men through their continuing involvement with domestic concerns.

The image of the soldier that they construct within letters reflects this duality. At once detailed and reassuring, letters home could contain a surprising amount of information about the conditions in which men found themselves and their reactions to the experiences they were living through. Enthusiasm for the experience of war, and the belief that such experiences were helping to transform them into healthy, broad-minded men were themes of many letters. At the same time, letters home were also spaces in which men could expose their physical and emotional frailty, and potential inability to live up to the social standards of the heroic male.

If letters home were spaces in which men both presented and interrogated their claims to heroic masculinity, they were equally spaces in which they continued to assert their claims to domesticity. By using the language of home to describe their living conditions and the experiences they were undergoing, men sought to forge connections of familiarity with their audience. At the same time, they highlighted both the ways in which their experiences of war reflected on their domesticity and in which their domestic identities influenced the way they waged war. Above all, they placed the home and its protection at the centre of their justifications of warfare, making domesticity a central element of their developing heroic identities.

In letters home the domestic and the heroic facets of ideal masculinity often converged, reflecting the importance of both the intended audience and the subject matter. Yet despite the detail and honesty of many of the letters, there was much about the experience of war that men did not include. These aspects of the war, the points at which not only the heroic and domestic diverged, but the ideal of the heroic diverged from the reality of warfare, were the subjects of men's wartime diaries, the documents examined in the next chapter.

2
Wartime Diaries

While letters home were some of the most common written narratives produced by British soldiers, they were by no means the only form. Men also found expression for their experiences through poems, short stories, cartoons and articles some of which were published in the press, other of which found their way into the numerous trench journals that circulated throughout the armed forces.[1] These forms of written expression covered a similar range of emotions and attitudes towards the war as letters home, from idealistic enthusiasm through disillusioned grousing at the dangers and discomforts of warfare to the angry satire of poets such as Siegfried Sassoon.

The publication of such narratives had a number of purposes, depending on the audience they were intended for. The short stories written by 'Sapper', a Regular officer, published in *The Daily Mail* and *Blackwood's Magazine*, were intended to amuse, hearten and, above all, inform the civilian population through tales of life at the front.[2] The satirical and potentially insubordinate submissions to trench journals, by contrast, were aimed at an audience of servicemen for whom they served as a safety valve for discontents, allowing soldiers to criticize authority without imperilling military discipline.[3] All, however, circulated in public domains and were thus limited in their range of expression by the expectations of their intended audience, just as men were restrained in writing letters home by the need to protect their family or their own inarticulacy.

Men did, however, have another form of written narrative that they could turn to as an outlet, the personal diary. Such records were not forbidden under military regulations, although they were classified as 'personal documents' and, if sent through the military postal service, as some were,[4] could be subject to censorship. Like letters home they were not supposed to contain any information referring:

> to the place from which they were written and despatched; to plans of future operations, whether rumoured, surmised or known; to orga- nization, numbers and movements of troops; the armaments of ships or fortresses; to defensive works; the moral or physical condition of the troops; to casualties previous to the publication of official lists; to the service of maintenance; or in case the writer is one of the garrison of besieged fortress, to the effects of hostile fire.[5]

Nonetheless, men who kept diaries were able to record a great deal of information and express their opinions about the war, its conduct and the nature of their comrades and superiors.

In comparison to the number of men who wrote home, those who kept personal diaries form a much smaller group. This was not only because the ideal of a reflective life was predominantly a middle-class one, meaning that the group who kept diaries was far more self-selecting than those who wrote letters home. The number who did so was also affected by the ease with which regular records could be kept and the survival of such records over long periods of time. The number of diaries kept may have been far larger than the number that have survived, with many disappearing, along with much else, during attacks and retreats, the disorganization of troop movements, or due to the death of diarists whose belongings were lost with the man. Of those that do survive, a large percentage were written by officers who were in relatively reserved positions. A particularly large number were written by medical officers, while others were kept by those with Staff positions or attached to trans- port. Such men were more likely to have the time and relative comfort in which to reflect on and record their experiences, although there are also examples of diaries kept by ordinary soldiers of the line.

As records of war experience, personal diaries share many similarities with letters home. They attempt to record the experiences that men lived through, from day-to-day occupations of cooking and cleaning through the discomforts of bad weather to the horrors of shelling and the experience of battle. Two significant differences are evident, how- ever. The first is how rarely home appears in these documents, with the exception of the occasional note referring to the arrival of letters. Even then, the contents of the letters are rarely noted or discussed in the diaries. Unlike letters home, in which men strove to form a link between their domestic and martial identities, diaries form a record of predominantly military experience, domestic concerns going, for the most part, unrecorded. In diaries, men's constructions of their martial identities are dominant, with narratives focussing on qualities of heroic masculinity, including endurance and adaptability.

The second significant difference between the two forms of narrative is the level of complaint and disappointment found in the diaries. Discomfort, fear, illness and horror appear far more regularly in these documents than in letters home, often without the comforting reassurances that men attached when writing to their families. If letters formed a space in which men attempted to comprehend their experiences of war in terms of their civilian lives, diaries formed an outlet for them to come to terms with the strangeness and horror of those experiences compared with their expectations both of military life and of themselves as soldiers. They were spaces in which men could admit to behaving fearfully or weakly, could grouse about bad weather, poor living conditions and boring food, and criticize the progress of the war from their personal perspective. Diaries thus expressed the ways in which men constructed martial identities, separate from their domestic identities, that differed significantly from cultural ideals of the soldier as courageous, enthusiastic and resourceful.

Discomfort

The primary purpose of most wartime diaries appear to have been to record the facts of day-to-day life as a soldier, including the conditions that they lived in and the dangers that they faced. The weather, trench condition and cleanliness all formed regular topics in diaries, both as vivid descriptions and as the subject of that endless activity of the soldier, grousing. Such grousing often represented reactions to the particular circumstances that individual diarists found themselves in. G. W. Broadhead commented at one point, with regards to a particular set of trenches that he was 'about fed up with seeing these death traps.' Later, a period of rainy weather prompted him to write, 'I am heartily fed up of this war.'[6]

One of the most common conditions noted and discussed by diarists was the weather. Almost all diarists recorded the weather conditions on a regular basis, often reflecting on its relationship to their attitude towards the war. Fine weather could create good moods, but it was bad weather and its attendant miseries that caused the most comment in diaries. H. J. Hayward, for instance, noted on 30 January 1918, 'Very cold and fed up.'[7] O. P. Taylor recorded how, in the winter of 1917–18:

washing & shaving [were] an awful job, and there was nothing but
icy water. My fingers were so cold, I could hardly hold the razor. The
mud outside is appalling. We had only been here an hour or so, when
a man's boot was sucked right off his feet and we had to dig for it.
One is constantly up to the calves in thick slimy ooze.[8]

Even lack of danger could not necessarily compensate for the discomforts caused by cold. 'Quiet trench,' F. S. Collings noted of one posting,
'but rotten, chilly all night.'[9]

Of all the weather conditions that men complained of in their diaries,
the most prevalent was rain and, by extension, the mud it created.[10]
'Very bad day Raining continually all day Trenches 1 ft deep in Mud,'
recorded A. Beevers on 22 July 1915.[11] Broadhead connected the weather
to morale with the comment, 'More rain & therefore more misery',[12]
while J. C. Tait noted in April 1916 that it had been 'Raining every day
since we have been in the trenches. Mud worse than ever in this part.
We stand in the open trench all night. Everyone is so miserable.'[13] As
these entries indicate, rain's demoralizing power derived as much from
its effect on trench conditions as the dampness it created in the men
themselves. Broadhead found the 'trenches in a rotten condition' after a
day of hard rain. He complained of having to dig 'in support trenches all
day and wet through again . . . . it was up to the knees in some places in
water. Fell in it twice.'[14] F. P. J. Glover also found his sector 'in a ghastly
state. Water and mud over one's knees, and there is every prospect of
more rain,'[15] while May feared that 'our next tour will be a thing to
remember', given that 'parts of the trenches are now waist deep in water.
No pumps can keep pace with a [rain] fall of this rate.'[16] Indeed, some
of the trenches were so bad that, as J. H. Mahon reported:

the men had to work from morning till night to keep the trenches
in a state fit to occupy. Many places were nearly up to the middle &
these parts had to be pumped out each day. Dugouts leaked & fell
in & the sides of most of the main trenches caved in a made things
worse. Oh yes! we had mud all right.[17]

Part of the problem with mud was that it was extremely difficult to
walk through, as Mahon noted after having to 'wade through mud &
water, in many places up to the knees . . . . I had the pleasure of carrying nearly half the way, pick-a-back, a young fellow shot through the
knee, who the stretcher bearers found it impossible to convey on the
stretcher, owing to the turns and the mud.'[18] May commented that 'No
one who has not experienced it can realise what a fatiguing business

movement under such conditions is.... One's progress is a laboured wallow through a shifting quag.' Such conditions, as he noted on an earlier occasion, were 'all dirty and strenuous like the war one reads about but seldom sees.'[19]

Nor was mud the only factor that caused men to complain of the condition of trenches. Collings pointed out that there were 'water-rats galore, rather uncanny dead men etc.'[20] The cramped nature of living conditions was also a common cause of comment. K. H. Young described one dugout as 'a hellish place 3 ft high with five men crowded at the bottom & quite six on each of the stairs.'[21] A later billet proved slightly more satisfactory, despite being described as a:

> very poor dugout, four men all sleeping on stairs as the bottom is too foul for human habitation. Very [illegible] smell but one soon gets used to it, you can almost cut the atmosphere with a knife but I can now sleep anywhere & under any conditions as long as I have the time so pass [illegible] restful night.[22]

Young was not alone in his complaints. H. Wilson described a dugout in some support trenches which 'held 20 men & was only big enough for about 12.'[23] A. Anderson described how:

> Three of us managed to crush into the small recess and find the atmosphere pretty thick, whilst six men are huddled together on the floor of the dug-out itself and another three find accommodation on the steps. I will certainly try to pinch a place on the steps next time, as it will be a bit easier to breathe there.[24]

Nonetheless, men were able to find some comfort in their living quarters. As R. W. Wilson commented of one shelter, it was 'Some ordeal to be cooped up in there any length of time, but a grand shelter from the terrors of the night and a useful shelter while working in this vicinity.'[25] Billets, however uncomfortable, were also a source of relief in comparison to the discomforts of marching. H. T. Clements, for instance, recorded marches undertaken while transferring from Ypres to the Somme as:

> the most awfull [sic] thing we have to undergo. At first everyone marches in fine style then gradually getting worse and worse until [sic] at last one looses [sic] all sense of time and is conscious of nothing but plod-plod. Heads hang down and all one sees are feet and

endless miles of road. The pack seems to weigh a ton and every limb aches. At last the billet is reached and then everyone flings themselves down for ten to twenty minutes.[26]

Glover recorded a similar trip out of the line which 'seemed endless and when we eventually left the trench on the far side the track along which we plodded was in an awful state. We eventually reached camp thoroughly exhausted had breakfast and then – BED.'[27]

Marching was not the only source of exhaustion men complained of in their diaries. R. W. Wilson wrote of one particular period in 1918 when 'There has been great scarcity of water through frost, the dug out is very "lousy", and continual attention to shirts necessary to deep these filthy pests under [*sic*]. Nights rendered sleepless from this cause.'[28] This particular discomfort was one that men described in their diaries but which was seldom written about in letters home, although it was as universally experienced by soldiers as mud. As H. Wilson commented, 'It is impossible to go for more than a few weeks without becoming full of vermin. Like lots of other things this is distinctly unpleasant, but can be got used to in time.'[29] C. C. May, however, claimed that 'If cleanliness is next to Godliness, I think lousiness is next to Hell.'[30] Most diaries deal with the particular discomforts of dirtiness and lousiness matter-of-factly, but it is noticeable that men appear able to discuss the subject of personal cleanliness and the uncomfortable results of its lack only in their most personal and private documents. Diaries were spaces in which issues of bodily discomfort could be discussed with propriety, discussions which served to construct the diarists as physical beings in ways that they were unable to be in other forms of written narratives.[31]

The complaints that men made in their diaries about discomfort were usually specific, concerning immediate circumstances rather than wider political criticisms of the conduct of the war as a whole. Thus K. C. Leslie felt disappointment about reverses at Ypres in 1915, because it meant that 'we should not be able to go down to the house for our rest.'[32] Tait complained about being forced to parade for fatigues on a 'miserable night, – result tired out. Parading for kit bags is practically unnecessary tonight and I think it ridiculous, to say nothing of disheartening.'[33] He was even more annoyed when he found himself forced to undertake the 'unwelcome task of cleaning buttons and equipment. What an absurd idea for active service! Why, the Battn. did not do this even in England! Our officers are very erratic and everything will have to alter before we are under fire.'[34] K. H. Young was similarly irritated by the rigorous daily routine of repairing trenches that he felt did not need it. 'The folly of this,' he wrote:

is that there is no necessity & it results in just messing about & nothing being done with any enthusiasm, more would be done if each man worked in a shift of 6 or 8 hrs besides there is the strain of being under shell fire & again all to no purpose. Some one must be mad! Do they want to wear us out now! We have to obey orders but all is done in a half hearted manner.[35]

For R. B. Wilkinson, it was the failure to learn tactical lessons that prompted him to describe the first day of the Battle of the Somme as 'Another awful blunder of the Staff in sending men across open country to face machine gun fire.'[36] Diaries served as spaces in which men could reflect the negative aspects of their war experiences but usually from a limited, personal and often physical perspective.

In voicing such complaints and criticisms, even in the privacy of diaries, diarists were staking a claim as individual actors within the depersonalizing context of military service. As Gary Sheffield notes, 'Even after being socialised into military life, working-class temporary soldiers did not abandon civilian patterns of behaviour or thought, and were liable to react to what they perceived as unfair treatment by their military superiors by going on strike.'[37] Where they felt the social contract was being ignored by the authorities, middle-class citizen soldiers were equally willing to say so in no uncertain terms, often using their diaries as private spaces in which to express their irritation within the stupidities, discomforts and unnecessary dangers imposed upon them by life in the military.[38]

Fear

Using diaries as an outlet for frustrations with the discomforts of war was not, however, always sufficient, with many men using them as spaces to express a growing sense of fatalism. J. W. Barnett found himself 'indifferent whether am killed or not. Much safer up front lines & bullets are cleaner anyway.' Even death by shellfire appeared not to concern him too much, however, as on one occasion when he recorded hearing 'shells coming to dug outs. Put down pipe & prepared to die. Curious but when realised that end was inevitable had no fear.'[39] J. H. Fordham was more flippant in his attitude to being shelled by Turks: 'There are two wagon loads of explosive just behind us, if one of those Turk shells hit them, well, there is a happy land far, far away.' Rather more seriously he noted on 14 May 1915, 'I've reached my 24th Birthday, but I don't feel at all certain about my 25th.'[40]

Such fatalism is unsurprising given the ubiquity of shellfire, a subject that dominates diarists' narratives as much as those of letter writers. For some men, this ubiquity led to their records of shellfire taking on an almost casual tone. On 31 May 1916, G. W. Broadhead noted that 'Fritz spotted us coming in and shelled us all day so we had a pretty rotten time.'[41] H. J. Hayward experienced 'a terrific bombardment big guns awful row all night.'[42] M. W. Littlewood was equally casual about the bombs and shells that came over at night, merely noting, 'This is a very active life.'[43]

The reason for Littlewood's attitude, compared with that of Fordham, a Regular infantryman, may have derived from his ability, as an R.A.M.C. officer attached to a Field Ambulance, to treat the experience of bombardment as something observed as much as lived through. Seventeen months earlier, he had described a British artillery barrage which resulted in the 'Frightful destruction of OG1 & complete destruction of five trenches' as 'one of the sights of the war.'[44] C. K. McKerrow, also an officer in the R.A.M.C., wrote of how 'Red and green rockets went up continuously, and that, combined with the yellow burst of the shrapnel and the crash of big shells, made a fearful but fascinating spectacle.'[45] As in letters, such observations were often described using metaphors to reinforce a sense of familiarity. R. B. Wilkinson found that bombardment 'reminds one ludicrously of a 5th November night',[46] while J. C. Tait described a bombardment as 'an interesting sight. Like some great firework display.'[47] Observational language served to distance the observer and from the danger that these spectacles actually represented.

The distance from the danger of shellfire that such descriptions created allowed some men to narrate their experiences of shell and gunfire as impressive or uncomfortable but not necessarily frightening. Thus F. P. J. Glover noted of his first experience of a 'strafe', 'I was somewhat awed... [but] As soon as I realised how local it all was (a matter of experience) I could quite enjoy the spectacle.'[48] C. C. May was equally nonchalant about a strafe which he and his companion 'watched... with interest. It is remarkable what an impartial view one takes of such things out here. One is foolish enough not to think even of taking cover. Ram remarked, "Some 'strafe'. And they've such a nice day for it." Thereupon we continued fishing.'[49] Even for diarists who were working under bombardment rather than simply observing it, the experience could be treated casually. A close shave, such as having a building ten yards away hit by a shell, could be dismissed as a 'Loud noise, that was all.'[50] As in letters, this ability to endure shellfire through familiarity with it was seen as a skill worth recording.

Despite the insouciant responses to shellfire that a number of men recorded, for others the experience of shellfire provoked a very different and far more fearful reaction. For these men, diaries provided spaces in which to describe specific experiences of fear in great detail. J. C. Tait, for instance, wrote of one British bombardment:

> No one who has not been through such hell can possibly con-ceive any idea of its devastation. It was very hell upon earth. The shells screech overhead creating a weird sensation.... You hear an approaching shell screeching through the air. It comes overhead & then one calls up one's utmost nerve power to withstand the shock. There is a flash across the eye and then a deafening report followed by part of the parapet falling on top of one.[51]

Such descriptions not only give the specific details of the physical expe-rience of being under shellfire, but also of men's emotional reactions to it. Tait's comments that the bombardment was 'a hell on earth' gives some indication of the fear he felt, emotions which allowed him to 'pity the poor devils in the front line' even when only observing a bombard-ment as 'a pleasing spectacle.'[52] J. W. Barnett felt similar empathy for the fearful reactions of others noting that 'Men simply scream when the grenade comes in & I don't wonder poor devils.'[53] It is unsurpris-ing, therefore, to find that Barnett, on a later occasion, wrote of how he 'Could have cried when out of shell range.... Relief from tension indescribable.'[54]

Through such descriptions, diaries became spaces in which men could record those reactions to war experiences in which they displayed fear and weakness. H. T. Clements could write that when 'Suddenly Fritz began to send coal-box over,...I felt rather windy!... It was altogether one of the worst experiences I have ever had.'[55] M. W. Littlewood described HE shrapnel as 'Windy stuff',[56] while F. S. Collings found his 'nerves a little shaken'[57] following a bombardment. Even quiet periods could cause nervous responses. 'I certainly am now feeling a bit weak at the knees,' wrote A. Anderson on one occasion, going on to wonder, 'If this is a sample of "quietness", what is it going to be like when they get busy?'[58]

Fearful responses were recorded as being both physical and emotional. Anderson's response to the shelling of a road behind his position was to 'begin to feel like looking for a nice deep hole to get into'.[59] Little-wood, on being caught by some sudden shelling with 8" shells, 'got the wind up badly & grovelled. Raced back through a sort of barrage.... Altogether a most trying experience.'[60] J. H. Fordham and J. Colinsky both responded by running away. Fordham, a Regular soldier who had served in India and Ireland before the war, reported how he 'went to a well about 100 yds in rear just as I bent down to get the water a sniper knocked a piece out of the [illegible] about 6 inches above my head, I didn't wait for a second one',[61] while Colinsky noted that, when ordered to leave one heavily shelled position, 'Could not see me for dust down the road.'[62] Colinsky was particularly explicit about the fears that shellfire engendered in him. His reactions to various experiences included 'feeling unimaginable', 'worst 10 mins. of life', 'made me shake' and 'wind up.'[63] On one occasion he even recorded that he 'Cried like a baby', although this was probably in response to the tear gas that had been released as much as in reaction to the fear of the 446 tonnes of explosive sent over by the Germans which made Colinsky feel that the 'Earth had come to an end.'[64]

Unsurprisingly, men recorded feeling fear most often in the days or hours preceding a major offensive. On the eve of the first day of the Battle of the Somme, Clements noted:

> We were all anxious for none of us want to go west and we all expect to have the wind up but we are afraid of being afraid. This was the worst part, every few minutes seemed an hour – all thinking of the past – what was the future to bring – death or blighty?[65]

This fear of seeming afraid appears in other diaries. McKerrow boasted that, during one walk with his commanding officer, he 'was not particularly happy, as the shells flew round, but did not shew it',[66] while J. W. Barnett recorded one incident when a bullet hit 'the ground between my feet & caused me to give a smothered gasp of fright. Had to stand behind tree to recover equilibrium as found I was getting rather confused with a tendency to bolt. Forced myself on.'[67] R. W. Wilson also forced himself to hide his fear, noting that he 'Felt nervous at being in open at first, but soon realised it had to be faced. (Started saying now "Be strong and of good courage" and then leaving at that).'[68] This desire to appear unafraid exposes the pressures that men felt under to conform to a particular ideal of soldierly behaviour.[69] While they were clearly proud of their ability to face the terrors of shellfire, men needed diaries as spaces to record their potential failures of courage as a comparison to emphasize their ultimate success in conquering fear.

Horror

Diaries not only provided spaces in which men could express the fear that experiences of warfare induced; they were also spaces in which they could write about the horrors of war. Death and injury appear in diaries far more often than in letters home, and in greater detail. Some descriptions were of the already dead, as in J. H. Fordham's description of one trench as 'a perfect cemetery every few yds either a pair of boots, the remains of hands or a skull...showing',[70] while J. W. Barnett noted an occasion when he 'saw a sepoy sitting on a dead German & eating food his ration tin resting on the dead man's back.'[71]

More common than observations of the already dead, however, were the records that diarists made of men being killed. McKerrow observed an advance on Vimy Ridge where 'One shell landed in a party of about 12 and only 3 were left.'[72] He had a later contact with death from shellfire when, during the Battle of the Somme he recorded how 'One man [was] killed next to me and another (Webster) badly wounded.'[73] Anderson observed death at similar proximity: 'A shell burst with a terrific din in the next bay and two of our men are blown to pieces. We, in our bay, pick ourselves up, and wipe the earth off our faces.'[74] Nor could death be escaped behind the lines. M. W. Littlewood was '2 feet away from a policeman [when] he was hit by AA shrapnel far behind the line. Really in the midst of life we are in death!'[75]

The wounded appear in diaries almost as often as the dead. Tait, for instance, described the aftermath of one bombardment in great detail including both:

> Dead and wounded...strewn everywhere. Their front line is blown to hell. Some wounded were being carried out – some on stretchers, others struggling along with the help of a comrade. Very few stretchers were available. The dead are thrown aside until the wounded are all away. It was a veritable nightmare.[76]

Barnett's experience of the aftermath of a shell explosion was similar:

> Hear screams...Gunner with both legs shattered to pieces lying. Dragged into Cellar to dress. Shall not forget that night. Cellar packed with gravefaced Tommies. Candledip & man with hideously smashed

legs – crying for chloroform. Gave it in end & sent off on door to hospital. Other man with shell piece in lung coughing life out on my blankets.[77]

For J. H. Mahon the aftermath of an attack on Festubert was also considered memorable enough to record in his diary, although he found it less easy to describe what he saw:

A very sad sight five minutes after the first lot went over, wounded men coming back by the dozen, full of grit most of them, but many dazed and wounded so badly that they cared for little but to be carried back. I care not to recall individual cases in writing, they are to be seen but one cannot read about them.[78]

Mourning

As in letters home, men struggled with their own inarticulateness to convey the strangeness of what they were witnessing in writing. Yet, the attempt clearly needed to be made by these men to record the physical cost of the war to men's bodies and minds. Diaries not only provided space to write about death and injury in terms of the observed horrors of war, however; they were also places in which deaths were recorded as a ritual of mourning. Some diarists simply kept lists of those in their unit or mess who had died. Others went into great detail, including observations about the manner of the death or the character of the man. Tait recorded how, on entering the trenches for the first time, 'we see Wells of C coy being carried out dead, (our second casualty). This upsets us a great deal, as he is a terrible sight.'[79] McKerrow similarly noted the death of Wilson, a fellow medical officer, as 'First to go of our lot.' Bott, a later casualty, was remembered because he 'came to me complaining of nerves' two days before his death, while Botham, who died of wounds, was mentioned as a 'Lesson to judge gently of one's fellow man. Band and I were crabbing him only yesterday.'[80]

Others were more valedictory in their recording of the deaths of comrades. Collings recorded news of the death of a former commanding officer with the comment, 'A good soldier and a true friend and gentleman.'[81] Mahon commemorated Drake, who he had nursed when injured, as 'a man every inch of him...he died well, although close to our parapet, bravely leading his boys.'[82] McKerrow, too, could be moved to praise the dead. After the death of his friend Joicey he wrote, 'What an

unnecessary waste of a good life. Made one feel quite sick.'[83] In recording their emotions about the death of a comrade, diarists helped to
reconstruct the dead as men with identities that encompassed comradeship and courage, as well as the fact of the physical destruction of their
bodies. The dead thus retained in memory the status of men.

The sight of so much injury and death could make men's records of
mourning appear perfunctory. Barnett, for instance, recorded the death
of McKay, a sapper, with a note that he 'Had to take over his kit & all
his girl's letters stained with blood. Very sad – but there seems no time
for regrets. One forgets at once.'[84] Following the death of a friend ten
days later he wrote, 'Had pheasant for dinner – it was good but it stuck
in my throat at times – But must steel ones heart to this – many times
will it happen.'[85] McKerrow tried to be similarly philosophical about
the death of a French airman: 'There was the same feeling when one
saw him as there is in looking at a pheasant or a grouse one has shot.
A pathetic remorse. However, it is war and someone has to die some
day.'[86] It was this sort of reaction to death that prompted R. B. Wilkinson
to observe:

> Men die and pass into the great unknown yet others live and eat
> and drink. Human nature is very forgetful. There is something about
> some men which cannot be defined. I speak of those who have lived
> and fought in the trenches. It is a sort of subdued preparedness. One
> cannot call it callousness or even indifference – they are too seri-
> ous for that. Men who wrestle constantly with death become more
> silent. Yet there is no doubt that war coarsens and brutalises the finest
> natures.[87]

Yet, men were moved enough by individual deaths to record them, mir-
roring the need to name the dead that was so central to First World War
memorials.[88]

Brutalization was, therefore, not universal. Many were not able to forget the dead. Collings, for instance, was buried alive by the same shell
that killed his brother Sid. Although, after being dug out, he wrote in his
diary that he took the news of Sid's death 'like a soldier',[89] in 1917, when
copying out his diary after being discharged wounded, he added that:

> the memory of it all is deep printed on my memory especially 30
> September 1915 when I parted for a while from my beloved brother.
> He was a true soldier a christian [*sic*] and highly esteemed by all
> who knew him. To me he will always be 21 yrs. and cut off for the

purpose of stamping the hand of militarism and lifting this World nearer Peace and Love.[90]

It was mass deaths, however, that appear to have had the greatest emotional impact. C. C. May 'saw the killed go down the line. It was a pitiful sight. Poor English soldiers battered to pieces.'[91] For Barnett, it was not the sight of the dead but the size of the losses that affected him 'like a shock waking up'.[92] Even the efficient replacement of forces could not stem the sense of loss. According to May, 'there are so many new faces with us now and so many old ones missing that the battalion hardly seems the same – an one cannot let oneself go with the new like one loves to with the old boys.'[93] May thus used his diary as a site of memory in which to mourn the dead of the 22nd Battalion of the Manchester Regiment in which he served as a captain throughout the war.

Enthusiasm and pleasure

Despite descriptions of fear and horror and expressions of mourning, servicemen's diaries are not unremittingly bleak records. Fine weather, with its attendant effect on morale, was recorded alongside bad weather, good food and regular mail deliveries were noted and celebrated. Entertainments such as pierrot troupes were appreciated and described, sometimes in great detail.[94] There were also expressions of genuine enthusiasm for war as an adventure and unique experience. These tend to occur early in the diaries. During training, for instance, C. C. May observed that if you 'Promise... [the men] a regular hell of a time in France and you can't please them better. Their keenness to go is marvellous and I trust will hold when they get there.'[95] For some, such as H. T. Clements, any overseas service was viewed enthusiastically. When 'Captain Scott turned up at 11 and asked if we would go to garrison Gib. Malta or Egypt: We all volunteered. We returned along the line singing and shouting enough to wake the dead and we were almost too excited to sleep,' he recorded on 29 August 1914.[96] For others, enthusiasm was expressed at the prospect of seeing action. A. E. Bundy, serving in Salonika in 1918, requested a transfer up the line because he was:

getting tired of the humdrum monotony of life here. Had a talk with the C. O.... He was not at all pleased and after expressing the view that I was doing invaluable work plainly told me that he would refuse to let me go. I was disappointed but not shaken in my determination to get away as soon as possible.[97]

This enthusiasm for direct experience of warfare often persisted as men prepared to enter the trenches. Clements wrote that, during the march towards the trenches, 'the nearer we reached the firing line, the higher our spirits rose.'[98] Such enthusiasm reflected a desire for the new experiences that war offered civilian soldiers and for the action in that men associated with adventure. J. H. Fordham's first entry in his diary expressed the wish that 'In future I hope to record something more exciting',[99] while C. K. McKerrow wrote, following one attack, 'This is a great adventure and the Fates are, no doubt counting the slain. May I have courage and gaiety and the quiet mind.'[100] For K. H. Young, observing a bombardment of the enemy, it was 'good to be here to witness these sights.'[101] This view of the war as a unique adventure that it was exciting and desirable to experience can even be seen in the efforts made by men such as H. J. Hayward to experience technological developments first hand. On 23 May 1918 Hayward recorded that he 'Had a ride on a tank; unique experience, "took" a tree; some bump!'[102]

Men's enthusiasm was not simply for the experience of war as a whole but specifically for the experience of action in warfare through which their soldiering might be defined as heroic. Waiting was thus portrayed as a considerable source of tension for many. C. C. May noted three days before the beginning of the Somme, 'we're all ready and anxious to get away, to get up and moving and done with waiting. Waiting is rotten. I think it tries the nerve more than the actual moment of assault.'[103] R. W. Wilson similarly found his trips up the line as a pioneer with the Royal Engineers were nerve-wracking: 'Each evening feel very nervous before and on way up, but on the scene of action manage to recover mental balance. The anticipation seems the worst of it.'[104] For Anderson, waiting for a trench raid to take place had a similar effect, causing him to write, 'I believe that all of us would be willing to go over any time and get it finished with',[105] while McKerrow, on hearing that 'a biff is coming off,' commented, 'Hope we are in it. This sitting down becomes tedious.'[106] The static nature of trench warfare was portrayed in diaries as both frightening and frustrating, with the active aspects of soldiering, for all their potential danger, appearing much more desirable.

Praise

Despite the fears and frustrations that much of the experience of trench warfare engendered, men found satisfaction in their ability to withstand the horrors of war. As C. C. May noted:

The war is a war of endurance, of human bodies against machines and against the elements. It is an unlovely war in detail yet there is something grand and inspiring about it. I think it is the stolid, uncomplaining endurance of the men under the utter discomforts they are called upon to put up with, their sober pluck and quiet good-heartedness which contributes very largely to this.[107]

Such praise of the heroism of endurance, both observed and received, was a regular feature of soldiers' diaries, allowing them to offset records of the horrors and discomforts of war with a sense of pride in their achievements both as individuals and as part of a unit. Direct praise received from others was recorded by many diarists. This often took the form of formal congratulations from commanders, such as J. Colinsky's record on 7 August 1917 that 'Wireless Boys [were] Personally congratulated by Major Gen. Trenchard C/O R.F.C. on Western Front.'[108] F. P. J. Glover similarly copied out the official orders in which the work of the artillery at Passchendaele was praised as 'admirable and the Divisional Commander cannot too highly praise the courage and endurance of our gunners, who, in spite of heavy enemy shelling, never failed to support an attack or to respond to the frequent calls which were made on them.'[109]

Praise of others in diaries often came from officers in relation to their own men, allowing them to reflect their own ability to train men as successful soldiers. McKerrow recorded the fact that he congratulated the stretcher bearers attached to his field ambulance 'on fine work done [on the Somme] and said we must keep up the reputation of the Battalion.'[110] In the paternalistic regimental system that formed the structure of the British Army, commendable behaviour reflected well not only on the men observed but also on the commanding officer who was observing them.[111] The record that McKerrow made thus served as consolation and inspiration in face of the fears and horrors that both he and his men faced in war.

Similarly the ability to endure shellfire through familiarity with it, already noted in letters home, was also recorded in diaries. As McKerrow noted 'It is very strange how indifferent one becomes to shells.'[112] M. W. Littlewood was agreeably surprised to find that, upon emerging from some cellars during a bombardment, 'After a few seconds I did no feel acutely windy & in five minutes felt almost careless.'[113] H. Wilson found that 'My first feelings on going into a front line trench under fire, were not nearly so terrible as I imagined. Once the din is got used to one looks upon it as a kind of Brock's Benefit night.'[114] May felt that 'one never gets to like [war] or even to cease to regard it with interest' despite the fact that one becomes accustomed to the life, to expecting danger.[115] Men might use their diaries to describe their fear of shellfire, but they also used them to record the moments when they conquered that fear, indicating both the extent to which men's reactions varied according to the mood and conditions in which they found themselves and the importance of enduring danger to their construction of their soldierly identities.

Stoic endurance of shellfire was not, however, the only character-istic the praise of which men recorded in their diaries. Cheerfulness, especially under difficult conditions was similarly noted in terms of admiration. McKerrow commented in early July 1916 that he 'found our men playing football, as happy as Kings. They are wonderfully well considering everything. The British Tommy is magnificent.'[116] R. W. Wilson reported, on a night when shellfire kept everyone awake, that 'Boys [were] singing in spite of it all',[117] while May 'came upon poor Carr…lying on the floor of the trench with a bullet through his leg. He was quite cheerful and the other men calm. They had been out wiring and a sniper had hit Carr, but the others carried on.'[118] As he noted on an earlier occasion, 'It is marvellous that the men can raise a smile at all. Yet they can and do. They are always cheery.'[119]

Diarists provided a number of explanations for this cheerfulness. McKerrow felt, towards the end of the Somme offensive, that men were simply 'very pleased to be alive.'[120] May, however, felt that cheerful-ness had a broader application, arguing that 'A laugh here is of such value. Bland has come on so through that. He grins from morn to eve, swears he is enjoying himself top-hole and, I believe, really is. Good luck to him.'[121] J. C. Tait agreed, noting that 'we optimistic beg-gars find optimism brings us through.'[122] Cheerfulness thus allowed men to endure, proving themselves, in doing so, to be appropriately soldierly.

Adaptability was another quality that men recorded in their diaries as helping them to define themselves as soldiers through descriptions of how they adjusted to the physical discomforts of war. H. J. Hayward wrote of marching five miles despite feeling 'very fatigued & weak.'[123] Littlewood similarly 'Hung on' despite contracting Spanish 'flu.[124] As May noted in November 1915, 'Six months ago and half these fellows would have been half dead with less than half this dampness and now here we are as happy as Larry and busily preparing for sleep. And all because it is war!'[125] He felt that war 'teaches one how little a man can rub along on,' a lesson he clearly felt that many in the army could use:

> We all find amusement in the grouses and grumbles of those who still soldier at home. If they only knew it what a bed of roses they are on. They do not yet know that they're alive. There a man does an eight hour day, has eight hours sleep and eight hours to himself. And then he grouses! The poor fool. Here, in addition to being under fire all and every day, in the line and out, he does hard manual slogging for about 14 hours out of the 24 and averages about five hours sleep per diem. I am afraid there will be a bitter awakening for some of the lads at home. No, I am not afraid, I am glad. It will make men of them – or they will go under. And the sort that go under are better there.[126]

Physical adaptation to harsh conditions was thus, for May, a symbol of appropriate martial masculinity. Men who endured war had earned their right to grumble, as those who had not suffered war's hardships and adapted to them had not.

Such adaptability was practical as well as physical. As May noted:

> One thing … worthy of note is the way in which the men have come on in the way of making themselves comfortable. Mostly townbred, they were slow at first to see that a man can live in comparative comfort in the most unpromising circumstances but they learn with avidity and in another week or so the oldest campaigner will be able to tell them little indeed.[127]

Despite the complaints that they made about poor living conditions, men used their diaries to record their triumphs over such conditions. K. C. Leslie, for instance, recorded being 'Billeted in an [illegible] barn – 20 of us in a space for about 8 or 10 notwithstanding which we all adapted very well.'[128] H. T. Clements was more proactive in adapting the barn he found himself in, making a den with two comrades that included cupboards and shelves as well as pegs for their rifles.[129] F. P. J. Glover showed similar initiative and ingenuity in improving his bivouac: 'by making the sides corrugated iron we thus had tremendously increased the floor space'.[130] These descriptions are less elaborate than the reassuringly domestic ones that men included in their letters home. Their inclusion in the more private space of diaries, however, indicates the importance that men placed on their ability to create comfortable living conditions for themselves in recording their lives as soldiers.

As important as home-building to men's identities as constructed in their diaries was the emphasis that men placed on cleanliness in order to combat the morale-sapping effects of mud and lice. Opportunities to bathe were hailed in diaries as red letter days. 'Paul's birthday was made notable by the fact that we had hot baths and a change of clothing,' Clements reported. 'This is the first since Feby 7!!! But we have managed to wash ourselves all over in cold water from a biscuit tin.'[131] The use of cold water and unusual methods for washing were both themes. A. Anderson found that 'the morning shave can be accomplished fairly comfortably with hot coffee although it takes a fair amount of work to get a decent lather.'[132] By recording the efforts they made to wash and shave, men indicated the extent to which the civilian symbols of masculinity, such as cleanliness and being clean-shaven, continued to influence their behaviour under wartime conditions.[133]

Food

One interest that matched, if it did not exceed, men's preoccupation with cleanliness was that which they took in food.[134] In many ways, attitudes to food can be read as microcosms of men's varying responses to the exigencies of war. Food was a boost to men's morale when in plentiful supply. Broadhead, for instance, felt 'perfectly satisfied' with life having 'Had a good feed.'[135] Littlewood noted 'the joy of a whisky and soda and ham sandwiches and a flea bag once more.'[136] Clements was moved to record the discovery of 'a large piece of cheese wrapped in a dirty sack ... Although muddy it was very good.'[137] Drink was also good for morale. R. W. Wilson found himself 'Very done up' one November night 'but bucked-up by rum issue'.[138]

By contrast, lack of food and drink caused men to grouse to their diaries as Anderson did on more than one occasion. While still in training, he noted that:

> What seems to be on everyone's mind ... is the food which, although plentiful enough, is of doubtful quality and atrociously cooked. It becomes, obvious, at any rate, that the term 'regimental mess' is peculiarly appropriate and is administered as a preliminary to the general hardening process which we discover is evidently to be applied internally as well as externally.[139]

Rather more soberly, he later reported that:

> Rations are none too plentiful these days and water is especially
> scarce, which is rather ironical considering that we are wading in it
> all the time.... There is no fresh food whatever and we have to sub-
> sist solely on tinned rations and hard biscuits. The latter can only be
> consumed after having been soaked in water.[140]

Such difficulties, however, forced men to adapt. Faced with a lack of
water on a winter march, Clements and his unit 'At each halt...sat in
the snow and ate it.'[141] Anderson described how 'those of us not fortunate enough to possess a Primus cooker light small fires of wood chips,
and contrive to do the best we can'.[142]

The best could be quite good, a fact that men were quick to point out.
R. W. Wilson, for instance, recorded a 'famous supper of Welsh Rarebit
and pickles',[143] while Littlewood boasted of making 'a wonderful potato
salad, pronounced very fine by the gourmand'.[144] Even McKerrow discovered that 'with my mess tin I can manage to make sundry savoury
messes.'[145] These comments and boasts were brief remarks in comparison with the more elaborate descriptions of domestic creativity
seen in letters written home. Nonetheless, by including such details in
their diaries, men were constructing themselves in these more private
documents as capable men, able to adapt to harsh physical circumstances, although they also used the space to complain about just how
uncomfortable these circumstances were.

Resignation

The tone of the diaries can thus be seen to be one of resignation rather
than outright disillusion. McKerrow, for instance, when informed that
his leave had been cancelled, shortly after receiving a letter from his
wife celebrating the news of his upcoming leave, wrote, 'It is annoying
but one must accept Fortuna Belli. After all is not the R.A.M.C. motto
"In Arduis Fidelis"?'[146] J. H. Fordham noted receiving orders to stand to
one night with the wry comment, 'No rest for the wicked.'[147] The war
as a whole was viewed as an unpleasant job that had to be done. As
McKerrow put it: 'One must...push on.'[148]

Such an attitude did not, as diarists noted, define men as heroic.
'One is supposed to have, as a soldier going into action,' C. C. May
commented:

no other desire than some high-souled ambition to do or die for one's country. Reality I am afraid falls far short. We go because it is right and proper that we should. But I do not think there is one high-souled amongst us. On the contrary we are all rather bored with the job, the thought of the bally mud and water is quite sufficient to extinguish keenness, and we are all so painfully ordinary that we think of leave a great deal more than we do of the nobleness of our present calling. When one is tired and unwashed I think one is legitimately entitled to refuse to feel noble, if one so desires.[149]

It was this attitude, however, that defined men as soldiers and, therefore, as men. 'It was a perfect morning,' McKerrow wrote on 10 November 1916:

Rosy red, changing through every shade of pink and green to fine amethyst. Looking from St. Peter's trench towards the East, it seemed vain and foolish to sit in trenches and try to kill each other. Only, behind it all, one felt the urgent demand for man to make the most of his circumstances, for these circumstances are but the screen on which the life of the spirit moves like a shadow, but still is the only reality.[150]

A. M. McGrigor

The extensive diaries of A. M. McGrigor (Figure 2) serve as an excellent example of how a tone of resignation towards the war could develop over time. Written between September 1915 and January 1919, the surviving volumes, which McGrigor sent home at regular intervals,[151] cover almost every day of McGrigor's war service. Now transcribed, they fill five volumes and cover over a thousand pages. McGrigor was able to write so regularly and at such length due to the fact that, although he served in the Royal Gloucestershire Hussars, he spent much of the war as an aide de camp (A.D.C.), first to General Sir Ian Hamilton, then Commander-in-Chief of the Mediterranean Expeditionary Force, and Lieutenant-General Birdwood, Commander-in-Chief of ANZAC, during the Gallipoli campaign and, from the end of 1917 until his demobilization in January 1919, to General Birdwood again in France. Between the evacuation of the Gallipoli peninsula and his transfer to France, McGrigor served in Egypt with his regiment where, despite extensive scouting and occasional skirmishes with Turkish troops, he saw

Figure 2   A. M. McGrigor

relatively little action. This distance from many of the dangers and discomforts of trench warfare gave McGrigor time and resources to record his experiences and observations of the war.

One of the results of this distance was that McGrigor's enthusiasm for action in warfare remained unabated throughout his service. While serving as A.D.C. he looked forward to accompanying Hamilton on tours of the trenches, commenting in 1915, 'wish I could get over [to Gallipoli] more. Will, no doubt, have more than enough before I am finished.'[152] He enjoyed new experiences, reporting that flying 'was a most fascinating experience for me, never having been up before, and I do hope I am able to repeat it.'[153] It is in his enthusiasm during his posting to Egypt, however, that McGrigor's longing for action as part of his war experience can be fully seen. He initially recorded that he was 'quite enjoying' being a scout because 'although hard work' it was 'very interesting.'[154] He expressed disappointment, however, when one expedition, intended to culminate in an encounter with Turkish troops, came to nothing: 'Allowance had been made for 100 wounded: a good job, of course, there were none, but still everyone would have liked a little bit of scrap, and we all came back rather disgusted.'[155] He was even more annoyed when, a week later, the Worcesters 'managed to have a bit of a skirmish, which we were dying for and did not get.'[156] His frustration at not seeing action was such that he eventually approached his commanding officer and:

> told him I was very keen to get to France, and asked him that as we seemed like fixtures hereabouts for the summer, and as this was my fifth hot weather running, whether he would allow me to look round for a job that might land me there, or possibly, if that was not possible, go Home and transfer into an infantry Regiment. I also pointed out that chances of promotion in the Regiment seemed extra-ordinary faint as far as I was concerned.[157]

For McGrigor, action was a chance to prove himself as a soldier and, in doing so, improve his status within the Regiment through promotion. Even when the dangers of war were made manifest, he retained his enthusiasm. On 23 April 1916 'A' Company was destroyed by Turkish forces at Katia. McGrigor wrote, 'What an awful business this is – who could have imagined that the scrap we were all hoping for could have turned out like this.'[158] Yet he later reported being 'awfully glad I was back now with the regiment for this show although it has been such a tragedy.'[159]

Despite his on-going enthusiasm for the experience of fighting, McGrigor's diaries also record his awareness of the horrors and fears that warfare involved. In November 1915, for instance, he recorded witnessing:

> a gruesome sight in of one of our new saps being dug – one of own fellows killed and buried in July – his body was found across the line of the sap; he, or rather what remained of him, was just lying to one side covered by a piece of wood, as there had not been time to bury him properly again.[160]

Later, during the Battle of the Somme, he noted the 'Perfectly appalling casualty lists coming in as a result of the fighting in France. It is inevitable I suppose but it is frightful to think of the loss of life necessary to make any advance possible at all.'[161] His own experience of participating in an attack on El Arish was of running 100 yards or so through gun fire. As he noted, 'I certainly don't want to have to do another advance such as that. It would be childish to say one did not mind it, one loathed it really but we were all well worked up to it; however it was good to get off with a whole skin.'[162]

It was, however, during his service in France that the fears and horrors of war were fully reflected in McGrigor's experiences. Unlike Gallipoli, where headquarters were located on an island at a distance from the line, in France McGrigor found himself, even as a staff officer, under shellfire. On 5 October 1917, for example, he experienced:

> my first … real barrage going over my head. It only lasted about 20 minutes and cease almost as suddenly as it began, but apart from the terrific din of the firing what lovely sound these hundreds of shells made passing over one, a regular sort of crackling mingled with a sort of noise of rushing trains. One could see the ground be thrown sky high where these masses of shells were falling, presumably where some Bosche had been reported missing.[163]

He was rather less sanguine upon finding himself the target of German 'high velocity stuff, one unfortunate Officer being killed. It was rather unpleasant'. Three weeks later he was still writing about 'that beastly high velocity stuff coming over. It gives one no warning and comes like a rocket.'[164] While never explicitly describing fearful reactions, as other diarists did, McGrigor did note on one occasion that he was 'far from unpleased to get under cover' while being strafed on the road to Bethune.[165]

Despite these experiences of being under fire, McGrigor's position continued to keep him relatively safe from the dangers experienced by the majority of British soldiers. However, he was aware of this fact and of the greater discomforts faced by men in the line. During a gale in Gallipoli, he wondered 'what it is like on the Peninsula. Infernal simply for the poor devils in the trenches…. A sorry plight some of them will be in with no food or accommodation of any sort.'[166] He felt similarly about the men in France during an August storm which 'didn't worry me much…wretched though for the poor devils who have to be out…. They never have over much room…poor chaps, and I don't suppose want too much at nights as just now they have only one blanket each, so even with their overcoats they can't be too warm.'[167] Even worse was the 'The awful gruesome part…when the Bosche puts his barrage down which often turns up newly buried bodies. There is no doubt that anyone living up in the front line for long, Officer or man, must grow inordinately calous [*sic*], it can't be otherwise.'[168] Despite his relative distance from the front, which allowed him to observe shellfire as interesting as much as dangerous, McGrigor was nonetheless aware of the danger and uncanniness of the war and the effect that both could have on men's bodies and minds.

While McGrigor was sheltered from some of the discomforts of front-line warfare, one that he shared with other soldiers, and which formed the principle source of grumbling in his diaries, was lack of cleanliness. In 1915, while on an extended visit to line, he wrote of how he:

> Would have liked to have gone over to Imbros, if for nothing less than a wash; on the Peninsula the matter of keeping clean is still a difficulty, with the shortage of water so acute. All the fresh water, bar drinking water, one gets is half a glass to shave in, otherwise salt water is rule, and ordinary soap in that is worse than useless, and no one seems to have any salt water soap.[169]

The situation in Egypt was as bad: 'all our water has to be brought from about 3 miles off in our one water cart, so we are down to a gallon of water a day for washing, drinking, and cooking purposes, that means only about a cupful for shaving in, no chance of course of baths.'[170] Opportunities for cleanliness were, therefore, to be celebrated by being specially noted in the diary. 'Managed to get my hair cut – feel very much better for it,' he wrote on 6 April 1916.[171] Similarly, a bath in January 1917 meant he 'felt like a new man in consequence' while a 'shave and a good wash makes a new man of one especially when one has not had much sleep.'[172] Cleanliness thus became rhetorically tied to McGrigor's understanding of himself as man, serving as a source of regeneration.

Food had a similar effect on McGrigor's morale: 'Got back to regimental headquarters at 4:00 p.m. and was very ready for some grub … What a different person I felt after performing ablutions and refreshing the inner man.'[173] Other small causes for celebration were also noted, among them the arrival of the mail. 'Received a big mail,' he wrote on 9 December 1915, 'they are coming out fairly regularly once more, which does make such a difference. Mails are worth more than anything out here.'[174] Indeed, he believed that 'most men would rather get their mails and do without food rather than vice versa'.[175] Other minor pleasures he felt worth recording included the pride he took in constructing a table out of two boxes and a visit to a pierrot show where 'their "girl" is undoubtedly the best that has been produced so far, and has that very rare thing in a man a true girlish voice'.[176] He also noted with pleasure the books that he read, including *Daddy Long Legs* (1912)and *The Strayings of Sandy* (1908).

War for McGrigor can thus be seen to have been an interesting experience, despite its dangers and discomforts. He may have complained of boredom, writing at one point, 'This diary is going to stop for the present, as there is not enough going on to make it worthwhile writing daily', and the work, noting that 'The ADC's job . . . is not a very enviable one, but it is all in a day's work.'[177] Nonetheless, his feelings at the end were ambiguous. On receiving his discharge papers he wrote, 'Although I am glad to be finished, I could not leave without a good many regrets, and I am certain it will be difficult at times to settle down into civilian live once more.'[178] As with so many men who kept diaries of their experiences of war, McGrigor's attitude varied over time, depending on the weather, the level of danger, the amount of work and the ability to stay clean, among other variables. The narrative of war that emerges from his diary is thus an ambiguous one, acknowledging both the terrible experiences and their impacts on men's minds and bodies, but also the excitements and consolations which had the potential to shape men.

Conclusion

What servicemen's wartime diaries reflect is a complex understanding of the war as terrible but ultimately worthwhile experience that shaped men's identities, with the diarist's specific attitude often shifting in response to the level of danger, the weather and the availability of food. The frustrations and fears that war engendered were complained about bitterly, but pleasures and the perceived development of qualities associated with masculinity were also recorded. In the private spaces of their diaries, men could record their doubts about the war's purpose and conduct, and the indignities of their physical and emotional condition, including aspects which were unmentionable in other documents. Diaries were also, however, spaces in which they could record sources of pride, including praise of their own adaptability and ability to endure.

Some aspects of men's boasting in their diaries, such as the desire to shave under any circumstances and their loving descriptions of living quarters, reflect more domestic identities. Yet war was, in these documents, if not the only, then certainly the predominant reality with all its fear, discomfort, consolation and reward. It is thus within the framework of this reality, rather than that of civilian life, that men's identities were constructed in these narratives. The ambiguities of the war as it was experienced by individual servicemen is reflected in these documents, and the martial identities that men constructed within them are equally ambiguous. Neither entirely jingoistic nor completely disillusioned, the soldiers of the diaries are neither heroes nor cowards but usually a mixture of both depending on the level of danger, the weather, the quantity of food and rum and how recently they have taken a bath. It was this mixture of attitudes and emotions, from enthusiasm to grousing, experienced over a length of time, that allowed diarists to view the exigencies of war with resignation rather than disillusion and their own role as soldiers in it as necessary, even purposeful. This sense of purpose was central to men's ability to construct a coherent masculine identity in their letters home, as well as in their diaries. It was even more central to the reconstruction of the identities of the dead, as we shall see in the next chapter on letters of condolence.

3
Remembering the Heroic Dead: Letters of Condolence

Letters and diaries were narrative spaces in which men could construct their own identities as soldiers at war. They were also, however, particularly diaries, spaces in which others could be observed and, in the case of the dead, commemorated. In diaries, such commemorations constructed the remembered dead in heroic terms, as good comrades, brave leaders or simply good men. These were not, however, the only form of written narrative through which the dead were commemorated or in which their identities were retrospectively constructed. Letters of condolence written to the families of the dead fulfilled a similar function, although the fact that such letters were written by civilian acquaintances of the dead as well as their military colleagues meant that the masculine identities constructed in such letters had the potential to encompass a wider range of qualities and signifiers.

The writing of letters of condolence was only one of a large number of commemorative practices, ranging from the creation of street shrines through to the erection of national memorials, that British society engaged in response to the mass deaths of the First World War. These acts of commemoration were communal in terms of both the method of their creation and the social spaces that they occupied. Whether created by schools, local governments or other civic bodies, who raised the funds for memorials through local communities,[1] or by the unification of social groups through bonds of 'fictive kinship',[2] the physical memorials to the First World War that proliferated throughout Britain were the result and focus of community activity. Letters of condolence were, of course, more private by their nature, being created by an individual for individual consumption, although they too could be incorporated into more public acts of memorialization. Letters were circulated within the extended family, appropriate quotations were selected for inclusion in obituaries published in local papers or sent to friends and relatives, and the letters themselves could form the basis of commemorative volumes such as the ones created by A. R. Williams's father and W. J. C. Sangster's parents.[3] Unlike public memorials, which located the dead within nego- tiations between the state and society over appropriate expressions of grief,[4] letters of condolence located the dead individual within a net- work of family, friends and associates who grieved the loss of a member of their community, becoming what Carol Acton has termed 'dynamic sites of mourning.'[5] In their writing, reception and circulation among groups of mourners, letters of condolence served as spaces in which images of the remembered dead were constructed and communicated, thereby forming written memorials to named individuals.

The two main communities who used letters of condolence to cre- ate such memorials were the civil community of family, friends and business associates, and the military community of officers and men who formed the unit, platoon or even regiment in which the dead man had served. There was a certain amount of overlap between these two groupings. Friends and school fellows of the dead were often serving themselves. Soldiers in the Regular Army were mourned by others as both comrades and colleagues. Both groups constructed their relation- ships with the dead in terms of kinship, although claims to personal relations with the dead man were sometimes tenuous. However, there are also distinctions to be seen between the letters written by the two groups, primarily in the meaning ascribed to the man's death and the virtues that such a death implied. Where civil mourners offered the consolation of a worthy cause and noble sacrifice, military letters of condolence were more likely to commemorate the qualities of the sol- dier, such as martial ability and bravery, that the individual was claimed to have embodied. The masculine identity embodied by an individual could thus encompass a range of meanings wide enough to blur the distinctiveness of the individual commemorated. For both communi- ties, the language of condolence served to construct the dead in heroic images that may have offered comfort but also served to reduce the individual to a simplified ideal of what it meant to be both a soldier and a man.

Communities of mourning

Evidence of the communal nature of letters of condolence can be found in the manner in which many of the letter writers sought to justify their expressions of grief through laying claim to a connection with the dead.

Obvious connections could be made through family, allowing distant relatives such as J. H. MacGregor's cousin Mary to feel 'proud to be able to count a hero in the family.'[6] G. B. Buxton's cousin created a connection in her letter by recalling his final visit to her: 'he came in all the glory of his joy of flying... We have never seen the like. I congratulate you on such a brother, and we fell the better for being close cousins to you and to such as he.'[7]

Business associations were also important in creating connections that could allow for expressions of condolence. Employers and teachers were common correspondents, sharing their memories of the dead and reflecting on the promise of a future cut short. In a long letter, L. H. Powell, director of the firm where F. Henley was employed as a stockbroker's clerk prior to enlistment, wrote:

> He was a delightful boy in every way and during the time he was with us performed his duties in a most exemplary manner. In fact, the firm considered him to be one of the most promising junior members of staff, and there is no doubt, had his life been spared, he would have had a highly successful career.[8]

Knowledge of the dead individual was not, however, a prerequisite for the writing of a letter based on a professional relationship. E. Nicholson's wife received a letter from the Chief Constable of Stockport, the force in which her husband had served as a constable.[9] Professional acquaintances of the father of T. M. Field, an admiral, wrote to condole over the loss of a young man they had never met. Letters of condolence thus allowed the civil community of mourners to spread beyond the immediate family to encompass much of middle-class society. Even if only a minority of the British population had lost a close family member or friend,[10] those for whom loss was more distant could participate in the rituals of mourning, thereby honouring the sacrifices of the dead.

Indeed, absence, as well as death, could form a connection through which grief and sympathy could be expressed. William Stagg wrote to Mrs Henley in sympathy because 'My brother has been missing since July 1st, and we do not know whether he is dead or alive, so I can enter, to some extent, into your feelings.'[11] Similarly, J. M. Greer, W. M. Anderson's commanding officer, 'asked [his] future wife to write [Mrs Anderson] a few lines, as I know, one woman can understand another woman's feelings better than any man'.[12] The anxiety of parting that his fiancée's letter expresses[13] was viewed by Greer as equivalent to the grief of loss through death. Nor did loss have to be in warfare for correspondents to gain access to the community of the bereaved. 'I know how you feel, or, at any rate, have some idea,' C. D. Linnell, whose own son had died of illness, wrote to Gerald Stewart's mother.[14] J. R. Wolkley similarly told W. H. J. St. L. Atkinson's parents that, 'Having lost a child myself I know a little of your trial.'[15] It was, however, the bereaved of wartime who formed the core of the civil community of mourning and who were able to express sympathy without equivocation. 'I can so well enter into your feelings as we have made the same sacrifice,' T. P. Wilsmhurst wrote to Henley's father, while Jean Thompson, the mother of a soldier in MacGregor's unit wrote bitterly:

> It is all very well for others to be pleased by the advance in Mesopotamia but you & I are paying the price in the loss of our best & bravest, & in the wearing anxiety over the living, & it is difficult to see where the glory comes in.[16]

The civil communities of family, friends and associates were not, however, the only ones with cause to mourn the dead. As soldiers, these men were part of a military organization based on a paternalistic regimental system that emphasized the community links among soldiers.[17] Men were mourned as deeply by their fellow soldiers as by their family and colleagues, although not always for the same reasons. There were some clear connections with the civilian bereaved, particularly that of parenthood. W. J. C. Sangster's battalion chaplain mourned him because, 'In many ways he reminded me of my own soldier son who was accidentally killed some 18 months ago, and this fact together with the attractions of his own delightful personality drew me very close to him.'[18] E. K. Smith's platoon sergeant was 'only too pleased to tell [his father] what had actually happened, & being as you say a parent myself, I know you would like to know even the smallest detail concerning the sad event.'[19] As H. Adams wrote to Gerald Stewart's parents, 'who can feel more for the parents than we who see our brave heroes and comrades falling every day knowing as we do what few familys [*sic*] there are but who mourn the loss of someone dear to them.'[20] The closeness of the military unit encouraged men to lay claim to ties of affection as close as that of a parent.[21]

It was, however, not as parents but as brothers that men were most often mourned by their fellow soldiers. Horace Waterall mourned the death of R. P. Harker because, 'for the last six month we have done everything together and been more than brothers to each other and there will be an awful blank in my life.'[22] For N. L. Woodroffe's soldier servant there was:

> one thing I can never forget & that is my late master....If it had been my own brother I would not feel so sorry as he was more like a brother to me than an Officer.i.C. of me. I hope you will not be offended with this letter as I am but a Pte. Soldier.[23]

The language of these letters was often that of love, emphasizing the closeness and kinship with the dead and, by extension, the family that mourned them. Indeed, some soldiers kept up long correspondences with the families of their dead comrades, receiving parcels and letters from them in place of the dead son or brother.[24]

Not all military relations with the dead were so close, however. As the war continued and casualties mounted, regiments were amalgamated and survivors reassigned to new units. Some men were promoted away from their units or underwent specialist training that entailed new assignments. In addition, the short life expectancy of junior officers on the Western Front,[25] meant that a man could be almost unknown to the superior officer writing to inform the family of his death. As Lt.-Col. Falbe explained to R. P. Harker's sister, 'I of course have had very little opportunity of seeing your brother but in our short acquaintance he made me feel he was just the right sort and we all sympathise with you in your loss.'[26] E. Mannering, F. Henley's regimental chaplain similarly told Mr Henley, 'Your son had only been with us some three months but we had learnt to appreciate his good qualities as a soldier and a man.'[27] As with the letters of business associates, such letters were written more at a professional level than a personal one. They nonetheless indicate the extent to which the rituals of mourning spread throughout British society, military, as well as civil, during the war.

In particular, the war saw the spread of the ritual of writing letters of condolence from the middle classes to a wider community. The letter of condolence was part of the extensive ritual of mourning which had dominated middle-class Victorian society.[28] For civilian society during the First World War, this continued to be true, with most letters being written by and in response to the death of those from professional backgrounds. Within the military community of mourning, however, the practice spread far beyond the ranks of officers, although the majority of letters of mourning continued to be written by officers. Commanding officers were responsible for informing the family of the deceased of the fact and manner of his death through a letter of condolence, in addition to the official telegram. The result was that the family of every man who died, whatever his background, would receive at least one letter of condolence, however formal and impersonal.

Many, however, received more than this, as non-commissioned officers (N.C.O.) and comrades also wrote to express their sorrow. Sometimes these letters were spontaneous expressions of emotion; often they came as the response to a family's desire for further information concerning the service and death of a loved one. The bereaved could engage in long correspondences in their attempts to establish precisely what had happened, writing to anyone remotely connected to the time and place of death. Men of all backgrounds were thus called upon to write letters of condolence so that the practice spread to include soldier servants, platoon sergeants and many others who had served alongside the dead. Chaplains, orderlies and nurses who had tended men at the moment of death were other common correspondents. Association with the dead drew disparate individuals into communities of mourning that found expression and solace through the ritual provided by letters of condolence.

Expressing grief

The extent of the communities of mourning who wrote letters of condolence had significant implications for the ways in which grief was expressed. Lack of specific knowledge of the individual being mourned could mean that the consolation offered was couched in generalized terms which drew upon traditional imagery and associations to describe the dead and the process of mourning them. F. Henley's parents, for instance, were comforted by their local vicar with the assurance that 'You must feel very proud of him.' He went on to write, with no apparent irony, '*Dulce et decorum est pro patria mori* Horace wrote many centuries ago, and those words still hold good, and must to some extent alleviate one's sorrows.'[29] In general, however, allusions to the classics were to be found not in letters of condolence but in obituaries, such as the one for W. B. P. Spencer that appeared in his school's Old Boys' newsletter, quoting the epitaph for the 300 at Thermopylae, 'Go tell my country those that passeth by/ That here, obedient to her call, I lie.'[30] Chivalry could also appear in such memorial forms, as it did in the memorial speech that described W. J. C. Sangster and his school fellows as 'Like the legendary Knights of King Arthur [who] . . . went forth to redress the wrong . . . . They went forth in the same chivalrous spirit as Sir Galahad and Sir Percivale, but they met danger more stupendous and foes far more redoubtable.'[31]

In alluding to popular classical and chivalric imagery, these public memorials, which commemorated groups rather than specific individuals, were tapping into common cultural tropes of the middle classes that they aimed to console through the evocation of familiar narratives of heroic death that had been on the increase in British culture from the 1880s. George Mosse notes that in Victorian England 'Heroism, death, and sacrifice on behalf of a higher purpose in life became set attributes of manliness',[32] while David Cannadine argues that:

> from the 1880s onwards, the *glorification* of death – of death on active service, in battle, in the front line, for one's country – was markedly on the increase. The growing international tensions of these years, combined with the ever-widening appeal of ideas of social Darwinism, and the stridently athletic ethos of the late-Victorian and Edwardian public school, produced an atmosphere in which death was seen as unlikely, but where, if it happened, it could not fail to be glorious.[33]

It is important to note that both Mosse and Cannadine identify the glorified and heroic death as sacrificial, as serving a purpose. There was an additional association of the death of youth with sacrifice, even if no obvious purpose is laid claim to.[34] According to Max Jones, the ideal of sacrifice:

> reached its apogee before the First World War. A resonant language of heroic sacrifice emerged, which drew on classical, chivalric, and religious models, Roman warriors, Arthurian knights, and Christ himself. This language of sacrifice, in which failure was redeemed by the exhibition of heroism in the face of death, rang out after the sinking of the *Titanic*, but found its most sonorous expression in the response to the death of Captain Scott.[35]

Letters of condolence, in seeking to mourn and comprehend the death of individual men, used these images of sacrifice, focusing in particular on religion, sportsmanship, patriotism and the worthiness of the cause for which men died.

Of all the forms of consolation offered by letters of condolence, religion, specifically Christianity, was undoubtedly the most central.[36]

G. B. Buxton's brother wrote to their father that he was 'indeed a wonderful brother and a Christian. How can we but praise God for him.'[37] It was not only pride in the individual man's life as a Christian one, as in Buxton's letter, that was cited as consolation, but also the assurance that dead were going to a better place and a higher role. Lady Adam Smith assured Lt. Sangster's mother that the dead:

> have run another race now – a straight, clean race – and they have finished their course, and we have nothing but thankfulness for all that they were, and all that they did. One cannot think of this as death...for spirits like theirs there must surely be life beyond and work still to do.[38]

Such assurances of spiritual homecoming were extremely common. As Arthur Evans told Mrs MacGregor, the knowledge that her son 'has died a noble & glorious death, & is at rest now with our Dear Lord and Master in Paradise...I am certain consoles you'.[39] David Potts's family placed this idea at the centre of their commemoration of their son's death as a prisoner of war in 1917. The card produced in his memory contained two poems, entitled 'For our Dead' and 'Looking Forward'. The first is an unremarkable commemorative verse. The second, however, does not commemorate the dead but rather prisoners of war. Its final lines, written in the voice of the captive, read 'So we wait till the guns are silent;/ Till the game is played to the end;/ To pass from the enemy's borders/ and enter those of the friend.' This ending is repeated at the foot of the card but altered slightly to give it an explicitly religious meaning: 'He has passed from the enemy's borders and entered those of his Friend.'[40] Death became a form of spiritual repatriation, in the face of official policy not to repatriate the temporal bodies of the dead.[41] The poem, and the circulation of the cards on which it was printed, act as a substitute for the rituals of mourning of a funeral that was denied to the families of those who died overseas. It is unsurprising, therefore, to find religion at the centre of the ritual.

While religious imagery was the most important source of consolation offered in letters of condolence, other concepts were also used to attempt to comprehend the deaths of men in wartime. As the Potts commemorative poem indicates, the idea of war as a game was also an important one.[42] R. S. Smylie's N.C.O. described him as 'a perfect Gentleman & a thorough sportsman.'[43] F. Henley's superior officer expressed a similar understanding of the war when he described him as 'one of the many brave fellows who has lost his life playing the game for his side, and our hearts thrill with pride when we realise the great sacrifice he made.'[44] This comment links the concept of war as a game to the importance of patriotism in the construction of the identity of the dead. Henley did not merely play the game, he played it specifically for *his side*. W. Nicholson was similarly praised as 'a boy to be proud of, for beneath that smiling infectious humour, there lay the spirit of a true British gentleman, & this is the highest praise a man can ever attain.'[45] This Britishness was offered as a source of consolation to Nicholson's wife, as it was to the family of Gerald Stewart by T. Bacon who felt that 'you have some consolation that he died for his home and country'.[46]

It was not, however, simply the 'eager patriotism' of the individual that gave consolation. It was also 'the noble cause for which he gave his life,' as C. H. Greene assured J. H. MacGregor's father.[47] Letters of condolence constructed the dead man as not merely patriotic but also selfless in his willingness to die. 'The great solace,' commented Grace Bowie of MacGregor, 'is that he among so many others was ready at once when his country needed him & that he gave his life in so great a cause – a thousand times better than to die like shirker'.[48] W. J. C. Sangster was similarly praised for having 'died nobly and gloriously for his country, and perhaps there is nothing in the way of sacrifice more noble and fine than that of a young life given in defence of a righteous cause.'[49] Nor was defence of home and country the only cause for which men were seen to have died, particularly in the early years of the war. N. L. Woodroffe, a Regular officer in the Irish Guards killed at Ypres in 1914, was commemorated for having died helping 'to put an end once and for all to the threatening shadow of German brute force, which has been overhanging the world.'[50]

The manner of death

By constructing men as good Christians, sportsmen and self-sacrificing patriots, letters of condolence idealized the dead through the fact of their service, which was given as evidence of the virtues of religious faith, sporting spirit and patriotic sensibility. These in turn could be offered as consolation for the death. However, it was the nature of the death itself that was presented as the greatest source of consolation, particularly the confirmation that death in military action gave of the heroism of the dead. 'I am sure he has died a noble death (A Soldier's Death) whilst fighting for his King and Country and it is a Death of Victory,' George Greenwood told H. Henfrey's mother.[51] Mary Woodforde joined Mrs MacGregor in her 'thanks to the Almighty that your boy died in Action…His young life was taken from him in a moment, without suffering, and that moment was one of heroic Action for his Country'.[52] E. Mannering hoped that, 'even in you sorrow', F. Henley's father would 'feel proud of your son's gallant end, for he played his part like a man.'[53]

The dead were not, however, simply heroes with who could claim manhood through death. Masculinity, after all, could be proved simply through service in the armed forces, according to recruitment propaganda.[54] The dead were greater than this. Through their deaths they had proved themselves to be superior to all other men, including those still serving, even members of their own families. W. B. P. Spencer's school obituary, for instance, claimed that 'his sorrowful parents…are saying at this instant of their youngest-born: "Ah, how little is all the rest compared with the memory of thee," '[55] despite the fact that two of his elder brothers were still serving overseas. Similarly, J. H. MacGregor's cousin wrote to his father, 'I remember your saying that he was the ablest of your boys',[56] while Fanny Beames wrote to his sister Edith that 'This terrible war takes toll of the *best*, and your brother has died a heroes [*sic*] death.' [My emphasis].[57] Jasper Davidson felt that 'We can never probe the obscurity that surrounds the fact that a man like Will should be taken while others with little to their credit are left.'[58] The act of dying in battle thus marked men out as the best of men, becoming, for civilian mourners in particular, the key marker of heroic masculinity on the part of the individual.

By dying in action, men were constructed not merely as virtuous but as a source of pride for the bereaved. 'Certainly, it is a glorious end to his young life!' S. McCall wrote to the 20-year-old W. J. C. Sangster's mother, 'and even in the midst of your great sorrow you must indeed be proud of having had such a son.'[59] One correspondent assured Lady Field that 'Amidst all there is some consolation and just pride in the assurance that you son met his death in the way that you & Sir Arthur & the young fellow himself would have first chosen in his Country's cause',[60] while Robert Wright felt that Mrs Stewart's 'pride in you dear son will help you to bear the awful blank he will leave, & the knowledge that he died the most glorious death possible'.[61]

Such a death could also be cited as a source of inspiration for those left behind. W. B. P. Spencer, for instance, served as inspiration for his school community, according to Harold Dehry, who wrote that 'In him we see, all of us here in Weymouth, an example of splendid cheerfulness & efficiency. May we all follow the example of the friend of whom we are so proud.'[62] The principal of Aberdeen University used similar language in relation to the death of W. J. C. Sangster: 'Your son has gallantly served his country and the sacred cause committed to her and we of the University are proud of him – proud and grateful.'[63] Such emotion imposed a duty on the bereaved to endure as the dead had done. As David explained to W. Nicholson's mother, 'All around us we see the lads we have watched grow into manhood drop away. It is heart-rending but we should be unworthy to be the relatives of these grand soldiers if we failed to bear their loss with the same fortitude and courage as they themselves showed.'[64] This role as source of inspiration added to the dead men's claims to ideal masculinity. As John Tosh has pointed out, a key aspect of Victorian masculinity was the father's role as an educator of his sons.[65] While the dead could no longer father children and educate them to maturity, as sources of moral inspiration to the communities they had left behind they could still attain the role of educator and, therefore, the moral authority that was part of the ideal of mature masculinity.

Knowledge

It was not, however, only the civilian community of mourning that offered the consolation of the manner of death to the bereaved. The manner of death was, if anything, of even more importance in the letters of condolence written by officers and men who had served alongside the dead. In these letters, however, the consolation derived not from the general context of a heroic death in active service for the nation but from the specific details of how men died. Unlike the letters of the civil community, which offered forms of consolation that constructed the dead in terms of traditional masculine ideals of chivalry, sportsmanship and patriotism, letters of condolence from the military could provide the more concrete consolation of knowledge.

The importance of knowledge as a form of consolation derived from the practical problems presented to a large civilian armed force by the death in action of its members overseas and in conditions that could make their bodies unrecoverable. During the First World War British soldiers died in ways that are often unimaginable to civilians. The fact that the dead were not and, in many cases, could not be repatriated reinforced the unimaginability of the death for the family left behind. Having no body to confirm the reality of loss, families were forced to turn to eye-witness accounts of those who fought alongside their loved ones.[66] Battles, however, were often confusing and eye-witness accounts, even at the best of times, could be contradictory. Some men simply failed to return from attacks or night-time raids, their loss unnoticed by their comrades, leaving open, at least initially, the possibility that they had been injured or captured rather than killed.[67] Many collections of letters of condolence contain a number of letters offering the hope that news will soon be heard of the man's captivity followed by correspondence confirming the reality of death through the testimony of witnesses. Specific knowledge was thus used to bring home the reality of death to the bereaved.

Two aspects of knowledge about the manner of death were particularly important to military offers of consolation – the fact that death was instantaneous and without suffering and the fact that death occurred in action. W. M. Anderson's senior officer was 'relieved in the thought that he did not suffer at all.'[68] Gerald Weston's parents were similarly assured that 'Your son was killed by a bullet and died without suffering any pain. He was not one whit mutilated, and as I looked down at his face as he lay in the battle field I remarked how bonny he looked.'[69] N. L. Woodroffe's fellow office felt that it would be of comfort to his parents to 'know that Capt Orr Ewing who was close by him is certain that he was shot through the head and that death was instantaneous.'[70] Such assurances allowed the unknown death to be imagined as quick and painless and the dead to be remembered as physically intact and unmutilated. The emphasis on death by gun shot rather than shrapnel with its ability to mutilate emphasizes this point. As Alan Wilson commented of J. H. MacGregor, 'Thank God he died so clean'.[71]

Similarly important to the imagined deaths presented in these letters were the assurances that men had died in action, described in explicitly heroic terms.[72] W. Lindsay's fellow officer felt that 'it will be a gratification for [his father] to know that he was at the time of being wounded splendidly advanced and skilfully leading his men, and was then worthy of the best traditions of our Glorious Army.'[73] J. Matthews's officer was more specific in his praise. 'I am so glad you have written to me,' he told Mrs Matthews:

> as it enables me to let you know what a hero's death your husband met. I thought so highly of the part he played in the capture of the German trenches at Hooge that I recommended him for the Victoria Cross.... He died instantaneously and never spoke, but those around him spoke, his comrades. Others were hit but none of that band of fighters paused to comment only when Matthews fell they spoke 'Oh! They've got him!' Him - the man we had all come to look to, the man who could by his throwing and courage drive back the enemy. And he had done it. They never advanced again.[74]

Nor was aggressive bravery the only form that men were said to have displayed at the moment of death. Lt. Collinson invoked chivalric traditions of compassionate bravery when he assured A. R. Williams's father 'your son...died a soldier's death giving his life while saving the lives of his comrades.'[75] C. K. McKerrow also 'yielded up his life nobly and grandly ministering to the wounded and dying, that mothers might have their sons back and wives their husbands.'[76] By describing the scene of death and men's actions at the time of their death, such letters allowed the bereaved the consolation of imagining some of the specifics of the death that they had had no part in. As David Waddell wrote to Mr Sangster, 'I sincerely hope that my poor account of the glorious work you son did on that fateful day will make your burden a little lighter to carry.'[77]

By constructing the dead men in heroic language and imagery, these letters of condolence, like those of the civilian community, memorialized the dead in stock terms of heroism. The figure of the heroic dead in these letters, however, differs in important ways from that evoked by the civilian community of mourning. Where the civil image was of a figure representative of the virtues of religious faith, sportsmanship and patriotism, military letters of condolence concentrated on soldierly qualities of military ability, courage, and cheerfulness in the face of adversity.

Ability

The letters that emphasized ability tended to be written by senior or superior officers who noted military skills including efficiency, leadership and reliability. The fact that F. Henley had been 'selected...to command a Company when [another officer] was wounded two days ago, on account of the very high opinion I had of his ability and bravery' was offered by his commanding officer as a source of pride and consolation for his family.[78] C. H. Rowe described W. B. P. Spencer as 'my right hand man in everything and of the greatest imaginable value.'[79] Both R. S. Smylie and E. Nicholson were described as 'conscientious', while H. Henfrey 'always did his work admirably and never wanted telling twice and a straighter young man I never saw.'[80] Despite the seemingly prosaic nature of these qualities, they were valourized in these letters as an aspect of fulfilling one's duty, an increasingly important quality in the definition of heroic masculinities.[81] After all, as A. R. Williams's civilian employer noted, 'a most efficient officer...was just the type of effective well-trained man the Army required.'[82]

Unlike the potential ability praised by civilian letters, however, military letters of condolence were able to draw on specific examples of military ability and its rewards. For example, Captain A. MacDougall wrote of R. Farley:

> I made him a Sergeant and no one deserved the promotion better. He was always cheerful, always willing, and his ability was far above what one looks for in an ordinary Sergeant. He was one of those rare N.C.O.s who have ideas of their own and good reasons for holding them.[83]

The honour due to such men was expressed by Private William Troup who found W. J. C. Sangster, as an officer, 'one to be relied upon, one who knew how to and discharged his duties. He fell in the fulfilment of these duties and we soldiers know how to honour him dead.'[84]

Courage

Such honour was offered not only for ability as a soldier but also for more abstract qualities of bravery that all the dead were identified as having. 2nd Lt. G. S. Halliwell reported of A. R. Williams 'that the whole section of which he was in charge vow that he was the best and bravest officer they have ever had.'[85] Captain James Oag considered C. K. McKerrow to be 'one of the bravest men I have ever known – a man such as one would like to be oneself.'[86] The idea of what courage meant in these letters was related to men's ability to do a job effectively. Thus McKerrow, a medical officer, was noted as having:

> showed an absolute disregard for danger in the performance of his duty and no man in the Battalion was more loved, admired and respected. I believe he had the 'Medical History' of every man in the Battalion who had passed through his hands, written down in his private diary, and I know he had compiled a lot of valuable notes on the medical side of the war.[87]

It was, however, coolness under fire that was regarded as the epitome of courage. Major George Ashton regarded McKerrow as 'one of the bravest and coolest men I have seen in Action',[88] while E. H. Owen was described as 'most brave in the advance and those of us who saw him could not help but notice his coolness and unconcern.'[89] Like McKerrow, Gerald Stewart was commemorated for combining coolness with duty.

According to Captain C. E. Fysh, 'Gerald died nobly doing his duty and leading his company on to a splendid victory, but at an awful cost ... he was splendidly cool and another officer tells em that it was splendid to see the way in which he got his company into position.'[90] Similarly, R. S. Smylie's fellow officers were of the opinion that:

> 'if that ridge over there had to be taken & Smylie knew it meant his death he would go straight for it.' Just before the action he said to the Colonel 'I would rather be here now, sir, than on any other spot on God's earth.' ... He had an extraordinarily keen sense of duty & neglected nothing that would make his company efficient. Everyone loved and respected him.[91]

Ability, coolness and a sense of duty combined to form the figure of the ideal soldier in these letters.

Cheerfulness

One of the symbols of coolness under fire that was particularly respected by fellow soldiers was, as we have seen in their diaries, the cheerfulness that men exhibited. Thus S. MacDonald recalled Weston Stewart, Gerald's brother, as 'a splendid young man and the bravest among our officers. I think I can see him again on that fateful day, rallying and leading his men and full of great happiness and cheer.'[92] G. W. Colebrook was deemed very brave by his friend and fellow officer Hugh Blyde because 'all the time I saw him, he was very bright and smiling and did not fear anything',[93] while H. Henfrey was considered by George Greenwood to be 'a very brave boy, he was always jolly and bright, he used to be singing while the Turks were firing there [*sic*] Jack Johnsons (shells) .... There was not a better hearted man our Battn than your son.'[94] This cheerfulness saw Henfrey promoted to band President, 'as he always led the singing on the march, which was a good help especially when we were fagged out.'[95]

Cheerfulness was also an important component of a final quality of masculinity memorialized in military letters of condolence, that of popularity. All the dead looked at here were described as being popular with their comrades and men, reflecting the importance placed on comradeship to understandings of ideal martial masculinity. W. J. C. Sangster, for instance, 'was a great favourite both in the Mess and with the men'.[96] R. Farley's 'officers liked and trusted him, the men loved him', while A. R. Williams's section 'adored him'.[97] E. K. Smith's wife received assurance of his popularity directly from one of his men who wrote, 'He was as brave a man as ever walked, & anyone in difficulties he was first to lend a hand can anyone wonder why we worshipped him, & will continue to worship his memory.'[98] W. B. P. Spencer, meanwhile:

> had endeared himself to us all by his fearlessness in action & his never-failing cheerfulness & devotion to the men at all times. So fond were they of him that some of them actually wept when they heard of his death – & these were strong brave fellows who afterwards earned the commendation of the commanding officer by their courage & steadiness under heavy fire & in very difficult circumstances.[99]

The devotion of such hardened types was, at least for Douglas Hodgson-Jones, evidence of masculinity. As he told F. Henley's father, 'We used to call him "Baby" but he was a man amongst men. The men of his platoon, some of them nearly 40 years of age, looked up to him and loved him.'[100] These men would appear to embody a traditional form of masculinity, defined by their maturity, but it was trumped by a more important form, defined by the comradeship of fighting men. Spencer and Henley's ability to command such affection implied their own possession of the masculinity of martial comradeship.

It is hard to know how many of these military letters of condolence hid a less ideal reality of the bravery and popularity of the dead, satirized viciously by Siegfried Sassoon in 'The Hero'.[101] Despite the specific details of the death that such letters offered as consolation to the bereaved, their celebration of the dead as able, brave and popular commemorated them as idealized figures in the same way that civilian letters constructed the dead as devout and patriotic. In all these letters we can see, from the early years of the war, constructions of martial ideals which were to continue to resonate long after the Armistice. The duty owed by the living to the dead and the fact of death conferring heroic identity would shape commemoration of the First World War in Britain throughout the 20th century.[102] Similarly the definitions of heroism as efficiency, coolness and cheerfulness would be echoed in ex-servicemen's postwar constructions of themselves as heroes, as will be seen in the next chapter. In letters of condolence, therefore, from the earliest years of the war, the ways the ideal heroic male was constructed as a military figure by both civilian and military communities, often at the expense of the more complex identity in which civilian experiences exposed in letters home played as great a role as military ones.

R. C. Trench[103]

Figure 3   R. C. Trench

When Reginald Chenevix Trench (Figure 3), acting Major with the 2/5 Sherwood Foresters was killed on the Western Front on 21 March 1918 during the German spring offensive, he left behind a family that included his mother Isabelle, wife Clare and a baby daughter, Delle. The engagement in which Trench was killed all but wiped out his regiment, with many men taken prisoners, as well as killed. Trench's own fate was unclear. He was initially reported missing, with his death only being confirmed to his family a week after the battle and following several letters of enquiry from Clare Trench to surviving members of the battalion.

Confirmation of Trench's death resulted in an outpouring of letters of condolence to his wife and mother. Most were written in the first three weeks after his death, although letters expressing sorrow at his loss continued to arrive until early 1919, and one ex-serviceman even wrote to Clare with his memories of Trench as late as in 1930.[104] The community of mourning that the 169 letters received by Clare and Isabelle represented was a wide one.[105] It encompassed school and university friends, work colleagues, fellow servicemen, the families of fellow officers, relatives, both close and distant, and even a few strangers. As William Swan wrote to Clare, 'Personally we are entire strangers, and yet in a sort of kinship of trouble we do not quite feel that to be so.'[106] He claimed kinship through the death of his son Wilke, a fellow officer who 'often spoke to us of your husband ... and they appear to have been very good friends. When my son was killed in December last year Major Trench wrote us a letter which we appreciated very much & he also gave us particulars which were not in the Colonel's letter.'[107] Isabelle Davis similarly wrote about the death of her son, on whose death 'Major Chenevix Trench in the goodness of his heart, wrote the enclosed .... My son was in the N. [illegible] R.E. 470th Field Coy. & evidently working with Major Trench it was therefore remarkably nice of him to have written & we greatly valued his kind sympathy.'[108] Even before the confirmation of Trench's death, Maud Alibon, the mother of his second-in-command who had died in 1917, wrote, 'I know so well just the helplessness of it all, the suspense of waiting day by day for news!'[109] For all these correspondents, the experience of loss and the receipt of letters of condolence created a connection through which mourning could appropriately be expressed.

As with other soldiers, Trench was mourned by both civilian acquaintances and military comrades. For the former, God and religion were central to the consolation that they offered, both through the assurance of salvation for a man of Trench's character and the Christ-like manner of his death.[110] Isabelle Davis felt that both Trench and her son had 'proved themselves worthy of another work &...God needs them',[111] while Muriel Steel assured Clare that, far from having left her, Reggie was 'really nearer us than ever before.'[112] Guy Beech called him 'one of the pure of heart on whom Our Lord pronounced this blessing: upright & sincere, with a profound sense of duty, righteous in all his ways.'[113] For George Fearn, however, consolation lay in the thought that 'It is a wholly Christlike thing to suffer & die for others.'[114] This idea of soldiers' sufferings as the suffering of Christ was also central to Charles Ovenden's letter to Isabelle Trench, although it was not only the dead whose sufferings he equated with those of Jesus. 'Our sufferings,' he wrote:

> are...the evidence of our actual partnership with Christ. In Du Maurier's pre-war pictures of Society as it was then, there is not a trace of this partnership. We might as well have been citizens of ancient pagan Rome. But now life has another and a nobler meaning. Apart from Christ it is from beginning to end an effort doomed to final failure, a hope which must end in disappointment. With Him it is a school in which we are learning out lessons for the eternal life.[115]

Religious belief was thus able to endow the losses suffered by both the dead and the bereaved with a sense of meaning and consolation.

It was not only the lesson of Christ's suffering that Trench's death was seen as offering by writers of these letters. His ability to inspire went far wider. Walter Wood, for instance, called him:

> one of the strong influences for good in my life and he will always remain so. He always strove unhesitatingly for the right and his strength of character must have helped directly and indirectly hundreds of young men .... Reggie will never be forgotten by me. I have a hundred things to remember him by but the most precious of all is my ideal of his as a Christian gentleman.[116]

Edward Burney called the memory of 'a personality true, loyal & loveable beyond compare...an inspiration, and my one anxiety is that I may not live unworthy of it.'[117] Walter Howard felt that 'If ever I have sons, I shall be well satisfied if they can in a small degree mould themselves on him',[118] while Muriel Steel assured Clare that 'he must have had a splendid influence on all around him which will never be forgotten...with their glorious of examples of courage & endurance before us, we mustn't fail them but live up to them & be worthy of them.'[119]

This need for the civilian population to be worthy of the sacrifice of the dead was another important theme in these letters. Ethel Gore Booth worried that 'we can never be worthy of all this sacrifice of the very best.'[120] Burney also felt that living up to the memory of the dead would be difficult. 'I cannot of course know,' he wrote to Clare, 'whether it is to be my honour to join Reggie and other brave and noble spirits in the world beyond, or my heavy task to live in a manner worthy of them and their sacrifice in this world.'[121] Through his death, Trench had become one of the best, having proved his manhood through sacrifice and sanctified his life as an example to others.

Trench's qualities were not, however, simply created through the fact of his dying. As Burney pointed out, 'He is not one of those who have to die to be praised.'[122] Praise was nonetheless lavished on him after his death, principally with regards to his devotion to duty which, according to Burney, 'was an example to all of us.' In addition, 'his conduct was … perfectly straightforward and honourable. I think that it has been the quality, that and his entire devotion to whatever work, civil or military has fallen to him, that has struck me most in him.'[123] His employers at the accounting firm of Deloitte, Plender, Griffiths & Co., where he had been working prior to enlistment, also felt that he 'had been cut off in the freshness of youth from a career of great promise. No one had a higher sense of duty than he, and no one inspired more affectionate feelings among those with whom he came into contact.'[124] E. W. S. Maconachy, a fellow officer, assured Clare in the days when Reggie was listed as missing, 'I know whatever happened he will have done his duty nobly.'[125] William Swan spelled out the consolation that such assurances offered. 'The great consoling thought you have,' he told Clare, 'is that those who have gone served willingly before Derby Schemes or Conscription were even thought of. They did their duty.'[126]

An equally important form of knowledge for the bereaved was the knowledge of the manner in which Trench had died. For civilian writers, the nobility of his death in action, having already been wounded twice, was viewed as consoling. 'The Times today told us of your man's death "facing overwhelming odds"', wrote Joyce Shipley. 'It is glorious to read that & I think when the awful gnawing … pain passes you will be able to feel the pride which is yours & which Delle must know in later years.'[127] Ethel Gore Booth similarly felt that 'Reggie had lived so gloriously and died so gloriously – I know how proud you will feel when you can forget your own irreparable loss'.[128] Dorothy G. Horsford simply stated, 'He was such a fine man, who died a hero's death',[129] while his Aunt Ida found that 'every thought of him is full of thankfulness for the beautiful life and the way in which given.'[130] For R. A. Copleson, the glory of Trench's death had as much to do with the timing as the manner of it:

> He seems to have been called away in the supreme moment of re-dedication of himself; just returned – was he not? – after dressing his wound, to [illegible] in the field. What could be nobler? Whether it was with a weary sense of going back to all the horror, or (as I think more likely) with the eager 'light of battle in his eyes', either way it was in the very moment of re-consecration.[131]

In this interpretation, the ideas of religious self-sacrifice and duty are fused to give meaning both to the manner of his death and the death itself.

As in other collections of letters of condolence, those from Trench's fellow soldiers were also concerned with the manner of his death but more with the specifics of what happened than with its wider meaning. In part, this was due to the virtual destruction of the Sherwood Foresters in the attack in which Trench died, leaving those who could confirm his death in hospital or as prisoners of war.[132] It took several weeks for Clare to receive eyewitness confirmation, during which time she kept up a correspondence with a number of officers and men who appeared capable of giving her information. This included three long letters from A. J. Lane, Trench's servant, written from a prisoner-of-war camp and detailing what information Lane had about the moments leading up to Trench's death. Other letters came from privates, N.C.O.s and officers who had served alongside Trench, some clearly in response to specific enquiries.[133] Friends such as Walter Howard gleaned information from 'a soldier who should have been with Reggie when he was hit. My informant, who I saw in hospital here since I last wrote to you, told me that Reggie was hit in the head by a trench mortar & killed instantly.'[134] This news of the instantaneousness of Trench's death was later contradicted by reports that he lay unconscious on a stretcher before dying. In both versions, however, lack of suffering was emphasized, allowing Ethel Gore Booth to write, following an interview with a casualty from the Sherwood Foresters who had known Reggie:

> I am sure you will feel thankful for his quick passing – to think of them suffering long is always more hard to bear – & now he is beyond all the struggle & sorrow of the world having done the utmost a man can do in laying down his life for his friends.[135]

In Trench's case, the need to communicate knowledge of the dead man and the manner of his death in order to express a sense of mourning was not limited to the months immediately after his death. Close friends such as Edward Burney continued to write to Clare about Reggie for several months, and she herself kept up a correspondence with Lane who wrote with reminiscences of Reggie long after his repatriation from Germany.[136] Even strangers felt the need to write. Robert W. Lloyd placed an advertisement in the *Daily Sketch* in 1930 requesting information concerning Major Trench's relatives. When Clare responded, he wrote her a long letter praising Trench for his care for his men and describing him as 'Decent to the very backbone without ever sacrificing one ounce of dignity.' 'I feel honoured even to have know him,' Lloyd wrote. 'That is why I write. I feel I would like to tell somebody near him how he made himself loved by the rank and file.'[137] As one of Trench's junior officers had noted 12 years earlier:

> Had there been any of the 2/5 left, I know no officer would be more missed & the officers and men alike would mourn the death of one who always shewed himself most fearless in his care of their safety and comfort. He never spared himself any amount of trouble to ensure that we were all looked after well & his work while second-in-command made him loved by us all in a way only a soldier can be.[138]

In his death, Trench, who showed himself in his letters to his wife and mother to be a devoted husband and son,[139] was mourned specifically as soldier for the same qualities of duty and inspirational masculinity that his civilian acquaintances highlighted. Despite the memories of men like Burney, E. D. White, a friend from Oxford, or his colleagues at Delloite, Plender, Griffiths, the manner of his death in battle meant that in the memorial that letters of condolence formed, Trench was constructed by both civilian and military mourners as a soldier whose masculine qualities were associated primarily with that identity.

Conclusion

In a society overwhelmed by death and mourning, letters of condolence provided private spaces within which individuals could be commemorated. Both civilians and fellow soldiers participated in such commemorations, writing letters that sought to both remember the dead and offer consolation for their loss.

There are clear differences between letters written by civilians and those written by soldiers. The letters of the civilian bereaved turned to images derived from the classics and tales of chivalry and utilized abstract qualities of religious sacrifice, sportsmanship and patriotism in their commemoration of the dead and justifications of their loss. Letters written by soldiers, by contrast, focussed on more specific details both of men's service and the manner of their deaths.

What both types of letter did, however, was construct the dead as specifically heroic. There is none of the ambivalence about war and men's participation in it that we have seen in wartime diaries. Doubts as to the worthiness of the cause for which men died would throw the death itself into question, thereby denying an important source of consolation. Nor was the domestic identity that was such a form of justification for fighting in men's letters home a feature of letters of condolence. While kinship with the dead was emphasized, the fictive kinship of military relations was as, if not more, important to the identities of the dead as civilian ties.

The dead were thus constructed in letters of condolence as entirely military figures, defined by their deaths as much as by their lives. These constructions were based on the concepts of sacrifice, patriotism, courage and duty so that the dead came to embody the masculine ideal of the hero. A countervailing form of embodiment can be seen in the narratives of disabled ex-servicemen examined in the next chapter, for whom the inscription of war experience on their bodies and minds served to undermine their attempts to construct postwar identities as successful domestic men.

4
'Fit only for Light Work': Disabled Ex-servicemen and the Struggle for a Domestic Masculinity

Despite the immense loss of life suffered by the British armed forces during four years of total war, the majority of servicemen survived the war, although many bore its scars upon their bodies and minds in the form of wounds, amputations and psychological disorders.[1] By 1929, 1,600,000 men had been awarded a pension or gratuity by the British government for disabilities incurred during the war.[2] Of these 71,433 were diagnosed with a psychological disorder either attributable to or aggravated by the war, 495,545 were in receipt of an artificial limb, mobility aid or other surgical appliance, and 1,331,486 had received institutional treatment for their disability.[3] While reintegration into postwar society was a struggle for all ex-servicemen,[4] the disabled faced particular hurdles as their experiences of disability often directly challenged the expectations of the masculine roles they had anticipated inhabiting upon their return to civilian life. Among the disabled, those with psychological disabilities faced particular struggles due to the contested nature of their disability.

The position of ex-servicemen in the postwar world was not an easy one, whether or not they had acquired disabilities during their service. Despite policies to rehire ex-servicemen that saw some reassertion of the gender order in the workplace,[5] the postwar economic situation in Britain worked against men's swift reintegration into the workforce. Similarly, despite men's efforts at maintaining domestic ties, four years of absence from home and the changes wrought by war had distanced many returning soldiers from their families, while the communities they had left had often been permanently changed by the absence of those who did not return. The patterns of remembrance that developed in Britain through the memorial movement and the Armistice Day ceremonies served to further distance ex-servicemen from the communities they returned to through the emphasis placed on mourning and comfort for the bereaved, as opposed to the celebration of survival that some ex-servicemen desired.[6] As the years went by, many ex-service groups found themselves marking the memory of the war in their own way, apart from the ceremonies developing in the broader culture.[7]

Within the main body of ex-servicemen, those disabled by the war faced particular difficulties in reintegrating. Some disabilities, such as shell shock or disfigurement, had the potential to alienate loved ones.[8] Physical disablement also meant that men were often unable to return to the jobs they had left or aspired to upon enlistment, entailing a loss of income or, in the most extreme cases, the ability to support themselves independently. The British government failed to provide enough resources for the retraining of the disabled, forcing them to rely instead on a network of voluntary organisations which also could provide treatment and shelter.[9] By placing such men in the stigmatizing position of recipients of charity, these policies isolated disabled men from the able-bodied world in which economic independence remained a key ideal.[10] They also forced these men to accept definitions of appropriate disabled masculinity imposed by charitable donors, definitions which included cheerful endurance, willingness to work towards recovery and a-sexuality.[11] While many disabled men did attempt to challenge these impositions and reassert their own sense of independent masculinity, their political isolation, both as disabled and as ex-servicemen, undermined such attempts.

If disabled ex-servicemen in general suffered from political and social isolation, no set of disabled men was more isolated than those suffering from psychological disabilities. The physically maimed could provide clear visual evidence of their war service and willingness to sacrifice themselves and their bodily integrity in the service of the state.[12] Those with disease, even though the question of attribution to war service might be contested, at least had a named, diagnosable illness that came within the authority of the medical profession. For men suffering from any of the numerous symptoms associated with the condition known as shell shock, however, the position was less clear. By the end of the war the reality of psychological disorders caused by the traumas of warfare was generally accepted, as can be seen by the adoption of 'shell shock' into common usage. Nonetheless, the accusations of malingering that had accompanied early diagnoses of these conditions remained, reinforced by the generally accepted view that the condition was curable.[13] Thus men who continued to suffer symptoms after several years of treatment were cast not as sufferers of wartime traumas but rather as lazy indigents attempting to rely on the state for support. For men whose mental health broke down after the Armistice, questions were raised as to whether the condition was attributable to war service or merely aggravated by it, allowing some psychiatric doctors to argue that men's family backgrounds of mental weakness made them unsuitable as soldiers in the first place. This argument denied men claims to heroic masculinity through the sacrifice of health that could be claimed by the physically disabled.[14]

Nowhere can these conflicts over the status of disabled men in postwar society be seen more clearly than in their treatment by the Ministry of Pensions. Established in 1917, the Ministry co-ordinated the diagnosis and treatment of war disabilities, as well as administering the assessment and payment of gratuities and pensions. It thus became the focus of pensioners' complaints about their treatment, both medical and financial, by the state which the Ministry represented. In letters to the Ministry, pensioners sought to reconstruct their masculine identities as socially appropriate domestic men despite their physical and economic disabilities.

The pensioners examined in this chapter suffered from a variety of forms of disability, ranging from lack of mobility to complete mental collapse. Some managed to return to their pre-war employment; others never found employment after the war or else were forced to change jobs, and even professions, several times. Some men waited several years before applying for a pension, others were dependent on the Ministry from the moment they found themselves in hospital. Some were able to renew or create family ties and domestic relationships. Others suffered as much from the collapse of domestic structures as their wounds. Their letters and other documents held in Ministry files describe struggles, both financial and emotional, feelings of injustice and of pride in the ability to survive in the face of many obstacles. Many letters are incoherent, angry or simply badly written. All bear witness to how these pensioners struggled to come to terms with their new identities as war-damaged men.

By their nature, many of these documents relate to men who continued to communicate with ministerial officials because they were dissatisfied with their treatment by the Ministry. As Helen Bettinson has noted, many men were either satisfied enough with their treatment not to bother appealing to the Ministry or else did not have the time, energy, wealth or support to argue their cases.[15] However, men who did continue to engage with the Ministry gave a voice to those struggling with their masculine identity and place in society as defined both by themselves and Ministry officials.

The Ministry of Pensions

Prior to the establishment of the Ministry of Pensions, pensions had been awarded by the different branches of the armed services on a discretionary, rather than a statutory, basis. With the introduction of conscription in 1916, however, questions arose over the state's responsibility to men disabled in its defence. The 1917 Royal Warrant set up a centralized ministry whose purpose was to co-ordinate the medical treatment and economic reintegration of men discharged from the military due to disability.

The warrant introduced a radical change to the way in which pensions were assessed through the introduction of the idea of pensions as compensation specifically for physical impairment. This policy reflected the belief that men had value to the state primarily as units of labour, whether in the armed forces during the war or as part of the national economy during peace. A central aim of Ministry policy was, therefore, to increase industrial capacity by encouraging men to work to their fullest physical capacity. In being detached from socio-economic standing, disability pensions could be used to encourage men to work to support themselves rather than relying on government funds. Disabilities were thus assessed 'with sole reference to the effect of war service on the condition,'[16] based on set schedules of disability. These schedules divided disabilities into percentage ranges, 1–5% for a minor, temporary disability through to 100% for permanent, total disability. Although these schedules were defined in terms of physical disablement, with 70% equating to the 'Short Amputation of leg or right arm above or through elbow, [or] total deafness,'[17] they were applied to all forms of disability, including psychological disorders and disease. The non-visual nature of many of these disabilities,[18] combined with the fact that 'the rate of compensation derived solely from scientific/medical factors, not from any attempt to restore the body to its socio-economic position prior to injury',[19] meant that the opinions of the doctors who assessed pensioners through medical boards had a great deal of influence in determining an individual's pension.

If the 1917 Warrant altered the way in which disabilities were assessed, the 1919 War Pensions Act altered the criteria for judging who was entitled to a pension by making the right to a pension statutory and introducing a right of appeal against Ministry decisions. Anyone who could show that their disability was attributable to service in the armed forces had a right of state compensation for the impairment caused by their disability. In addition, because pensions were to be awarded on the basis of physical impairment, as opposed to moral judgements of desert, a disability assessed as aggravated by war service would be granted at the same level as one attributable to it. Such cases were not uncommon. Cursory medical inspections on enlistment, particularly during the early years of the war, led to a number of men being invalided out of the armed forces due to medical complaints that had been aggravated rather than caused by their experiences of warfare.[20]

The 1919 act was the high point of state generosity towards First World War pensioners.[21] In the years that followed, the Ministry came under pressure from several sources that forced it to modify its stance. The first of these pressures was the steep rise in the number of men claiming war pensions immediately following the war, as men claimed for disabilities upon demobilization and the army began to discharge men under treatment once the war ended. At the same time, the Ministry was coming under increasing political and economic pressure from the Treasury which, in response to postwar economic gloom, sought to limit government spending. The Ministry was one of the victims of the 'Gedes' Axe', forcing it to cuts services to pensioners who turned instead to the voluntary sector for care and support.[22]

One of the first attempts by the government to reduce the pension bill was the 1921 War Pensions Act which sought to reduce the roll of pensioners by introducing both a Final Awards Scheme, designed to cut down on the expense of repeated medical assessments, and a seven-year time limit on pension claims. These measures did help to reduce the number of pensions awarded, with approximately 250,000 men being awarded a final one-off gratuity by 1925 and 500 having their awards stopped following a review of claims to entitlement to a pension.[23] However, a number of 'discretionary safety-valves' were also developed over this period, including the strengthening of the appeals process and increased use of Article 9 of the 1921 Act, which allowed pensioners to claim for disabilities even after the expiry of the time limit. Thus, although the financial pressures of the interwar period forced the Ministry to 'see its job as primarily one of limiting state liabilities,'[24] the administration of pensions provided space for both discretion on the part of the bureaucracy and complaint on the part of the pensioner.

Throughout this period, the Ministry was driven by two primary imperatives, the political need to be seen to be recompensing the heroic victims of the war and the economic need to rebuild those victims as independent economic players so that they no longer had to rely on ever-tighter state funds.[25] These imperatives led ministerial officials to construct two different and sometimes conflicting discourses of appropriate masculinity for disabled ex-servicemen. The first discourse was that of the heroic cripple, whose heroism was defined by his uncomplaining sacrifice for the state.[26] The original pressure brought to bear on Parliament to amend the pensions system arose from public opinion that men disabled through a service to the state made mandatory through conscription were heroes because of their physical sacrifices for the state.[27] The initial liberalism of the system that gave equal pensions to all those who had served, whether their disability was directly attributable to their service or merely aggravated by it, fed the discourse that those who served were heroes and thus deserved the gratitude and financial support of the state. There were, however, limits to heroism. Despite their statutory nature, pensions were never universal, with those viewed as morally unsuitable denied pensions. Wounds or diseases that were deemed to have been contracted through the sufferers' own behaviour, either by intention (self-inflicted wounds) or negligence (accidents) were refused pensions.[28] The state, through the Ministry, thus retained a level of control over who could be deemed a heroic cripple deserving of state support.

The second discourse that the Ministry created was that of the disabled ex-serviceman as independent worker.[29] This discourse arose out of the way in which pensions were allocated. Pensions were granted with reference to the effects of war on the physical or mental health of the pensioner rather than on his level of employability in the postwar economy, with the clear intention that pensioners should not be allowed to rely on the state for financial support. It was presumed that pensioners would seek and find work to the level of their percentage of health, the pension only acting as a supplement to a regular income. Thus a man who was assessed at 20% was assumed to be capable of earning 80% of his pre-war income, and it was considered his responsibility to do so. In order to achieve this aim, training was provided for ex-servicemen to prepare them as workers in the postwar economy.[30]

In addition to ensuring the reintegration of disabled men into the workforce, training was seen as a vital therapeutic tool. In an article for *Recalled to Life: A Journal Devoted to the Care, Re-education and Return to Civil Life of Disabled Sailors and Soldiers*, Sir Alfred Keogh, Director General of Army Medical Services during the war, wrote that the object of the

Curative Workshops schemes in government hospitals was 'to accelerate the men's recovery by providing them with congenial occupations, which serve to keep their minds occupied, and also to prevent them from losing touch with their active ways.' The result, he argued, was a:

> real satisfaction [that] does not lie in the fact that a man is able to augment his pension in so substantial a manner, but in the fact that he once more finds himself a capable citizen, competent, self-reliant, and able to regard [his disability] as it should be regarded, that is to say not as an affliction, but as a handicap, which, like a keen golfer, he can steadily reduce.[31]

In cases of neurasthenia, such mental activity was considered particularly important to treatment, in the form of 'ergotherapy,' or treatment through work in order to strengthen men's will-power, which had been pioneered at Craiglockhart War Hospital during the war by Dr A. J. Brock, Wilfred Owen's doctor.

While these two narratives of appropriate disabled masculinity could coincide, with the stoic disabled man who cheerfully underwent treatment and retraining retaining his status as heroic cripple, they also had the potential to conflict. At the political level, ministers and civil servants in the Pensions Ministry and the Treasury were involved in negotiations between themselves and the public over the amount of money to be committed to supporting pensioners. Conflicts were most common, however, between the Ministry and pensioners, who often viewed heroism and economic viability in different terms.[32] For pensioners, while heroic masculinity was located within their wartime experience, masculine identity was by no means limited to their time as soldiers or their ability to re-enter the workforce. It was also defined by their role as independent providers for the home. Their sacrifice of bodily health for the state thus entitled them to compensation not only as physical beings, as intended by the pension warrants, but also as economic individuals. While pensioners' own understanding of masculinity in economic terms supported ministerial discourses of the reintegration of the disabled into the economy, it also held the seeds of potential conflict when men failed to reintegrate at the level expected of them. Disability, for many, entailed losses of status, income and future in relation to employment, losses that pensioners often felt should be compensated for but which were not covered by the royal warrants.

Pensioner responses

Ex-servicemen's letters responded to the expectations of the Ministry of Pension through manipulation and contestation of these discourses of heroic and economic masculinity. In both their approaches to the Ministry and their responses to their treatment by the Ministry, men developed a number of rhetorical tactics designed to elicit sympathy for their own perceptions of their masculine status. These included identifying the war as the primary cause of their condition, reasserting the argument that the British government, in the form of the Ministry, had a duty of care to ex-servicemen because of the manner in which they had become disabled, and emphasizing their own ability to be self-reliant except in extremity. All three tactics served to place responsibility for the care of the war disabled with the state, while re-emphasizing the claimants' possession of the heroic qualities of endurance and resourcefulness that the Ministry desired the war disabled to display.

The tactic of identifying the war as the cause of disability was not intended only to appeal to the ideals of the state. Men applying for pensions, or appealing against the refusal of a pension, had to show their condition was either directly attributable to their war service or else due to a pre-existing condition that had been aggravated by war service. Neither conditions that were the result of postwar actions or experiences nor those that appeared during war service and which could not be shown to relate to that service were eligible for a pension. Men's declarations that their conditions were the result of the war were thus a necessary part of their application or appeal process.

The language that men used to make their cases, however, utilized discourses of heroism. By casting their appeals in the language of state responsibility, men and their advocates emphasized their heroic sacrifice for the state. Thus C. E. Evans's father pointed out that his son had 'faithfully and worthily done his duty to his King and Country and is now in need of their care.'[33] Similarly, C. J. Stanfield's doctor argued, 'The country has just as great a responsibility to the wounded of mind as it has to the wounded in body.'[34] Such comments emphasized disabled ex-servicemen's identities as soldiers to whom the state they had served owed a continuing duty of care.

Pensioners and their families reinforced their claims to state care by emphasizing that their disability was attributable to, rather than aggravated by, war. O. P. Allcock:

desire[d] to appeal against [the Medical Board's] decision to state that the disability (Neurasthenia) was 'aggravated by' my service in the R.A.F.... I can prove that I did not suffer from Neurasthenia before the war & that my speech was then good enough to make a speech in Latin at my school 'Speech Day' before an audience of several hundred.[35]

N. L. Corbet's brother acknowledged that he was 'suffering from mental derangement' but in the next sentence wrote that 'His trouble is undoubtedly due to his war experience.'[36] W. H. Botterill had a friend write to the Ministry in his support stating, 'He is now a bundle of nerves, and it is pitiful to see him so sadly changed – undoubtedly chiefly through the dreadful time of the war.'[37] For these men, there was no financial advantage to be gained in having their disabilities assessed as attributable to rather than aggravated by war. The attribution of disability to war service, however, gave the neurasthenic man a claim to masculine status that he otherwise forfeited through his apparent loss of self-control.[38]

Men suffering from other forms of disability also supported their arguments for attribution by pointing to their good health prior to the war service. 'I went overseas as fit as any man could go,' C. S. Bellamy asserted. 'I did what I was told to do while over there. I am now back and I cannot run even 100 ft without puffing and wheezing very badly and my heart going out of all reason.'[39] G. M. Hetherington's wife pointed out, 'he was a capable officer – also a strong healthy man, he returned in 1916 a physical wreck having lost 4 stone in weight, suffering from dysentery, frozen feet, acute rheumatism & general nervous prostration.'[40] F. Room similarly noted his categorisation as A1 on his enlistment compared with his Grade II categorisation upon demobilisation,[41] while R. J. R. Farrow's doctor also wrote of his patient being a different type of man following his war service: 'Until he entered the army, he was quite healthy & a very fine specimen of manhood as well as being unusually able. I also attended him after his war service & can certify that he was then a broken man.'[42]

If the tactic of making the state responsible for the disabled because disability was attributable to war experience emphasized men's identities as soldiers, other tactics emphasized qualities associated with appropriate domestic masculinities. One tactic that pensioners used, for instance, was claiming to refuse Ministry assistance except as a last resort. The point of this form of appeal was that it emphasized pensioners' desire to be self-reliant, a tenet of self-help that was central to pre-war concepts of the virtuous domestic masculine ideal.[43] 'I do not want a pension,' J. J. Holland told the Director General of Awards, 'I want to be clear of the whole thing, to go away and get well again.'[44] Many men felt as G. H. Birch did: 'It is a hell to write asking for this favour.'[45]

Work

Self-reliance was also highlighted by men's insistence that they would prefer a job to receiving a pension if only they could find work. As J. L. Campbell-White explained, 'I cannot get any work, I only wish that I could do so – I have tried hard enough through the Ministry of Appts. & also myself – If I could get a decent job, I should not trouble about the Pension.'[46] E. C. Booker similarly told the Ministry, 'I am trying to make myself and family self-supporting and thereby independent of any pension.'[47] The desire to be self-sufficient was also expressed by pensioners whose disability meant that they had to give up work. W. C. Greene's letter is a typical example: 'Following my doctor's advice and instructions I *had* to cease work as a printer, leave London and come to Leeds on the 12th November, 1921.' [My emphasis].[48] F. C. Gerard also used the imperative, writing that he was '*compelled* to give up my Business in London and come down to the country for the Benefit of my health, my Nervous System being shattered.' [My emphasis].[49] J. J. R. Larkin, having found a job in 1925 was, in 1930, also '*compelled* to cease my work owing to finding the effort of walking too painful' [My emphasis],[50] while J. W. B. Balfour was, 'owing to a very serious breakdown...*forced* to give up my business.' [My emphasis].[51]

The implication behind these imperative verbs was that the reason that men were not supporting themselves through independent work was due solely to their disability, rather than due to any desire to rely on the state to support them. Such word choice helped to create a sympathetic image when appealing to the Ministry. However, the desire to work was also genuine. The medical board that evaluated R. N. Barwell, a neurasthenic, reported that 'he gets very tired after hard work, but if he does not work he gets depressed.'[52] Such reaction to the inability to work grew out of the sense of obligation to support themselves that was impressed upon pensioners not only by the Ministry of Pensions but also by social prescriptions of appropriate domestic masculinity that encompassed ideals of self-help and the male breadwinner.[53]

Unemployment

Obtaining work in the postwar economy was not, however, easy for ex-servicemen. Unemployment in Britain between the wars was high, varying between 1.1 and 1.75 million between 1922 and 1929. By 1930, it had reached two million, a level which did not fall until 1936.[54] In such an economic climate, finding work was problematic for the able-bodied. For men suffering from a pensionable disability, the difficulty was substantially increased. As J. J. R. Larkin pointed out, 'disabled soldiers are not over popular as candidates for jobs.'[55] The glut of able-bodied workers on the market and the levels of unemployment that persisted throughout the interwar period meant that employers could be choosy. The government introduced and promoted schemes such as the King's Roll, whereby employers agreed that a certain percentage of their workforce would be made up of disabled employees.[56] Such schemes, however, were neither mandatory nor enforceable and tended to be limited to the larger employers such as the railways and the postal service. As one Ministry of Pensions Employment Sub-Committee noted, 'So long as the employer is desired to pay the same wages for a disabled man as for an able bodied man the chances are that the latter will be selected in preference.'[57]

Men with psychological disabilities, which were not understood particularly well, faced particular difficulties in obtaining and keeping employment. Norman Fenton, an American doctor, noted that:

[The] misconception of shell shock as related to insanity worked out often as a great difficulty for the men in finding employment... One employer seeing the magic words said, 'I'd like to reemploy you, but I'm afraid you'd get to breaking things and hugging the girls, etc.' Many employers refused to reemploy men – to say nothing of employing them for the first time – upon whose discharge there was any indication of shell shock or war neurosis.[58]

Similar problems faced British ex-servicemen with neurasthenia. A. Gear made sure that 'my present employers are not aware that I receive Retired Pay', explaining that he had 'already lost one post as the result of my service with H. M. Forces due to Neurasthenia and kindred ailments; [and] my services have been exploited by another employer because I have been in receipt of Disability Retired Pay'.[59] C. F. Ambler told the Ministry, 'I do not desire to go to my employers for anything as they are not aware that I am a pensioner, if they knew my job would not be secure',[60] while C. E. Evans:

> stated that when called upon by his employers for an explanation for his absences from duty he never urged that his war service was responsible, because he did not wish it to be known in the district that he suffered a mental disability. He preferred to allow his actions to be regarded as wilful.[61]

Here was a case of a man willing to risk his economic situation in favour of retaining his masculine reputation for self-control by hiding his disability. At a social level, mental disability, and the lack of self-control that it implied, continued to be seen by sufferers as a stigma. Hiding their disability was a way in which disabled men could attempt to reclaim a sense of normalcy in which they saw themselves as self-controlled individuals.

When they knew of adverse medical records, employers appeared to avoid employing disabled men. P. G. Eckersall 'put in 70 applications in working for [illegible] this year alone & ... received [not] the slightest consideration from anyone excepting in one case where I was told not to appear before the Committee unless I could produce a Medical Certificate certifying me absolutely fit.'[62] G. M. Hetherington also found that his medical record told against him. Having given up his medical practice when he lost his memory, he found he was 'quite unable to find any work owing to his having been in a mental asylum.'[63] Prejudice and the fear of prejudice against mental disability played a significant role in neurasthenic men's ability to reintegrate themselves into the postwar economy.

Problems with employment

The majority of the pensioners, however, were forced to work by their economic situation, a 100% permanent pension only being granted in cases of complete incapacity. Some were more successful at finding and maintaining employment than others. B. Harrison, whose right leg was amputated below the knee, worked down a mine for six years,[64] while R. F. Williams, deaf in one ear, returned to his pre-war job as the statistical manager of a large hosiery firm. He was so successful in living with his disability that, in 1933, he was 'appointed to the control of the staff of my firm ... [which] necessitates continual conversations and meetings.'[65] He attributed his ability to function so successfully as a businessman to the quality of his Ministry-supplied hearing aid.

Not all pensioners, however, were so lucky in adapting, even with Ministry assistance. For amputees, the necessity of mobility aids often caused difficulty. Although the Ministry was supposed to supply all amputees with either artificial limbs or tricycles, delays were common.[66] R. A. McCaffrey had problems when his artificial leg broke down in 1919: 'he applied personally at Thorney House, and was informed that his application for a second limb would be considered in about two months time from then. He is employed as a Storekeeper, which work he is unable to continue on crutches.'[67] A damaged or lost leg could, with some difficulty, be replaced. More complicated for ministerial bureaucracy were the cases of men such as F. J. Edwards who was 'unable to wear this [wooden] leg as a spare owing to the difference in weight as compared with his metal leg, also the leg is very uncomfortable and does not fit.' As his work as a Custom's official involved a 'considerable amount of walking and standing, ... [he found] he cannot carry on when repairs are necessary to his metal leg.'[68]

Although the Ministry was often bureaucratic in its approach to supplying men with suitable limbs, problems such as those faced by amputees in their employment tended to be comparatively easily solved through the supply of more appropriate or extra limbs or treatment for infected stumps.[69] For men suffering from neurasthenia and other psychological disorders, the problems were not always so easy to solve. The disabilities that these men suffered incapacitated them for work in ways that the Ministry's treatment programmes could not always address. W. Dewherst, for example, felt that:

he cannot carry on his job as a schoolmaster. His memory is getting worse & so is quite unable to concentrate on his work. He has brought to the Board a report from the Durham County Education Department expressing marked dissatisfaction with his work and a threat of dismissal if there is no improvement within the next six months.[70]

J. W. B. Balfour told an appeal board:

In leading up to reports in connection with my business, I often have to make statements contradicting experienced Engineers, and as these reports have been coming into meetings, they are argued at these times. I often break down and give way to emotions and very often have to leave these meetings.[71]

O. P. Allcock stuttered and 'had to give up one job as motor-driver owing to my nerves being unable to stand the strain of driving.'[72]

Another problem faced by neurasthenic pensioners was the fact that the pressures of work often served to exacerbate their condition. S. F. Luker told an interviewer from the Ministry that his work 'leaves him thoroughly exhausted',[73] while W. Dewherst was reported as having 'had a "bad time" since Christmas owing to his worry over his school experiences.'[74] In some cases, such strain was caused by the nature of the work chosen. R. K. Pillers acknowledged that 'the universal conditions of my profession – engineering – necessitate long hours and, as engineering work is invariably situated in non-residential environments, the day is further lengthened by the time taken in travelling to and fro. In my case the average working day is sometimes twelve hours.'[75] H. V. Elliot exacerbated his neurasthenia when 'he started a dance band in addition to his piano tuning. This employment in addition to his piano tuning made his meals irregular & constant insomnia.'[76] The nervous breakdown he eventually suffered was deemed to be attributable to post-war economic pressure rather than war service, and he was refused any further compensation from the Ministry.

Indeed, Ministry of Pensions officials tended to be suspicious of claims of nervous decline, especially when it was considered that such decline might be attributable factors other than the war. In the case of F. W. de Valda, the Appeal Board hearing the case was advised to:

> make due allowance for any persisting effects of the non-service illnesses, for economic and other non-service factors, and for any other constitutional weakness present, special regard being had to their effect in worsening or retarding the recovery from the pensioned disability, and the Board's assessment should reflect solely the disablement resulting from the accepted neurosis.[77]

In 1923, an Appeal Board declared in the case of R. J. R. Farrow that 'the Officer's present condition of anxiety hysteria and associated symptoms are entirely the outcome of civil and economic circumstances, quite unconnected with his military service which terminated in April 1919.'[78] Nonetheless, the doctors who examined pensioners were quite aware of the strain that civil employment could have on a man's condition. They noted, for instance, that F. J. Blackburn suffered from 'overwork & worry with sleeplessness...headaches following overwork',[79] that F. M. Brister had his sleep disturbed by worrying dreams about his work,[80] and that A. W. Beamand's 'work appears to be worrying him considerably & he is in an exceedingly nervous sensitive state.'[81] As these were factors unconnected with military service, however, they could play no part in assessing men's level of disability with regards to a pension.

Perhaps the most ironic example of how detrimental neurasthenia was to a man's ability to work was the case of G. H. Edwards. In 1919, a medical board reported that 'Since last board [he] has done six weeks work as clerk in Ministry of Labour. Gave up because of depression and fear that the work would finish.'[82] The responsibility that Edwards felt to keep working was the ultimate aggravating factor in his condition, forcing him to eventually give up work. As another pensioner put it, 'The struggle to try and keep going is hardly worth the constant anxiety.'[83]

Maintaining employment

Despite the difficulties that ex-servicemen face in finding work, the social pressures upon them as men to support themselves and their dependants was such that many were forced to compromise in finding and maintaining work. For some, this meant relying heavily on the assistance of others, often colleagues, to hide their inability to do their work properly. W. P. Gooding, a schoolmaster, was considered by his doctor to be:

> not in reality fit to earn his livelihood – his position in school is made possible only by the loyalty of his colleagues who are continually on the watch for his lapses & who relieve him as much as possible – He could not as he is at present obtain or keep a teaching billet among strangers.[84]

C. F. Ambler similarly found himself relying on 'a personal friend...who helps me a great deal and without this help I could not do my job.' He continued:

> By the end of the week I am absolutely worn out and have to rest the week-end to get sufficient energy to carry on the next weeks work. Of course the work as it is, is too much for me and if it wasn't for the position I am in being on a temporary pension I would not carry on.[85]

S. F. Luker, a pub manager, also found his work too much and felt that he only maintained his position due to the tolerance of his employer. An enquiry officer sent by the Ministry to assess his situation reported that:

> on occasions he breaks down completely for a week or so at a time, and [he was]...emphatic that not every employer would be

so indulgent as the present one, knowing full well that pensioner [*sic*] is without the capacity to normally undertake his full share of the responsibilities entailed, and that he is frequently of no use at all when he gets a bad spell.[86]

Another way in which neurasthenic ex-servicemen compromised in order to withstand some of the strain of civil employment was to obtain a more junior, and therefore less remunerative position than they would have otherwise held. J. Burdekin, for instance, 'was Branch Manager for "Electrolux" for 4 years, but had to resign this month as he found the work too worrying. Has been offered a junior position now.'[87] F. M. Brister similarly found himself:

> obliged to accept junior positions in business due to my health not being sufficient to bear strain of position as my training and previous abilities fitted me for.... This causes serious embarrassment to me in my profession inasmuch as I cannot place any confidence in myself or enjoy that of my superiors.[88]

By accepting a junior position, Brister maintained his employment but, in the process, felt himself forced by his disability to sacrifice an element of his self-respect as a man capable of working to his full pre-war capacity.

Finally, because of the postwar economic climate and the restrictions imposed by their health, disabled men often took work where they could find it, even if it meant that they were exploited by their employers. In his search for work, Eckersall told the Ministry, 'I have applied for over 30 posts as an engineering assistant & in some cases I have offered my services as low as £130.' '[T]oday,' he explained, 'I ought to be in a position to command more than three times that amount.'[89] J. S. Hardy, who also found his services as a draughtsman in low demand, complained that he was 'existing by working as an assistant in a tobacco store in Wolfville, Nova Scotia & at the same time endeavouring to secure employment as a draughtsman or in some capacity where my technical training would increase my earning capacity.'[90] Prior to the war he had specialized in the production of small arms for the Royal Ordinance Factories at Woolwich but 'The injury to my knee necessitated my retirement from the Civil Service & the loss of professional employment in which I had specialized for fifteen years.'[91] This reduction in status from professional to unskilled labourer was presented by Hardy as a loss that affected his masculine identity as it was defined by his work.

Loss

In addition to loss of income and status, pensioners also suffered a much deeper sense of loss, as hinted at in Hardy's comments. Disability meant the inability to return to the normalcy that pre-war careers exemplified, as well as the loss of a past dedicated to a career. Like Hardy, C. E. Evans cited the amount of time he had put into his career when bemoaning his loss of profession: 'I have no other profession than that of a soldier, having served close on 9 years with the Colours, and have no employment of any kind to go to.'[92] Being invalided out of military service was particularly difficult for Regular soldiers as it automatically debarred them from pursuing their chosen careers. They were certainly not alone, however. P. Ashe found that 'I cannot engage in General Practice and resume the work I had, prior to joining the R.A.M.C. . . . I am fit only for light work, which is difficult to get in the medical profession.'[93]

Men who lost the ability to pursue their pre-war professions did have the option of retraining, something that the Ministry was eager for them to do.[94] To do so, however, could mean loss of social status. Hardy's frustration at his inability to use his technical skills to earn his living was one example of this. Another was F. C. Gerrard who 'was passed unfit for pre-war occupation as a School Master; he was recommended for a course of poultry farming.'[95] Other occupations that the Ministry offered training in included basket making, massage and telephony.[96] This loss, of the past and the status earned in the past, could be very distressing. It was, after all, both a denial and inversion of the middle-class tenet of self-improvement that was central to the Victorian concept of masculinity[97] and a re-emphasis of the destruction of normalcy that the war had caused to these men's lives.

Reactions to such loss varied. Hardy, for example, asked for recompense for what he cast as a sacrifice of his masculine identity, namely his ability to do his job, in the service of the state. 'Practically my profession has been taken from me,' he wrote. 'I can only appeal for fair treatment from the greatest Empire in the World towards a man who offered all that life meant to him and lost practically half of it, both from the point of view of enjoyment and earning capacity.'[98]

For men beginning their careers when they went to war, the loss of their professional future was as distressing as the loss of professional standing was for men already established in professions when war broke out. For some, it meant the loss of the chance to improve professional status. J. J. Holland, for instance, was '[b]y profession . . . a schoolmaster, & just prior to the war was well on the way to obtain a university degree; but now, as I can study only at such time as my disability will allow me, my hopes of future scholastic attainment are poor.'[99] Similarly, R. J. R. Farrow claimed, 'had I not been suffering from my invaliding disability neurasthenia, I should have been granted a Certificate of Qualification'[100] which would have allowed him to obtain a permanent position as a civil servant. As it was, he was only offered temporary employment for two years.

For young men like G. M. Lawless, who had 'no profession to follow as my training was interrupted on my joining the army in 1914',[101] the loss of professional future could be equally severe. W. B. Hetherington claimed that:

> Previous to the war I was considered one of the brightest apprentices in the employ of my firm. I passed numerous examinations in Mathematics Mechanics etc. I was the head boy at school and a good debater.... Now I have lost confidence & in spite of my anxiety to get on I cannot keep a job requiring any brain effort.[102]

J. Burdekin found that 'I am now unable to resume my studies as my memory entirely fails me due to Neurasthenia.'[103] Although they had not put in the time to building their careers that older men had, young pensioners such as these were faced with the devastating loss of the future promise they had shown before the war. Under such circumstances, it is hardly surprising that some men had 'Lost self confidence and hope in [their] future.'[104]

Supporting the family

Loss of status and the ability to practise the tenets of self-help were not the only challenges that disability posed to ex-servicemen's sense of masculine identity. Equally threatened were the discourses of the male breadwinner and family wage that defined the respectable man as a family provider. Many pensioners considered themselves the family breadwinners. Whether the family was supported by the pension alone or by income from supplementary employment, the general assumption expressed in letters to the Ministry was that such support would be derived from the man's income, in line with the male breadwinner norm. Because of this, disabled men with families often assumed that they would receive special consideration. H. O. Bristow wrote in 1920, 'I feel sure that on stating my case the amount offered will be reconsidered in a favourable manner,' giving as his first reason, 'I am a married man with a wife and one child living.'[105] M. J. L. Daly argued 'that a disability which not only interferes with my office duties but affects me even in my marital relations and prevents me from leading a full married life deserves more generous consideration.'[106] R. J. R. Farrow also asked for special consideration when he asked to have part of his pension paid as a lump sum. 'I understand that this, my application is irregular,' he wrote, 'but I do pray that my appeal be granted as it means such an enormous lot to me, being, in fact, the difference between health & strength and permanent invalidism of my Wife.'[107]

Expectations that they would fulfil the masculine role of provider was a cause of concern for many men, particularly when the alternative was to suffer the humiliation of asking for charity.[108] E. C. Booker, for one, found that, 'living in the City, trying to earn enough to keep my family and send my boys to school, just drives one to distraction especially when rent alone costs $40 per month which leaves $2 per month for food clothing and schooling.'[109] When writing to request an allowance for his wife, M. L. J. Daly pointed out that:

> since July last I have had the extra responsibilities and expenditure necessitated by the birth of a child. Under these circumstances and also for the reason that my disability is aggravated by the struggle to make ends meet I trust you will give this application your sympathetic and early consideration.[110]

Despite the detrimental effect that he believed work had on his health, a moral imperative to support his family was clearly a strong driving force.

The result was that men could feel deeply aggrieved when perceived lack of Ministry support caused them to fail in their roles as family providers. C. E. Evans, for instance, complained:

> I am now living on my wife's people, being unable to follow employment, and having no means to carry on. I should be very grateful for a lump sum in payment immediately or I shall have to seek charity . . . .
>
> [T]he public would make a great outcry if the facts of my case were made known to them. And I shall feel compelled, unless something definite is done *this week*, to obtain help in a way which may cause publicity. I do not want Charity I want my rights.[111]

J. L. Campbell-White similarly asked, 'why cannot I get what is due to me?'[112] Campbell-White's accusation was that the Ministry was being unjust and parsimonious towards his innocent wife and children in their refusal of his request for financial assistance. 'How do you think I am to keep my wife & two children when I am receiving no money,' he demanded in early 1920.[113] Four months later he wrote again, expressing astonishment that 'the Ministry of Pensions think that a man can keep his wife self & two children on £87 a year, it seems too ridiculous for words.'[114]

Campbell-White was not alone in his complaint. 'How am I expected to keep a wife and one child, and live in these expensive times for six weeks on nothing I can't quite see,' Evans declared. 'It is absolutely impossible....'[115] F. V. Branford complained that 'during the past two years my pension has been lowered from £210 to £140 per annum and it is practically impossible to maintain a wife and child on this allowance.'[116] Even men with private incomes found that supporting a family was difficult. C. W. N. Fuller found:

> The little capital which my wife and I had, has gone during the strug-gle of the past 4 years, as owing to ill health, I have lost one job after another, and have had many long periods of unemployment. The result is that, now, my wife and child are entirely dependent on my pension and the position is desperate.[117]

R. J. R. Farrow complained that treatment for his disability had 'exhausted the small stock of capital, which I had. Consequently, I am now experiencing severe hardship and, not only does this apply to myself, but also to my Wife & family.'[118]

Responsibility

Men thus presented the duty of the Ministry as being not only towards themselves, the men who had sacrificed health in the service of their country, but also towards the families who looked to them for support. 'I regret that I am obliged to make this application but I find that it is absolutely necessary that I should do so in justice to my family,' wrote J. R. Hill.[119] Others appear to have taken a similar view of the Ministry's responsibilities towards the families of pensioners. A friend of H. A. Amiss wrote on his behalf explaining, 'Mr. Amiss has a wife and 3 children, and it is hoped that in *their* interest he will be afforded a medical examination at the earliest possible moment.' [My emphasis].[120] 'I am not looking for comfort,' E. C. Booker explained, 'but if you can-not give me my health, I have every right to expect sufficient to enable myself and family to get the bare necessities of life, that is food and clothes.'[121] The masculine role of supporting a family which disabled men could not fulfil was thus transferred to the state.

Some men demanded even greater levels of responsibility from the Ministry. Booker asked for 'official permission to work at the Lumber mills here or any other job sufficient to support my wife & family –, and acknowledging that the Ministry of Pensions will be responsible for any result to my condition brought about through not carrying out the Doctors orders,'[122] while C. W. N. Fuller demanded that, 'if he leaves here [a mental hospital] without a permanent pension, the Ministry will accept responsibility for any injury he may do his wife and children.'[123] These requests asked that the Ministry take moral as well as financial responsibility for the condition that the war had left pensioners in, a condition which, they argued, caused them to fail as breadwinners and good husbands and fathers. Ultimately, in seeking to justify their requests for support, pensioners demanded that the Ministry of Pensions, on behalf of the British government, accept responsibility for their failings as breadwinners, good husbands and fathers, and therefore men, which they saw as being a direct result of their service to the state. This claim, while it might serve as justification for their failures to support their families, undermined claims that disabled men were also trying to make to the masculine role of independent breadwinner.

Family support

The extent to which reliance on a pension for financial support undermined men's ability to see themselves as family breadwinners can best be seen in the cases of men who underwent residential treatment for their pensionable disability. As they were unable to work while undergoing treatment, men were placed on full pensions of £210 per year with a deduction of 7s.6d. per week for maintenance. Men still feared, however, that their families were not being provided for. J. L. Campbell-White complained bitterly when deductions for maintenance were made from his pension because 'I am married and have two children to keep, and am entirely dependent on my pension.'[124]

Treatment not only threatened men's domestic masculine identity as family breadwinners through the financial hardship it imposed but also challenged their roles as good husbands and fathers by distancing them from their families. The Ministry could instruct a man to report to any hospital for treatment, not always one that was close to their family. In cases of neurasthenia, separating men from their families was deliberate. Many specialists who worked with neurasthenic servicemen during and after the war believed that the presence of relatives had an adverse effect on the patient's ability to recover. In a 1918 article in *The Lancet*, Dr A. J. Brock argued:

> The neurasthenic is very apt to use his relatives merely as props or drugs, to pander to his feeling of helplessness; sometimes relations (and, of course, also other friends) become such a nuisance in this way that the patient has to be forcibly isolated from them by imposition of the 'Weir-Mitchell treatment.'[125]

Sir John Collie, Director General of Medical Service for the Ministry and later President of the Special Medical Boards that assessed neurasthenic ex-servicemen, also saw isolation as a solution, declaring, 'In the case of men earning no wages who are suffering from persistent and pronounced Neurasthenia, the only useful treatment consists of removal from the sympathetic environment of their homes to a suitable Institution where they will be subjected to Psycho-therapeutic treatment.'[126] The concern expressed by doctors such as Collie was that disabled men who were emotionally dependent on their families would become financially dependent on the state as emotional dependence would threaten the desire to be cured.[127] Many men, however, wanted to be close to their families,[128] presenting themselves as integral members of their families not only in the economic role of breadwinner but also in the more emotional role of husband and father.

Despite the disapproval of some specialists, families' support of disabled men, both emotional and financial, was often vital, even though such dependence could serve to further erode pensioners' understandings of themselves as mature men. A. C. Gilmer and E. C. Booker both turned to their relatives for financial support. '[M]y Father,' Gilmer wrote, 'is prepared to assist me financially to start in an outdoor way of business, providing I get assistance in the shape of a Gratuity.'[129] Booker reported, 'had it not been for relatives my wife and I both would have these last few years gone short, if not actually without'.[130]

The family member that many men turned to in the first instance was their wife. Wives were often the main source of care for disabled men. In the case of F. E. B. Feilman, his doctor actively encouraged his marriage as a source of care, telling a Medical Appeal Board that 'it seemed to me the best way of having some one permanently present who would be responsible for him.'[131] C. J. Stanfield similarly justified his proposed marriage to a nurse by pointing out that she 'thoroughly knows my case having nursed me at the Red Cross Hospital Brighton, on several occasions.' He express concern, however, over the question of his pension:

> Some time ago I was informed, that, being on the Alternative basis, it could not (at present) be made permanent. If, however, you could give me an assurance that, provided I complied with the Ministry's regulations regarding treatment my pension would remain on the present basis of £346 p.a., I should feel safe and justified in making the contemplated alteration to my life.[132]

The desire to be a good provider for the family was, again, a predominant concern.

Wives provided a great deal more support than simply medical care, however. W. Dewherst, whose work made him feel suicidal, told a Medical Board that 'when with his wife he feels safe from harm.'[133] E. C. Booker's wife provided her husband with a more concrete form of support in his management of a pub. A report on the couple noted that 'when trade is brisk he becomes too excited to be of any real assistance and that for this reason his wife takes sole charge from eight o'clock onwards when it is customary for him to go to his private apartments to rest.'[134] W. H. Botterill's wife used the £210s a week that she earned to 'keep our home going, support myself, and provide my husband's extra expenses, laundry, postage, etc.'[135] while he was undergoing treatment.

For Botterill himself, his wife's willingness and ability to earn her own living and support him was not entirely positive. He wrote to her from hospital, 'I'm sorry you are so tired & are having such a worrying time, it makes me so frightfully fed up being so absolutely useless.'[136] G. H. Birch found the fact that his wife needed to work not only frustrating but also shameful. 'You will understand my position,' he wrote to the Ministry:

> when I tell you that my poor wife went to work at the Manchester [illegible] as a librarian (as I thought) but really washing pots etc in the works canteen in order to help keep things going ....I don't like complaining and I hate to display my poverty which although due to incapacity is hateful to my wife & me ....It is hell to write asking for this favour ...but could I see my dear wife washing pots for a living.[137]

Birch expressed the humiliation that men felt when forced to admit their failures as family breadwinners.

Such humiliation was felt by most men forced to rely on the support of their families. A report on Booker noted, 'He is not getting on as well as he hoped in civil re-establishment and has had to have recourse to assistance from his people, to live, and this he feels is a constant injury to his self-regard.'[138] Charity was seen as humiliating, even when it came from within the family circle. In addition, families could not always afford to support the pensioners, adding a sense of guilt. A. C. H. Groom found himself 'entirely dependent on my fathers' [*sic*] generosity for a roof & food for my wife self & child. My father cannot afford this which knowledge naturally in view of my health only retards my progress.'[139] P. G. Eckersall, meanwhile, felt that 'I cannot live on my people who are themselves only in moderate circumstances.'[140]

Domestic breakdown

The frustration and humiliation felt by pensioners forced to rely on family members grew out of a role reversal that challenged the ideal of the independent male. Instead of supporting their wives and other dependants, men were forced to accept help from wives and parents, placing them in positions of medical, financial and emotional dependence akin to those of a child, undermining their claims to mature masculinity.[141] This could, in turn, place enough pressure on families that the very existence of the family unit was threatened. Families found themselves having to physically care for invalid men in ways that they had not anticipated. Wives who worked to support their husbands, for instance, could break down physically, as Mrs Botterill did in 1924. Her doctor reported that he 'found her suffering from overwork and strain. Upon enquiry, this was inevitable. She was carrying on business to support herself & husband, and was in much anxiety'.[142] The wife of J. F. Marshall, paralysed from the waist down, was reported as 'feeling the strain of constantly pushing me up these hills & her medical attendant has advised her not to subject herself to this strain unless absolutely unavoidable'.[143] O. C. Marris, who suffered from functional paralysis, required 'constant attention,' according to his father, '& is very helpless, requiring frequently two persons to move him in bed....At present I and my wife have to do all this in addition to our other duties.'[144] The result, as in Mrs Botterill's case, could be a breakdown on the part of the carer. Five days after Dr Alderson reported that J. E. Cornell, who suffered from tuberculosis, chronic asthma and bronchitis, was 'certainly in need of more care than his wife is able to provide,' the Area Deputy Commissioner of Medical Services reported that 'this officer's wife has broken down and was no longer able to look after her husband.'[145] Although no details are given as to what sort of breakdown Mrs Cornell suffered, it would appear, on the evidence of the earlier letter, that it was related to the physical and emotional strain of caring for a disabled husband, a child and a household.

Men's disabilities could also place their families under intense emotional pressure. W. P. Gooding's wife, for instance, 'became alarmed by his depressed spirits, lack of control etc.'[146] N. L. Corbet's brother 'state[d] that the Officer was...causing great anxiety at home on account of his behaviour. He wanders about at night, undressed, and attempts to go out.'[147] C. E. Evans's father expressed his family's concern over his 'fits of loss of memory [which] have occurred ever since he left the service in Jan 1919 and they have gradually become more severe making him forget his duty to himself and his home, forgetful of every thing but the Phantom which has guided him away for a week.'[148] The emotional suffering of the family was thus cast in terms of Evans's failure to fulfil the domestic ideal of the good husband through his inability to do his duty by his family.

It was not only anxiety that disabled men caused to their families. Men with neurasthenia could be actively disruptive to domestic health and happiness. E. C. Booker admitted 'that he is extremely irritable in his daily associations at home, and states that he finds it very difficult to prevent himself from making a great deal of unnecessary trouble.'[149] J. H. K. Barraclough also disrupted his family by frequently finding grievances against his parents, not all of them, the authorities implied, rational.[150] More obviously irrational were G. M. Lawless's accusations against his wife. As he descended further into the delusions that saw him certified in 1926, he claimed, 'that his wife is unfaithful to him and wants to get him out of the way.' Although he later recovered enough to be released to the care of his wife, six years later he again claimed, 'he wants to get rid of his wife as he cannot afford to keep her, and thinks she has another husband somewhere else.'[151] Lawless, in his delusions, gave voice to two dominant concerns of men as heads of households through his conflation of the sexual and the economic. His fears of his wife's imagined infidelity arose as much from his inability to support her, forcing her to find a husband who could, as from his fears over his lack of ability as a lover. Such delusions, however, ultimately betrayed Lawless's desire to act as a good husband, leading as they did to hospitalisation and the resultant fracturing of the family structure.

Financial pressure could also be a cause of family breakdown. This was particularly true in the cases of those families forced by financial strictures to live apart. In 1925, C. E. Evans complained, 'My wife & child are living with relatives, and I have not been able to support them all this year.'[152] J. L. Campbell-White informed the Ministry, 'I am writing from [the] above address as I am staying with my people, & my wife at her people at 49 North Street as we cannot get anywhere else to go.'[153] R. N. Gosling found himself in similar living arrangements: 'He was married in 1922 and has two children. He is living with his parents at present and his wife and children with hers, but there is no domestic trouble.'[154] As already noted, men felt strongly about not being separated from their families when undergoing treatment. To be separated from their families because they could not afford to give them a home only made such separation the more humiliating.

Unsurprisingly, such domestic arrangements could cause marriages to collapse. Despite the assurances concerning domestic troubles, by 1927 Gosling was separated from his wife and struggling to pay a court-ordered separation allowance. Nor was he not alone in his marital trouble. Men could become permanently separated from their families if sectioned under the mental health act and permanently institutionalized, while divorce was not uncommon. Even when separated, however, pensioners still appear to have viewed themselves as family providers. Gosling was one of only three cases known to the Ministry who had to have deductions automatically made from his pension to pay for his wife's maintenance.[155] Most men were quite happy to pay maintenance to their wives. W. J. Halifax argued that the only reason he was in arrears with his maintenance payments when separated was that he had been unemployed. He asked to commute '£10 of my pension whereby it would enable me to meet the demands now placed on my shoulders.'[156] The obligation to provide for families, and thus define themselves as men, persisted beyond the breakup of those families, even though the dreams of domestic felicity that so many men had expressed in their war-time letters had been shattered by the realities of postwar disability and economic struggle.

A. Harman

The case of Arthur Harman indicates some of the complexities of the relationship between war disablement, work and family breakdown. Born in 1899, Harman enlisted in the Royal Flying Corps at sixteen and a half, having run away from Sandhurst following the death of his father, an officer in the King's Royal Rifles.[157] He was commissioned in January 1918 as a second lieutenant before being demobilized in

February 1919 with a health grading of A1. Prior to his demobilization, however, he crashed twice, in May and October 1918, and was treated first for concussion and then for nervous debility. He applied for a pension for the latter disability in May 1919, although he withdrew the claim in September 'as his condition had greatly improved and he had been advised to go no further with the matter.'[158] He renewed his application in November 1919 and was awarded retired pay at the rate of 20% or £30 per year. An injury to his right leg was deemed unattributable to his war service as having been caused by a childhood illness.[159]

Harman's history with the Ministry of Pension continued long after this initial award was made, however, becoming increasingly complicated. Far from improving, his health deteriorated the following year to the point where he was assesed at 40% disabled. His condition, as traced through the bi-annual medical assessments in his records, improved to 20% in 1921 but had again deteriorated to the level of 30% by 1924, the level it was to remain until 1929 when Harman became dramatically worse. He was assessed at 50% disability in October and, by March 1932, had become 100% disabled. On 15 September 1932, following in-patient treatment at Orpington Hospital and an interview with the Essex Area Awards Office in which 'it is recorded that he was crying during the whole of the interview',[160] his award was made permanent at this level.

Throughout these changing assessments, the Ministry of Pensions kept a close eye on Harman's claim to disability. In a memorandum dated 28 November 1929, for instance, one official queried the raising of his level of disability to 50%:

> in view of the length of time since this officer's war service terminated (February 1919) and the fact that the assessment has remained at 20% and 30% since 1921. We are surprised to find an increased assessment recommended at this stage and after the consistent lower assessment . . . . Although the officer suffered from loss of memory in 1927 it would appear from treatment report dated 28th January, 1928 in D.O. file that officer recovered from this attack.[161]

Nor was it only the Ministry who were concerned with the legitimacy of Harman's claim to a pension. In September 1933 the Ministry received an anonymous letter alleging that:

> If you knew how Capt. Harmon [sic] of Orwell goes on you would not allow him to be kept at the country's expense, he drinks and

gives away his dope as he calls it to his friends .... he has got all the cunning of a lunatic and has no principle he can cry and moan at will and he makes a boast of getting round any Dr. in the Ministry by crying and having and emotional turn, and you are all so blind that you cant [*sic*] see that a course of disipline [*sic*] in hospital is what he needs, and moreover would save the country pounds besides doing Harmon himself the best turn you could do him, he drinks and gambles and causes disturbances at night .... He is fit to work he can play tennis and golf and walk miles and stop up half the night dancing so why cant you find him a post.[162]

Harman defended himself, accusing a neighbour of sending the letter as part of an ongoing feud and noting that, when interviewed by the police, the man 'stated ... that I suffered with mental aberrations.'[163] However, a special enquiry officer sent by the Ministry in response to the letter reported that one informant 'came to the conclusion that [Harman] was drinking heavily although he never saw him the worse for drink, but for many months ... he had, on occasions, displayed an uncontrollable temper. Sometimes he was quite normal and on other occasions he "talked absolutely idiotic." '[164] The charge of drunkenness was ultimately deemed not proven, but this case indicates the extent to which pensioners' behaviour continued to be policed by the Ministry to verify their worthiness for their country's support.[165]

Throughout these claims, appeals and investigations, Harman made regular references to his inability to work due to his disability. His leg injury, for instance, was presented as affecting his ability to work in a café, as was his neurasthenia which caused him to 'become subjected to severe fits of temper ... during these tempers, I have crashed crockery to the ground, locked my cousin in the Café for hours, and refused to serve customers, and when I realised what I had done, have burst into to tears'.[166]

Harman's café work was, in fact, one of a number of jobs that he held at various times during the interwar period. He also found work in the civil service, as a manager in the film industry and as a publican, the job listed on the marriage certificate of his second marriage in 1958. Immediately following his discharge from the military he claimed to have been employed by the Air Ministry 'but my health was such, that I had to attend at Lancaster Gate for treatment and thus relinquished my appointment.' He then moved to Eastbourne where he spent 12 months unemployed before drinking carbolic acid in an attempt to kill himself. Eventually, 'I decided I would be better if I had some occupation', so he opened a café with his cousin.[167] The emotional distress that had led to his suicide attempt was, however, exacerbated by business worries, resulting, in 1927, in a period of memory loss that meant he 'was not able to take active part in his business.'[168] By 1933, he was writing to the Ministry that 'My condition is such that I am not in a condition to work & am also forbidden to do so by my doctor.'[169] The Ministry Special Enquiry Officer felt, however, that 'the Officer's profound inertia, by reason of which he is content to loaf around doing nothing, reveals a degree of constitutional inadequacy which cannot be attributed to the effects of Great War Service.'[170] A revised assessment of 70% was recommended, although never implemented, and later medical reports concluded that it was 'doubtful whether he can interest himself in anything for long or is physically capable of any prolonged exertion.'[171] In this instance, the medical evaluation supported Harman's own assertion of the attributable nature of his sporadic employment as opposed to the construction of the Area Deputy Commissioner for Medical Services (D.C.M.S.), which put his unemployment down to personal inadequacy.

Harman, like many other pensioners, defended himself against such accusations of inadequacy by arguing that his requests for consideration from the Ministry were a last resort. 'Time after time,' he wrote:

> I wanted to tell [the Ministry] the utter failure, and the difficulty I have had in trying to surmount the many obstacles my disability caused me, but somehow I just could not, foolishly I did not want them to know, and that has been the reason that I have never submitted bills from my doctors, that I never applied for a deterioration board, after all, I had an income, and the pension was of secondary importance, I wanted to get fit, and have always availed myself of the treatment the Ministry has offered me, but today I find myself a sick man, three businesses have been swept away from me through my inability to carry on... and I now find myself practically penniless, and in a condition that I am worth nothing to anyone, and still less to myself.[172]

He also asked, 'who is going to employ a man who one day is well, and another, totally unfit for work, a man who through insomnia is a physical wreck.'[173] The future, he felt, was 'like a blank wall', the only comfort being his children. As he told one Ministry official, he would 'finish it all if he were not responsible for the children.'[174]

Even this domestic aspect of his life was affected by his disability, as trying to support his family created strains. His inability to find work meant that he was unable to continue paying the mortgage on his house, resulting in the loss of £200. His marriage in 1924 to Dorothy Holland eventually collapsed under the strain of his disability, his wife leaving him because of her fear of 'my periodical outbursts of temper, and the morbid fits of depression which overcame me, to say nothing of the insomnia to which I was a martyr.'[175] Although Harman asserted that 'my wife deserted me on three occasions [*sic*] and finally abandoned my little boy and girl aged 6 yrs & 4 yrs', he did note that 'at times she must have been very tolerant.... During the time we were living together I had the misfortune of a loss of memory for several days.'[176] By emphasizing his wife's abandonment of her feminine role as wife and mother, Harman implies his own responsible role as a good father seeking to support his children despite his disability.

Care of his children was a dominant theme in his letters as evidence of both his independence and his respectability. 'I have tried to work to save losing money which I intended for my children, that is now gone & should anything happen to me they will have nothing, for I've got nothing.'[177] He asserted his good character in response to the anonymous letter writer by noting, 'My only income is my pension and after paying my rent & furniture I have less than £7 per month to feed and cloth my children.'[178] Because of this situation, he was 'confident that [officials at the Ministry] will meet their obligation to me and my children.'[179]

Through the care of his children, Harman sought to lay claim to a respectable domestic masculinity that was thrown into doubt by the collapse of his marriage, his inability to gain employment and his reliance on the support of the Ministry of Pensions that lasted into the 1960s. Yet, as with so many other men disabled by their war service, he found himself caught in the paradox created by dual expectations of appropriate masculinity. For while he was forced to defend his record of service as sufficiently heroic and therefore deserving of support, the need for such support, created by his failure to successfully maintain his role as provider, undermined his claims to appropriate domestic masculinity. Thus for Harman, as for so many disabled ex-servicemen, the service for the state that allowed them to construct themselves as heroic soldiers even after the war was over also undermined their ability to define themselves as ideal domestic men in the interwar years.

Conclusion

Although the majority of men who served in the British armed forces during the First World War survived, many found that the war had been permanently inscribed on their bodies and minds in the form of disability. For these men, reintegration into civilian life after the war was to prove extremely difficult. Work was hard to find, particularly for the disabled, and the government, in the form of the Ministry of Pensions, was unwilling, and indeed unable, to provide the level of support that many disabled ex-servicemen felt they were entitled to.

In their correspondence with the Ministry, disabled ex-servicemen were forced to negotiate with two ideals of appropriate masculinity, the heroic cripple treating his disability with cheerful stoicism and the help offered him with gratitude, and the independent wage-earner, able to support himself and his dependants with minimal assistance from the state. For men writing to the Ministry, both these figures were unrealistic and unattainable ideals. Instead, ex-servicemen constructed alternative figures, the heroic citizen soldier who had willingly sacrificed health and future for the state, and the caring husband and father seeking what was best for his dependants at whatever cost to his own pride.

In presenting themselves in this fashion, however, disabled ex-servicemen undermined their own claims to a mature masculinity based on economic independence. Their claims for state support, and the evidence they provided as to its need, contradicted the desire that many expressed to be independent. In addition, family breakdown, a source of concern for many ex-servicemen, emphasized their inability to fulfil the role of good husband and father.

Thus disabled ex-servicemen's claims to both the heroic masculinity of war service and the mature domestic masculinity of financial independence were undermined by their disabilities. For these men, the effects of war service on their masculine identities was both long-lasting and almost entirely negative. However, such a negative view was not limited to the disabled in the years after the war. As we shall see in the next chapter, as ex-servicemen revisited their memories of war experience in memoirs, a more negative view of the war's impact on masculine identity more generally began to emerge.

5
'The Very Basic Test of Manhood': War Memoirs and the Remembering of Martial Masculinities

Despite Robert Graves and Alan Hodge's assertion that 'everyone who had served in the trenches for as much as five months, or who had been under two or three rolling barrages, was an invalid,'[1] not all those who served in the war were disabled by it. Nor were correspondences with government ministries the only form of written narrative produced by ex-servicemen. Almost as soon as the Armistice was declared, politicians and generals rushed to print their version of events. Other servicemen took longer to produce memoirs, but they were by no means silent. Collections of letters, edited diaries and the occasional memoir began to appear as early as 1919, although war memoirs only fully reached public consciousness in the 'war books boom' of 1928–1931.[2] Following a period during the Second World War and its aftermath when few memoirs were published, another spike in the writing of memoirs occurred in the late 1960 and 1970s, coinciding with the 50th anniversary of the conflict.[3]

Although there was a boom in the publication of war books in the interwar period, published memoirs formed only a fraction of the total number of written records of men's war experiences. Many men wrote memoirs that were never intended for publication but instead were meant to educate their children or simply record their experiences, even if no one else ever saw them.[4] A number of these were published during the period of renewed interest in the war in the '60s and '70s, either by men themselves or their children.[5] These years also saw the publication of a number of new memoirs by ex-servicemen, written in response to both the public interest sparked by the 50th anniversaries of wartime events and the authors' own awareness of ageing. As Dan Todman has noted, in the 1960s:

> the generation of men who had fought in the First World War reached an age where they retired from their jobs; in practical terms this gave them more time to write their memoirs. Being older meant that there were social expectations that they would remember in public: it had become their role to tell stories about the past. It also increased their awareness of their own mortality, encouraging them to look back and try to make sense of their own lives.[6]

Telling the story of their war service, one of the formative moments in these men's lives, became a way in which to comprehend their lives as a whole.

Todman goes on to point out that 'These books did not contain a single, monolithic view of the war. Rather, they continue to reflect the variety of veterans' experiences and subsequent reactions.'[7] Indeed, understandings of the war's meaning could alter over time even within the recollections of one man. Michael Roper has, for example, demonstrated how, in the multiple memoirs of Lyndal Urwick, there developed a 'tendency to incorporate aspects of experience that did not fit the wartime image of the soldier hero'.[8] Drafts of Urwick's war memoirs increasingly came to reflect his postwar experiences and identity as a salesmen, even if the narrative never strayed beyond the events of 1914–1918. Similarly, Charles Carrington wrote and rewrote his memoirs, first as *A Subaltern's War* (1929), then as *Soldiers from the Wars Returning* (1969), incorporating a longer historical view in the second book.

Despite the fact that memoirs changed over time, influenced as strongly by the context in which they were produced as by the individual memories that they narrated,[9] the narratives they present do bear strong relations to earlier written records of war experience such as letters and diaries.[10] They record the terrors and discomforts of war, with the emphasis placed on the experiences of shellfire. Domestic adaptability plays an important role, as does commemoration of dead comrades. The retrospective nature of these documents, however, introduces new elements, many of which reflect as much on ex-servicemen's postwar experiences as on their war service. The resignation of the diaries intensifies in many memoirs into disillusion with the postwar world, while an increased emphasis on comradeship as a form of consolation allows memoirists to construct an understanding of martial masculinity which acknowledges loss even as the war is presented as a life-changing event.

Discomfort

As in diaries and letters home, the bulk of the narratives presented in memoirs are recollections of the physical experiences of warfare focussing on the weather, exhaustion and shellfire. Memories of the trenches were intimately bound up with the sensory elements of trench life,[11] with the effects of rain being recalled with particular vividness. C. C. Miller recalled how:

> when the rain was coming down in buckets (and that seemed to be nine tenths of the time) trenches would become water logged, or rather mud logged. I have been in trenches in which the mud was indescribable – stagnant rivers of brown cohesive mud, and oh the weariness of getting round such trenches.[12]

Such conditions affected men's morale. W. Griffith found that 'four days...of hard weather were a severe trial to all our powers of resistance.'[13] S. H. Raggett wrote, 'When one was wet, cold and hungry the world seemed very grey, but when one was warm, life seemed more tolerable.'[14] And for most men war experience was remembered as being characterized more by being wet, cold and hungry than otherwise. The effect that this had on men was, as A. J. Turner recalled:

> demoralising; movement was restricted.... Standing day after day in water had the effect of turning one's feet a horrible grey colour and wrinkled like the skin of an elephant. Shell-holes became filled with water, mud was deep, duckboards floated or sank, tracks and paths disappeared, casualties ran a great risk of drowning. Mud and misery were synonymous. One experienced a feeling of degradation whilst wallowing in it.[15]

Turner was not alone in recalling living in mud as a degrading experience. W. Clarke told the story of how:

> I was once able, after about 4 weeks, to have a hot bath, and clean, dry, lice-free clothing. I was working my way back to the front-line when heavy shelling started. I crouched down in what was called a 'Funk Hole' and a shell burst just beyond me and I was covered

in mud and debris. I can remember weeping with fury. That lovely feeling of being dry and clean gone.[16]

Nor was it just the feeling of being dirty that made living in mud so degrading. There was also the exhaustion that it induced. E. B. Lord remembered how the mud at Passchendaele was so terrible that gumboots were sucked off and 'the men had to proceed in stocking feet. The troops were often completely stuck; the only remedy was to go crashing on, the physical strain was tremendous.'[17]

Mud was not, of course, the sole element of trench warfare that exhausted men, undermining their morale. The entire experience of trench life did so. According to Griffith:

Four days in the line can be written down as a rapid fall along the slope of vitality into a stupor of weariness; on the path, some sharp crests of fear, but the end was overwhelming fatigue. . . . to most of us who served in the infantry, the thought of a trench brings back that long span of damnable tiredness, broken here and there by a sudden dry-tongued spasm of fear. . . . but nothing can efface the memory of that all-conquering fatigue.[18]

For Lord, 'Relief from the trenches [was] a relief in more senses than one; days with very little or sometimes no hot food, exercise limited in a very confined space, sleep spasmodic, if any, and cleanliness almost impossible.' The result was that as men came out of line they:

drag along their weary feet, lurching from side to side, in twos or threes in a line of sorts. Officers, as weary as the men, disregard step . . . The prospect of a billet acts as spur, but on this occasion we were disappointed to find our billet was a field, the muddy grass our bed, and the sky our roof. Fortunately, our fatigue was so great that we dropped off in spite of the discomfort.[19]

One consolation of such exhaustion was the rapidly learned ability to sleep in very uncomfortable conditions. G. V. Dennis recalled one night on the Somme when 'the remnants of our battalion and some other units arrived back at Green Dump. . . . The early arrivals found any old spot in which to sleep – beside a broken ammo box against a smashed limber: in shell holes and old trenches.'[20] This ability to sleep wherever one found oneself could be very useful in dugouts that were recalled, as in diary descriptions, as being extremely uncomfortable.

Dennis described some as 'just big enough to crawl into and then sit up in. Each held four men and there was just enough room for them to lie down like pigs in a sty. Except for the fact that each day the men were dog tired after being up all night it was remarkable that they could sleep in such uncomfortable surroundings.'[21]

Despite this ability to sleep, exhaustion remained a central memory of trench life for most men. Turner described such exhaustion as 'the numbing weariness of mind and body, resulting from being too long under conditions bordering upon the fringes of human endurance [which] created a state of semi-coma.'[22] The effect of such exhaustion was the same as that of living in mud. It sapped men's morale. D. J. Polley found that 'lack of sleep pulls a man down quicker than most things.'[23] This can also be seen in the experiences of Raggett. He recalled a night when:

> The weather had been bad, the trenches were worse and the road along the canal bank was as black as pitch and we had to feel our way, step by step. Never before or never after was I so utterly exhausted, so absolutely done. It is a horrid feeling to get far beyond the tired stage to that of extreme exhaustion, and only those who have felt it know what it means. I remember sitting down by the side of the canal and crying like a child. I know on paper it sounds so stupid, but tears, even to a man are sometimes a consolation to over-wrought nerves. I have never felt like that again and I hope I never shall.[24]

It was at moments like these that men felt themselves to have been least manly, as Raggett's identification of his actions with those of a child shows. Exhaustion thus undermined memoirists' perceptions of themselves as men both physically and emotionally. The condition inverted the role of war as an arena in which to become a man or prove one's manhood, by causing, in memory at least, a regression to childhood through a loss of self-control.

Fear

While the physical discomforts of war were a common theme in memoirs, they were generally overshadowed by the memories of fear that so dominated war-time diaries. Being under shellfire made the deepest impression on most men because it 'was always there day and night.'[25] These were not necessarily continuous bombardments, but every morning and evening brought some shellfire making it the form which the enemy took on a day-to-day basis. Although engagement with a human enemy is described in a few memoirs, and others describe involvement in large assaults, most, like letters home, focus on the normal routine of trench life and contain little consciousness of an enemy except in relation to the shells that came over. Turner did note an 'awareness of the unseen enemy somewhere in the too near vicinity,' but he labels this, along with the sense of security given by being below ground level in the trenches, as 'false emotions.'[26] For him, as for all the memoirists looked at here, the reality of the enemy was defined by shellfire.

Despite this, as Polley commented:

> I have heard men say that one gets used to shell fire, but I am tempted to believe that these gentlemen have learned whatever they know on the subject from books, or perhaps the 'pictures'. Frankly I do not think it possible to come to regard screaming and blasting death with the contempt born of use. I know very well that I cannot truthfully say that I ever became blasé where shelling was concerned.[27]

Memoirists demonstrate this lack of complacency through the specificity of their descriptions of particularly heavy bombardments which stood out for their level of ferocity and terror. Raggett wrote of one such experience:

> I have seen and I have been through many 'barrages' during the war and, except for one, that was the worst of the whole lot for intensity and noise. It lasted about half an hour and every second of the half hour was and seemed a perfect hell. It literally rained shrapnel, pieces hit our steel helmets, chunks dropped all round us, people were hit, people were killed.[28]

Lord had similarly vivid memories of 'A battery of eighteen-pounders, four hundred yards to our rear, [which] fired directly over our heads, just clearing our parapet, and the noise was almost intolerable; not even the burst of fifteen inch shells could compare with the discomfort to our ears; I thought my ear drums would burst.'[29] Griffith also remembered noise as a key element of bombardment:

> a sudden fury of shell-fire turned our poor trench into a field of spouting volcanoes, spattering mud up into the air. The angry hiss of 77's, the ponderous whirr of 5.9's, the dull empty whack of bombs and the whipping crack of shrapnel all merged into a sea of noise.

Ten minutes of this drove us into a stupor of fear, and fear brought its terrible thirst; there was nothing we could do but sit still, half crouched against the wall of the trench, waiting, waiting....[30]

The 'hideous crash and scream of shell bursts and the whirring whine of red-hot razor-edged fragments of metal which would amputate, decapitate, or disembowel with impartiality'[31] was compounded by the sense of impotence generated by waiting helplessly with nothing to do to defend oneself as the shells fell. Kemp experienced one barrage where 'gradually it...boxed us in, those of us of 8 Platoon. For four hours we could only sit and hope that one wouldn't drop on top of us. This was the worst bombardment I have ever been under....We sat and waited and waited.'[32] Raggett commented, 'to be shelled with every prospect of getting hit or killed at any moment and not to have a run over for one's money is, as every Infantry man knows, one of the most unpleasant things possible.'[33] Miller claimed, 'you can do nothing except ask your own artillery to intervene with counter battery work on the enemy's artillery.'[34] In such memories, men were made passive by shellfire, forced to endure as there was nothing else that they could do.

A similar sense of passivity is evident in what J. F. B. O'Sullivan termed 'That horrible idle waiting for zero.'[35] The real horror of such wait was that 'You can do nothing but sit or stand or crouch, and think. One's brain races, but time seems to stand still.'[36] The waiting challenged men's desire to play an active part in the war, a desire and a challenge that they were able to fully consider and acknowledge only in retrospect. As Raggett commented:

To be laid out doing something is infinitely better than to be laid out whilst waiting. The mental stress before an attack, the strain of waiting and wondering what <u>will</u> happen is far more trying than the actual attack. For this reason: in an attack one forgets everything in the excitement of battle. One has no time to think, the same as one has in the hours and moments beforehand.[37]

This, in turn, affected morale. R. M. Luther recalled a sector of the trenches where 'we never advanced one yard or retreated – we were just bogged down, subject to gun-fire....The tension and effect upon the observer is terrific.'[38] Just as waiting had been recorded in diaries as a source of tension, so also it was recalled in men's later memoirs.

The result of the enforced passivity of trench life was that, while they could not necessarily act of their own volition, men did *react*, often through instinct. H. Sturdy recalled that new recruits 'make a bolt out of the salient but are soon turned back. Not cowardice, just this, no man will stand in the vacintiy [*sic*] of these things unless he is compelled by discipline, to do so.'[39] While Sturdy may have denied that such instinctive reactions signified cowardice, his recollections indicate that memoirs, like diaries, were spaces in which potentially unheroic and actions, both in others and in memoirists themselves, could be recorded.

Nor was it only new soldiers who experienced a physical response to shellfire. A. J. Heraty recalled several weeks of shells falling on his wagon line when:

> we had to dive for it anywhere, and as we found out later in bombardments from enemy shell fire you would dive down anywhere to avoid the blast of a shell, whether it was in mud or headlong into a shell-hole... as a matter of fact, I am not exaggerating when I say you were prepared to dodge behind a small bush or a clump of grass to try and save yourself when you come under direct machine-gun fire from the Jerry, as I have experienced on more than one occasion.[40]

This response was recalled as less an instinct than a calculated attempt at self-preservation, however hopeless. As Sturdy noted, 'How degrading and unmanly were the positions that one was forced to get into, to keep hanging on to that little bit of breath.'[41] In memoirs, fearful reactions to shellfire could be fully acknowledged as antithetical to appropriate masculine behaviours.

Men recalled and recorded not only their physical reactions to shellfire, but also their emotional ones. H. Clegg remembered how,

> as days went on, my nerves suffered, and I must admit that one very dark night... I completely lost my nerve; the heavy shelling and loneliness contributed to it I suppose. I could not get past a certain point where shells were dropping every two minutes; I tried several times in half an hour, but something had failed.[42]

What made such reactions comprehensible to most memoirists was the fact that, while they were acknowledged to be the result of fear, it was also acknowledged in the war's aftermath that most men who experienced war also experienced fear. As J. S. Y. Rogers told the 1921 War Office Committee of Enquiry into Shell-Shock, 'I think every man, no matter how brave out at the front, has experienced fear.'[43] For Sturdy, if a man 'has been under terrific shellfire, he knows the symptoms alright [*sic*], as most at times have had to fight against this madness caused by pure unadulterated fear.'[44] R. G. Dixon, who became a subaltern while in his late teens, acknowledged, 'most fellows were scared out their wits a lot of the time. I was, I know! The thing was, to try not to show it, especially to one's men.'[45] This was in itself a struggle that defined men as soldiers. As W. Griffith wrote, the man who experienced war 'fought against the tiger, no less than with his fellow man, against the overwhelming terror of sudden fear as implacably as he fought against danger. There had been no victory, no triumph.'[46]

Change

If memoirs provided spaces in which men could reflect more fully on the fear that had been exposed in both letters home and diaries, they also provided spaces in which men could comment on the challenges that war experience posed to their identities as soldiers. The extent to which conditions of service undermined men's sense of masculine identity can be seen in the sense of disillusionment and callousness about the war that many expressed in retrospect. The petty irritations of army life, for instance, were recalled by some not merely as day-to-day irritants but as the basis of complete disillusion. As C. W. Hughes pointed out, 'when one thinks about war and imagines its excitements and glory the idea that there are all sorts of minor wrongs and irritations does not enter your head.'[47] He found, however, 'We had been roused to hopes of exciting times, and found ourselves doing nothing more than we did at home, and under conditions far less comfortable.'[48] P. R. Hall didn't even need to get as far as Salonika, as Hughes did, to experience this form of disillusionment: 'Disillusionment began during training, there was a lot of unnecessary bloody mindedness on the part of some senior officers and some very foul mouthed bayonet fighting instructors. However, this was war and I was in it . . . so I must learn to be a clean fighter.'[49] The grousing of the diaries became transformed in memoirs into the source of outright disillusionment.

While the petty irritations of life as a soldier could undermine ideals of glory, it was the memories of the conditions of dirt, death and danger that most seriously affected men's understandings of the realities of warfare and their roles in it. E. B. Lord remembered one particular encounter with a unit decimated in an attack, that caused him to become disillusioned:

What a sight this small band presented when we met them; weary, haggard and drawn faces, bodies exhausted and legs that almost could not carry their burden, but their thoughts were too tragic for words. All had lost many friends on that awful day and as I marched along with them trying to cheer them on, I felt like a warder escorting a condemned prisoner. . . . I nearly wept with impotence and sadness. For the first time I fully appreciated the horrors of war, the futility and madness of it all and realised that nothing but dishonour could justify such senselessness.[50]

As S. H. Raggett commented, 'War to us [as recruits] was just a big game – then – but later, what disillusionment, how different to what we imagined.'[51] C. C. Miller said much the same thing when he wrote to his daughters:

I started out looking on war as a great adventure, but before I had finished I knew it for what it really is, a thing of filth and horror. . . . Modern warfare is simply an assembling of mechanical contrivances on which has been lavished all that God has given to man in the way of brains and intelligence with the sole object of destroying humanity, and with complete oblivion to the horror and suffering entailed thereby. The number of men killed in the war in hand to hand fighting, where there is the primitive joy of struggle and you can face your enemy, was infinitesimal beside the number of those killed or maimed by long distance slaughter from the guns. It is true that war brings out great qualities in men such as those of courage, devotion and self sacrifice; but people who stress this are apt to overlook the fact that in some people it also develops hideous traits of cruelty.[52]

Miller's letter was not simply disillusioned, however. It also acknowledged the war's ability to evoke both primitive joy in violence, particularly when fought hand-to-hand rather than at a distance, and more sophisticated emotions of devotion and self-sacrifice.[53] Nor was Miller alone in addressing such issues in his postwar writing. R. G. Dixon may have argued that war's 'results are so ghastly that inevitably there comes a time when war ceases to be an adventure, and the young regard it cynically, disillusioned and disenchanted,' but he also pointed out, '[w]ars are fought by young men, inexperienced and impressionable, to whom in large part the thing is seen in the light of an adventure. Indeed, it is in some degree an adventure, and no adventure is worth calling such without a degree of risk to life and limb.'[54] Dixon, like Miller, acknowledged that the war was dangerous, disagreeable and disheartening but, despite their declared disillusion, both men also remembered it as exciting.

In this, they echoed others who recorded their initial experience of war as too exciting to be frightening. S. H. Raggett, for instance, wrote in 1920, 'I shall never forget the day we went [to France], November 14th/15th – Monday – it was snowing, bitterly cold but we were not downhearted.'[55] Perhaps W. Kerr summed it up most succinctly when he recalled, 'My first turn of the front line was uneventful, but thrilling and exciting for all that,' pointing out that 'it was the greatest experience of my life up till then.'[56] For many memoirists, war was constructed as *the* moment of their lives, their chance to take part in a great adventure. This sense of excitement was remembered even after the full experience of war had shattered many of these men's illusions about the nature of war.

A more extreme effect of war on martial identity was the sense of fatalism that many men recalled. Such fatalism could exhibit itself in the sort of momentary brainstorm that Siegfried Sassoon apparently experienced when he won the Military Cross by storming a German trench single-handed. Sassoon described his actions as being characterized by the sensation of not caring whether he lived or died.[57] Although he won no medal for his actions, Dixon experienced a similar 'spell of to-hell-with-it-all-what-does-it-matter, and in the popular phrase of a later time, couldn't care less.... This particular spell lasted about six weeks, I remember, during which time I behaved like a complete idiot and did the silliest things and, though I had plenty of narrow shaves, I never got hit.'[58]

Such reactions involving the embracing of death might be seen as endorsing the pre-war cult of the dead hero that influenced the civilian bereaveds' constructions of the dead.[59] Unlike the ideas expressed by Victorian poets and Edwardian journalists, however, the fatalism that memoirists recalled undermined the idea of a sacrifice ennobling the death of youth that was so central to the Victorian ideal. There is no overriding cause for which these men are willing to die. Instead they embrace death as a preferable alternative to life, something that would have shocked proponents of youthful sacrifice, for whom such an attitude would mean giving in to despair, an act of cowardice rather than courage.

For memoirists, however, fatalism was presented primarily as a form of self-protection against constant fear. D. J. Polley felt, 'every soldier becomes more or less of a fatalist. How many times did one hear, "If a bullet or shell has my name on it, it will find me"? Spoken half in jest, but with a good dash of belief as well.'[60] F. de Margry remembered similar phrases:

> During the war I came across a good many men who more or less indifferently admitted to being fatalists and who often expressed their views by using expressions such as, 'You never hear the bullet meant for you, so what's the use trying to dodge it' – 'If it has your name on it you'll be hit in any case' – 'If you're for it, Chum, there's no dodging it.'[61]

Such views were a denial of the ability to exercise control over their fate, to act for themselves, and as such threatened the very root of those Victorian ideals of masculinity, self-help and self-reliance.[62]

The result could be, as it was in the case of R. G. Dixon, permanent. He felt, 'the Kaiser's war did something to my sensibilities – made me indifferent about death. Not callous, but so used to it that it stirred no emotion.'[63] Dixon may have denied that his reaction was callous. Nonetheless, fatalism was a form of emotional self-protection in the face of danger and the fear that such danger might cause. Callousness was a similar form of protection, not from fear but from horror and pity, two staple ingredients of a war in which:

> [w]herever you went in that nightmare country you saw obscene things protruding from the mud; grinning skulls, rotting buttocks, boots with feet inside them, or a hand grasping at nothing. One grew accustomed to these things, but I never grew accustomed to the all-pervading stench of decay and decaying flesh, mingled with that of high explosive fumes, that hung over miles and miles of what had been sweet countryside that was now one vast muck-heap of murder.[64]

Dixon may have grown accustomed enough to some sights that he was able to write about them later; he clearly never became so accustomed that he was able to forget them. Nor could C. C. Miller, who told his daughters, 'There are some horrible and unforgettable pictures there which I would rather turn over quickly, it is a terrible thing to see men die in agony, and to see dead men unburied and rotting.'[65] For Miller, these horrors of war were both unforgettable and indescribable.

This inability to describe the visual horrors of war is comparatively frequent in memoirs, as it was in letters home from the front. Some men, such as P. R. Hall, were simply too overwhelmed by events to form clear memories:

> I find it very difficult to have clear consecutive recollections of what happened in those battles [for Passchendaele] – the mind was stunned. The whole world seemed to have erupted like a volcano: one had to fix ones [*sic*] mind on the necessity of going forward to reach the objective at all costs.[66]

Many memoirists simply refused to try to describe their experiences. '[T]he difficulties [of a working party] were far greater than I am capable of describing,' E. B. Lord claimed.[67] Miller also excused his refusal to describe the scenes of war that he remembered saying, 'It must be very difficult for anyone who hasn't seen a trench to visualize trench life, and it is not very easy describe.'[68] These moments of inarticulateness, as much as Dixon's agonized description, indicate how memoirists did not become inured to the horrors they were forced to live with and through during the war, any more than they were able to forget them once the war was over.

Yet some memoirists believed that they became callous due to their experience of war and that such callousness denied them a level humanity. W. Griffith, a subaltern, noted this change in the way he treated his men and was treated by his superiors:

> No word came oftener to the lips than 'men', as one would say, 'Send three men to Sap B, and tell them to hold it at all cost....' A 'man', in this usage, was no more than the temporary overseer of a weapon of destruction, the indispensable, but imperfect, servant of a potential gas asleep in a powder. Man, to a Town Major, was the envelope of a ration of food, the tenant of a bed. In this way, and in no other, lay sanity, for no man could escape madness who turned the impersonal and desiccated 'man' into a living creature with a body to kill and a soul to hurt.[69]

W. Clarke similarly felt:

> You became hardened in the trenches.... Seeing so many corpses became just another sight. Often when you moved in the trenches you trod and slipped on rotting flesh. Your feelings only came to the

fore when it was a special mate who had been killed or wounded and then it would quickly go away. Because what you really wanted was to go to sleep, get warm, get clean and have a good meal. These seemed the main priorities.[70]

Given the space to reflect upon their experiences, memoirists recalled and reflected on the perceived damage that the horrors of war had done to their identity as civilized men.

For all their recollections of callousness towards human suffering, however, remarkably few men record any reaction at all to the main focus of any war effort, that of killing the enemy. Indeed, only one memoirist in this sample recorded any act of killing. In the moment before firing, D. J. Polley recalled that he 'caressed the grip of my trusty Vickers and felt a grim kind of satisfaction when I thought of the deadly stream of lead I should be directing on the oncoming Boche.'[71] Even then he recorded feeling guilt in the moments after firing.[72] As in letters home, memoirs were spaces in which it was not appropriate for men to describe their experiences of and feelings about battle and the act of killing. Instead, men chose to structure their memories of their own experience of war around a narrative in which callousness was acceptable but other emotions were not.

By giving callousness such primacy in their narratives, memoirists helped create and sustain what Leed has called the 'myth of the machine,'[73] the idea that men were parts of a machine of war rather than self-determining individuals. A. J. Turner certainly felt by the end of the war that 'we had...been cogs in the gigantic war machine, the machine now having ground to a halt in no way altered our status – we were still cogs.'[74] The sense of dehumanization that men presented in their memoirs served to illustrate how they perceived war experience as eroding their identity as heroic men by attacking their sense of self-determination.

Courage

Despite this undermining of martial masculinity by warfare, memoirs were not defined entirely by a sense of war's futility and damage. They were also spaces in which men were able to reconstruct their masculine identities as soldier through redefinitions of the masculine ideals that warfare challenged. Courage and cowardice were redefined retrospectively to accommodate the fact that all men felt fear and were perilously close to showing it. Indeed, cowardice remained ill-defined in many memoirs because the belief that experiencing fear denoted cowardice could not be maintained under circumstances in which all men felt fear, whether they showed it or not. As G. Fisher commented of a Guardsman he saw overcome by fear, 'We used to think it was cowardice but we learnt later that there *was* such a thing as shell-shock.'[75] Many memoirists agreed with the analysis of Lord Moran who wrote:

> Courage is will-power, whereof no man has an unlimited stock; and when in war it is used up, he is finished. A man's courage is his capital and he is always spending. The call on the bank may be only the daily drain of the front line or it may be a sudden draft which threatens to close the account. His will is perhaps almost destroyed by intensive shelling, by heavy bombing, or by bloody battle, or is gradually used up by monotony, by exposure, by the loss of the support of stauncher spirits on whom he has come to depend, by physical exhaustion, by a wrong attitude to danger, to casualties, to war, to death itself.[76]

This was a definition of war that required a new description of courage identified not simply by self-control, but also by the ability to regain self-control even after it had been lost. It was this understanding of courage in warfare that men put forward in their memoirs.

The definition of courage the memoirists constructed was one that allied self-control, a quality that was susceptible to the terrors of warfare, with that of endurance. Self-control had strong roots in the 19th-century definition of 'character'[77] and was much admired in other men that memoirists encountered. Raggett, for instance, expressed particular admiration for a group of men he saw marching towards the Somme battle line: 'they were singing away as if they were going to a picnic. . . . How *bravely* they were hiding the feelings that stirred them to the depths,' [My emphasis].[78] Lord was equally impressed by troops at a Christmas service: 'shells were crashing into nearby houses, but no one seemed to take the slightest notice, and I tried to emulate them.'[79] These men appeared to control their physical and emotional reactions to the dangers that they faced in ways that others such as Clegg admitted they could not.

Unlike self-control, a quality of masculinity that had its roots in Victorian prescriptions about masculinity, the quality of endurance, so much a part of the narratives of warfare constructed in letters and diaries, was more specifically the product of the war. R. G. Dixon, for instance, admired a battery of gunners he observed being shelled:

Coming on top of what the survivors had been through that day, gunners without their guns, and all that remained to them the personnel in their horse-lines away back, that five-nine ought to have struck the final blow. But it didn't. Those fellows were really tough nuts, and showed no sign of cracking. And when the shelling eased off, and we said our farewells, and departed, it was with something of a sense of wonder at how much human beings could stand.[80]

C. C. Miller similarly admired the 'grand men in that second battalion of the Royal Inniskilling Fusiliers, [who] however appalling things were there was always a laugh in them,'[81] while C. W. Hughes commented on the infantry, 'How your admiration for them increased the more you saw of them; they knew the difficulties, they knew the probability of death or wounds but few words of complaint were heard; they were content to do their best even if it cost them their lives.'[82] Men who endured were those who controlled their emotions not only in the moment of fear and stress but also when confronted with the on-going horrors of warfare.

However much men might admire groups, it was in their memories of individuals that admiration for the qualities of self-control and endurance were most explicitly expressed as qualities of courage. A. J. Turner, for instance, recalled:

An example of behaviour by another officer [which] made a lasting impression upon me and on my conduct under fire. Whilst still fairly new to trench life we were being heavily shelled, and many like me, were crouched in the bottom of the trench under the duckboard firestep. Glancing up I saw a young officer sitting quietly on the firestep and viewing me with tolerant amusement; shamefacedly I got up and sat by him – he offered me a cigarette. When noise permitted, we talked. I saw him several times after that and always he remained completely unruffled.... I regarded him with great respect and his example and death lived sadly in my memory for years.[83]

Dixon also knew a man who he described as:

one of those who truly won that decoration [the Military Cross] by sheer bravery.... Nothing seemed to scare him, and he treated Jerry's missiles with superb contempt, often ignoring them in a fashion that should have, by all the laws of probability, brought him wounds or death. I admired him tremendously, and wished I could be like him.[84]

Such men were admired for their emotional control rather than for specific acts of bravery. It was the lack of *re*action when faced with the dangers of war, specifically shellfire, that was recalled and admired.

Such lack of reaction can be seen in George Harbottle's description of his transport officer:

> a fine soldier whose courage and complete calm prevailed however difficult the conditions might be.... For much more than twelve months I walked behind those ration limbers led by him and I never once remembered him halting his transports because of shelling. Others might stop and seek shelter but he never did.[85]

Here, lack of reaction meant that the transport officer could do his job. Merely fulfilling one's allotted role, therefore, became a brave act to be admired. Similarly, C. C. Miller admired his commanding officer for the fact that 'He loathed and detested that life of mud and blood but he put a good face on it.'[86] Again, it was the ability to control fear and thus appear to endure that was remembered as one of the most admirable qualities a man could possess.

According to Lord Moran, a man's ability to endure could be maintained through the 'pride and habit of his race.'[87] Yet for most memoirists, the ability to endure seems to have come not from any sense of racial or national identity but from the expectation of doing their duty that they had of themselves as soldiers and, therefore, as men. As G. Fisher commented, 'at the time you either did your job or you didn't. There was no halfway house.'[88] In a world where simply doing one's job was courageous, simple acts of selflessness in response to a perceived duty could be cited as potential acts of heroism because they displayed endurance. Such acts could simply mean taking part, as they did for S. T. Kemp. Kemp refused to take a safe post at Divisional Headquarters, writing:

> I could not let my younger brother go to the trenches and I take an easy way of life, so again I refused and felt that I did the right thing. About a year later I met the chap who went to Divisional Head Quarters and he looked in perfect health, and was pleased he had got the job. Still, I kept faith with myself.[89]

Kemp felt he had displayed endurance in order to do his work. By presenting such acts as worthy of recollection and note, men constructed both themselves and others as heroic through their emphasis on duty and the endurance that fulfilling such duty required.

Doing one's job was thus a vital memory for memoirists. As S. H. Raggett wrote, 'There is the knowledge of having done something, having given something, without thought of self or gain. The knowledge of knowing that in after years one cannot be accused of having failed in the hour of need. There is consolation in that knowledge.'[90] Yet the desire to do one's duty could become a burdensome obligation. J. F. B. O'Sullivan certainly felt the pressure of a duty to endure after he was wounded during the Somme offensive: 'the Colonel had been killed whilst leading C Company over the top, and...Stuart had assumed command as Campbell had been badly wounded and was dying. My personal anguish now seemed trivial in face of such disasters and only Martin's insistence kept me heading for hospital.'[91] Similarly, when Max Plowman found himself in hospital, his sense of duty caused him to feel 'rather a fraud, for I've every limb intact and only a dull headache and a thick ear.'[92] As W. J. Adie told the War Office Committee of Enquiry into Shell-Shock, 'many of us were suffering more or less from "shell shock", which made us not so efficient, and yet we remained in the front line.'[93] Wounds and illness served as no excuse for men for whom duty had become synonymous with suffering alongside their fellow soldiers and thus displaying endurance to prove their masculinity.

Comradeship

While these changes to the meaning of courage were already emerging during the war, when duty and endurance were central to constructions of appropriate martial identities in both letters home and letters of condolence, retrospective memoirs emphasized another quality as even more vital to the ideal soldier, a sense of comradeship. One veteran claimed in a speech at his regiment's reunion luncheon in 1930, 'Comradeship was the most precious thing they had; it began at home, and the further away they got the stronger it became, and it happened that many a man gave his life for a comrade.'[94] Many memoirists used the ideal of comradeship to justify all their experiences of war, however terrible. For F. A. Shuffrey, the sense of adventure that he felt going into war was 'stimulated...by comradeship much more vital than is found in peace.'[95] R. Foot agreed, arguing:

It was such friendships, based on mutual individual respect, that made the 'horrors' of the war endurable. The good comradeship of male society...carries men through the most heavy trials of danger and physical exhaustion. And when good natured fun and humour cement that comradeship, it is the pleasant times that one remembered rather than the horrors.[96]

For many memoirists comradeship was recalled as a general feeling that existed throughout whatever unit they belonged to, including, for some, the entire army. After the war, one man wrote, 'I never meet a man now who served in our battalion without a feeling of very close affection springing up in me for him.'[97] S. T. Kemp similarly believed that, despite there being,

> so many fellows together from all walks of life, some rich, some poor, never were there quarrels. In fact all the time that I was in the army I never saw or heard chaps quarrelling. It seemed as if the common purpose was for everyone to try and get the job finished.[98]

It was this spirit of equality that the luncheon speaker cited as the prime importance of comradeship. 'In the old Army,' he wrote, 'there was plenty of comradeship, but in the new one got, in addition, men of every kind and rank all mixed up together; old barriers were broken down, and every man found his neighbour much like himself.'[99] Such comradeship, he argued, was a positive lesson that might be taken from the experience of war: 'We must keep down the barriers and spread the spirit of comradeship. We should be prepared to give ourselves up for our friends as we were in France. If we had that same comradeship now half our social problems would be solved.'[100] Comradeship thus not only justified war experience in retrospect. It was also presented as a solution to the disillusioning situation that many ex-servicemen found themselves in after the war.

Lessons in equality, and the positive light that such lessons cast on men's experience of war, were not, however, the only way in which comradeship defined appropriate martial masculinities. It also acted as an arbiter of courage in face of the tests that war presented to men's self-control and endurance. Max Plowman, for one, believed, 'Courage is a social quality. Out here I see it means caring for you pals more than yourself. For me it has no meaning apart from some degree of friendship.'[101] He wrote of one friend:

> One grows to love and hate men here according as one feels that in crucial moments they will be on the spot or absent. Whatever

happens I know that Hardy will be there, and this last quality of comradeship is worshipful: it seems to be the very basic test of manhood.[102]

In the face of the inability to act and the constant challenges to their endurance, men found that the ability to be a good friend under all circumstances became a signifier of courage.

Some, like Plowman, described other men in whom they admired the quality of comradeship as courage. More common, however were memoirs of those like J. McCauley, who felt himself to have been lacking in the ability to be a good comrade, and therefore lacking in courage. McCauley recalled that:

as I lay wounded on the battlefield, no further use for fighting in my condition, and free to make my escape from the hell we were enduring, I felt genuine regret at the thought of parting from my chums. Fine, loyal comrades they had been. Tested and proved steadfast and true to one another. I began to appreciate what the splendid spirit of comradeship, born out of the horrors and hardships we had faced together meant to me....I had a feeling that I was imposing on these splendid fellows; leaving them just when my help was most needed. Two dead and one wounded in our little group meant that extra burdens would be thrown on my pals, and I thought that I would like to stay with them, wounded though I was, to prove that I was as loyal as they had been to me.[103]

Raggett also felt that:

even after I knew war, shorn of its glamour, knew it as it was, I wanted to be there, even when in England in safety. When I thought later of what the men in the trenches were doing and going through, when I realised that the men who were men were in the line fighting for their lives, when I saw those who were home, fit, ... shirking, I wanted to go back and be with those who were doing so much.[104]

R. G. Dixon felt that, when he was wounded, he:

was 'letting the side down', of being safe while one's friends out there were sticking it out and one was not with them, sharing their life and toil, their hardships and dangers. One hated it, but wanted to be back in it, because it was shirking to be elsewhere. One was so much the less a man if one were not at the front; for us it was the one reality, and the old notorious names were a kind of home to us.

This sense of reality persisted in Dixon's memory, so that:

the very sound of their names to me now is like faint but clear echoes of a vanished world whose permanent inhabitants were terror and pain and violent death, but where tremendous qualities such as courage and comradeship and selflessness shone like stars. I know for myself I have known no such comradeship as those old years gave us who fought on the old Western Front.[105]

Such testimony stands in contrast to arguments that service comradeship collapsed in the face of interwar economic and social divisions.[106] While ex-servicemen's associations did fail to form a cohesive political voice to speak for veterans,[107] memoirists' retrospective celebration of comradeship suggests the continuing importance of a martial masculine identity defined primarily by male bonding rather than the act of killing. In comments such as Dixon's, the duty to endure, cast in the language of comradeship, imposed itself on memoirists as a remembered arbiter of their masculinity as defined by the experience of war. This was the new definition of heroic masculinity. To prove oneself a man in the eyes of memoirists one had to prove oneself not as an adventurer but as a good comrade.

The body

Courage was not the only masculine attribute that men sought to redefine in their memoirs. Physical strength and beauty, an important ideal of pre-war masculine identity throughout Europe,[108] was similarly redefined to fit the muddy conditions and shellfire that destroyed physical perfections. Memoirs provided the spaces in which men could express admiration of the physical strength of soldiers, a quality of masculinity that some recalled as inspiring them to enlist. D. J. Polley remembered 'longing to join [the new recruits he saw], especially when in a short time they donned their khaki. They looked so well, their faces browned, and each looked fit and full of hope.'[109] He was similarly impressed by a Guards regiment he saw going into battle: 'On they came with that long sweeping stride patent to the Guards, almost a slow march compared with the normal pace of a line regiment, they *looked* splendid. Young men of fine physique, trained in one of the finest Battalions in the world.' [My emphasis].[110] In both Polley's descriptions, it is the visible physical attributes that are remembered and described, standing as a symbol for less visible attributes of masculinity that these men were seen as embodying. Nor did memoirists only admire physical qualities in others. They were also extremely proud of it in themselves, regarding it as evidence of their manhood. Walkington, aged seventeen when he enlisted, judged himself 'as good a man as the rest [of his company]. I had never fallen out on a route march like some of the older men. I had even carried a man's rifle when he was nearly done.'[111] Walkington explicitly associates his strength with his identity as a man as opposed to a boy. War in this narrative thus retains the ability to turn boys into men.[112]

War, however, also challenged the idea of physical perfection as a symbol of heroic masculinity. Bodies were destroyed by bullets, shrapnel and decay, while living in a muddy trench proved a disillusioning antithesis to the smart uniforms and physical health and strength that Polley so admired. S. T. Kemp, for instance, recalled:

> the infantry had all been issued with a great coat on enlistment. This was all right but not much use to fellows who were getting up to their waists almost in mud and water in the trenches. The weather was getting very cold at nights and fellows reluctantly put their great coats on, but before long the lower half of the coat was just one mass of mud and water, as were their trousers and puttees.[113]

The visual symbols of war such as uniforms could thus fail when brought into contact with the actual experiences of war. The idealized vision that Polley had of healthy young men in smart uniforms could not last under these conditions. Mud was too common. The use of physical strength and beauty as a visual signifier of idealized masculinity could not survive it.

Despite this, memoirists could find a retrospective source of pride in their improved physical fitness. Jay Winter has pointed out that, 'the war, with all the suffering it caused, was the occasion of a completely unanticipated improvement in the life expectancy of the civilian population.'[114] While Winter notes that this effect was not necessarily felt by soldiers who were actively within harm's way, an echo of this paradox can be heard in the accounts that memoirists gave of their health during and after the war. Those who were not killed or permanently injured found that the experience of warfare could make them physically stronger.

This paradox was evident to men from their training onwards. 'Fitness – physical and moral – is necessary in war,' S. H. Raggett argued, 'and to become fit one must train and train and train. How well I remember how dog tired we used to get, and how fed up, so much so that we used to wish we were in France, and think the war would end before we ever got there.'[115] This training to exhaustion could be taken to extremes. A. J. Turner found:

> [o]n the pre-breakfast physical training 'jerks' the rarefied air of North Wales proved too much for some of the boys, and for a few mornings it was common for one or two to faint. As part of the psychology of toughness we were warned of the consequences should we attempt to help them.[116]

The training may have been brutal, both physically and psychologically, but it served to improve health and could even be recalled, as it was by G. V. Dennis, with pleasure: 'We were fit – open air and plenty of it, exercise not too strenuous to affect us were good for growing lads.'[117] The implication is clear: such physical exertion was turning boys into men.

The trenches, of course, were another matter. They did not directly improve fitness but living in the front line exerted a sort of Darwinian pressure, as R. M. Luther recalled. He suffered from Spanish 'flu at the end of the war but 'got over it, and was back on duty again in about four days' time. There had been no tender hand of love or care in that dug-out, but this was War – the survival of the fittest.'[118] The men who did survive without physical wounds often felt that their health had improved. Griffith recalled one night when he:

> stepped out of my [sleeping] bag to find the clothes I had slept in were wet. . . . Little wonder that I was cold and stiff. Had this happened two years earlier I would have waited for pneumonia, but all I did was change my underclothing and allow the rest to dry upon me.[119]

H. J. Hadlow similarly found, 'my health improved, before the War I was quite often getting swollen glands, sore throats, colds etc., and since the war I do not remember having any of these things except the occasional cold and so far have had no serious illness and my health has been good.'[120] The training that men received as soldiers and the exertion that warfare put them to improved their health, where it did not kill them. Thus participation in war helped some men improve a facet of their masculinity, one that had been part of their enthusiasm for war in the first place.

After the war

Despite the improvement in postwar health noted by several memoirists, many found that the experience of war had complicated the lives they returned to in ways unimagined by letter writers or diarists. Hadlow, for instance, found that, when he started work after demobilisation:

> I was very unsettled, I seemed cooped up and wanted to get out into the air, but after a time I got used to it and settled down. I found that at night I was getting nightmares and dreams of the fighting, I remember one night, at the time I was living in Woolwich and the Military Barracks were only about a couple of hundred yards away as the crow flies and I woke up to hear bugles sounding; there was I found out later a fire alarm, I was perspiring and shaking and it took some time to cool down. I expect that this was a reaction to Army life. This type of thing went on for some years but it eventually went away.[121]

For D. J. Polley, the nightmares never did go away. In his 1920 memoir, he wrote, 'Even all these years after, I sometimes dream of [Ypres], and thank God when I am awake that it was a dream.'[122] Men knew themselves to have been changed by war. W. Griffith believed that, after the war, 'In all that mattered, I was not the same person, a different way of thinking and of feeling had overwhelmed the traces of the old life. The past had become an ancient monument, buried deep, and covered from the mind's eye by the mud of the Low Country.'[123] R. G. Dixon similarly felt, 'I might have been a finer human being had the experiences of war not spoiled me, blunted my sensibilities, and coarsened my reactions.'[124] Indeed, Dixon believed that not only had the war made him different from the man he might have been, but also from the men who did not experience war:

> I am certainly not superior to other men because of what war has helped to make me, [he wrote,] I am not better than they nor are they worse than I. I do not despise them, though I may despise some of their ideas and values, and it is certain that it is not a matter of superiority or inferiority, of better or worse at all. It is simply that I exist on a different plane from that on which they live, and from

that plane I received a different view of life from that which they see. It is therefore a question of difference.[125]

It is this sense of difference that lies at the heart of how memoirists depicted their masculinity during and after the war. Some viewed their experience as making them better men – fitter, tougher, more loyal to their comrades. Others viewed themselves a weakened in body or mind, hardened in spirit, or as having proved themselves less worthy than those who had died. Whatever the effects individual men believed the war to have had on them, all memoirists believed that the war had changed them, as it changed their ideals of what made men heroic.

G. V. Dennis and T. P. Marks

For G. V. Dennis (Figure 4), the war began to change him as soon as he enlisted in the King's Royal Rifle's, straight out of teacher training college. Within a day, he found himself moving 'From white tablecloths, cups and saucers to – thick slices of bread and "Pheasant" margarine slid along the wet tables to each of us.... No turning up our noses at this fare and we showed the beginnings of good soldiers in being able to adapt ourselves straight away to changed conditions.'[126] By the end of the war, he had 'grown up and put on weight no doubt due to the fresh air, exercise and simple meals',[127] although he also found he was suffering from physical disabilities, including the fact that 'My eyesight was much worse owing to army service: my left ankle was never normal and like many other soldiers suffered some discomfort of legs through the constant wearing of tight puttees'.[128] Writing his memoir in 1928, however, Dennis argued that:

> Whatever impression the readers of this book draw, I should like to emphasise that I bear no resentment or bitterness. As far as I could I have drawn a true and honest picture of my army life. I have listened to rumours, grumbles, grousing and complaints.... Much of it was not meant.[129]

Dennis's recollections of the war are, like those of many others, are ambivalent. He clearly recalls the war as uncomfortable, particularly at moments such as the winter of 1917 when:

Figure 4   G. V. Dennis

snow had fallen very heavily and the frosts were very severe.... Shaving water froze before the task was finished. The pint of tea we received each morning froze almost immediately if it was not drunk straight away.... Water was scarce and it was a difficult job to get any for washing. We shared out the little we got – sometimes from a shell hole. As dirty as it was and perhaps only a pint or so we all used it – six or eight of us. I have known eight of us wash and shave in a cigarette tin full of water.... Were we dirty in so carrying on? Yes! No! No, because we did anything to keep clean and that water did help us look cleaner.[130]

The conditions in which Dennis fought may have been on occasion, 'a worse enemy than the Germans',[131] but he and his comrades were clearly determined to maintain what elements of normality they could through their efforts to keep clean.

Dennis also wrote about the dangers of war and the fears that they induced. On his second trip to the front line, for instance, he found himself in a 'part of the line much nearer to Jerry.... Being nearer to him meant that we suffered more from his daily small "Hymns of hate." Every morning at breakfast time there came the mortars: at dinner time a few whizz-bangs and at tea-time some rifle grenades.'[132] Out of the front line, life was also dangerous:

Runners and guides had to time their entrances and exits [to and from a dug out] to the second in order avoid being caught by a shell.... The best procedure to follow was to lie flat on the face as soon as the shell was heard: wait a few seconds whilst it exploded then move on and repeat these actions and be thankful when you stumbled down the rough hewn steps of the dug-out and got your breath back.[133]

Dennis recorded a range of reactions to these conditions. One man became fatalistically convinced that he would be killed in the next attack. 'I failed to cheer him up and I could not get him to change his mind – yet he was not miserable or even frightened.'[134] He also remembered two men encountered during the battle of the Somme who were crying. 'One was our beloved Wesleyan Padre, down whose face the tears rolled non-stop. The other was our "C" Company S.M.: a regular soldier, whose time was nearly up. He had served in the Boer War and in South Africa he had seen nothing like the Somme.'[135] The Sergeant Major's reaction to the battle was thus recalled in terms that directly challenge his identity as a stoic martial figure. Dennis also found himself affected, if rather less dramatically, by the immediate experience of war. 'Our initiation into the arts of trench warfare affected us in different ways,' he wrote, 'Perhaps we were not so happy go lucky as we had been in Helmsley [where he had trained]. A grey shadow now hovered over us and influenced us indirectly.'[136]

Dennis's narrative was not, however, one entirely of fear, discomfort and horror. Fear could be eased 'by the smoking of a fag…[which] helped a man with nerves…many men gambled – it seemed they must do something.…I wrote letters, sent off cards and played patience by the hour. The mind had to be occupied with something, according to one's taste.'[137] This remedy for nerves also worked during action as, for example, during an attack on Messine Ridge when Dennis found that the din faded because 'I was so busy getting on with the job in hand.'[138]

There were other compensations as well. Mail was 'as good a tonic as any man could wish for.'[139] Rest periods could be 'carefree days [of]…relaxation and freedom from strain'.[140] Above all, however, there was the comradeship of wartime. From the beginning, 'khaki made friendships. Whereas we had been reserved in civvies, now we spoke to any Tommy whatever his company.'[141] Such feelings persisted in Dennis's memory. 'No matter which was your company or specialist section the spirit of comradeship was everywhere. It characterised the whole battalion – all were very friendly to all others.'[142] Indeed, this aspect of the war was the most important in shaping Dennis's recollections. In the preface to his memoir he wrote, 'Those that came back from war's hell cannot forget, and in many instances do not want to forget because they made the acquaintance of men, met true friendships, saw the best in men, and realised that the other men were as good or better than themselves.'[143] The end of the war, he concluded, 'did not and could not terminate the friendships that were made and few were the men whom others wished to forget.' Dennis himself continued to meet regularly with other survivors, endeavouring, 'By such calls, visits and thought…to keep alive the goodness that was created amidst horror,'[144] as well as remembering 'those who did not return with us. Their memory lives with us for evermore and we are not likely to forget them for their spirit of self-sacrifice and comradeship was of the *best.*' [My emphasis].[145]

By using this superlative structure, Dennis constructed the men who died during the war as more manly than those who survived because of the evidence of their spirit of self-sacrifice provided by their deaths. Yet his understanding of his own identity as shaped by the war was by no means negative. Despite the physical injuries that he suffered, and the feeling of restlessness that took hold of him after the Armistice,[146] Dennis's strongest emotion about the war's effect on him as a man was one of pride. 'I know how fortunate I was and what a lot of the worst I missed,' he concluded, 'but I am very proud of that "bit": proud that I could have been marked "unfit" and did not accept it: proud that I met scores of boys and men and realised their worth...proud that they accepted me.'[147] For Dennis, the war provided an opportunity to integrate into a community of men that he admired for their specific qualities of comradeship and self-sacrifice. In being accepted by such men, he felt that he had proved himself to be a man as well.

By contrast, Thomas Penrose Marks's memoir paints a far bleaker picture of the effect of war experience on masculine identity. Written in 1936 with the encouragement of his wife, 'the manuscript...[lay] in a cupboard for forty years' before it was published in 1977 under the title *The Laughter Goes From Life*.[148] Written in the present tense, it is, unlike Dennis's more linear narrative, an episodic, atmospheric account of day-to-day experiences providing comparatively little contextual continuity.

Marks's view of the war, as reflected in his narrative, is of a process primarily of dehumanization by life in the army. '[W]e are not supposed to think,' he noted:

> Anyone who thinks cannot be a good soldier. A good soldier is one who always does what he is told to do. In our school days we had been told that the power to think differentiated man from beast. In the army there are other rules, and a completely different set of values.[149]

Among these values was a celebration of destruction which Marks viewed as the antithesis of humanity:

> We appear to be well on the way to becoming dehumanised. All our early training and education was aimed at creating and building up, but now we seek only to destroy. Pity seems to be going out of our nature. The more we can injure the other man, the more satisfied we become. Our aim is always to strike two blows to his one.[150]

These emotions are illustrated by Marks's description of an attack in a chapter entitled 'Going Over the Top': 'Ahead of us there are thirty or more of the enemy. My platoon engages the, and we fire shot for shot....It is like shooting rabbits. At such a distance it should be impossible to miss one's target....We get fifteen of the enemy.'

He concludes, 'We feel that we have done quite well. There are fifteen dead Germans for the loss of our lance-sergeant and four men in the attack.'[151] Here both friend and enemy are reduced to numbers in a calculation. As Marks notes of an earlier experience of watching a bombardment destroying a cavalry unit, 'One must become callous in order that we may carry on.'[152]

Elements of Marks's narrative, however, contradict any simple reading of the war as an entirely dehumanizing and disillusioning process. In one incident, for instance, when he and three comrades discover their platoon officer lying on the edge of a shell hole with his head and hand nearly severed, they 'find a stretcher and put him on it. The ground has been torn up and it is heavy work even with four men. But we would willingly have carried him twenty miles.'[153] Similarly he observes and records the death of a man in his unit with great compassion, remembering that 'He spoke with a peculiar drawl. One front tooth projected forwards and a wisp of hair would not be brushed backwards. To live with horses, and always near to the earth, was all that he asked in life.'[154] Despite his military training and experiences of battle, war experience clearly failed to render Marks entirely callous to the tragedy of individual deaths.

Perhaps more destructive to Marks's identity than experiences of battle and killing, was, as it was for so many men, the experience of living day-to-day with the threat of death. 'It is,' he noted of being under barrage, 'luck, sheer luck, that you find yourself uninjured from moment to moment.'[155] As he pointed out earlier, 'Life at the Front destroys our nerves. There is danger about us, and below us, and above us. It is always present'.[156] The result both of the danger themselves and the fears they produce are deeply destructive to masculine identity in Marks's narrative. Of men buried alive by an explosion he writes, 'They are not injured, by very badly shocked. . . . It will be many weeks before the three men rejoin us. They are in a bad way. . . . When any man has had such and experience he becomes transformed, and is never more than half a soldier afterwards.'[157] Similarly, following a bombardment, 'There will be half-men and quarter-men and no men at all left where little groups now huddle together with a few planks or a sheet of elephant iron over them in the trench.'[158] Such destruction of masculine identity was not limited to those who suffered specific moments danger:

As rocks will, in time, will become eroded by falling water, so men's nerves become frayed from being too long in the line at a stretch. The last straw breaks the camel's back and anything can happen to a man when he has to put up with the explosion of bursting shells, and the hideous sight of his best friend being dismembered. To these can be added confinement for weeks on end within a few yards, prolonged periods of sleeplessness, a monotonous and inefficient diet, and whatever inclement weather the gods may choose to send.[159]

The experience of war is viewed in retrospect by Marks as simply destructive of men, body and soul.

Unlike Dennis, there are few consolations in Marks's recollection of the war. While there are recollections of pleasant meals at estaminets behind the lines and interesting discussions with other members of his unit, these memories appear to have little effect on Marks's attitude towards the war. Marks was the youngest member of his platoon, having enlisted straight out of school. He indicates his level of integration into the military unit by a consistent use of the plural pronoun 'we' throughout the book, yet the joys of comradeship play little role in his memories. Even when his battalion is decimated by gas, leaving Marks himself temporarily blind, his primary emotion is that of gratitude that, unlike two of his companions, he has not been killed:

> I think of Polly and Bill, and decide that it is better to live a blind man than to die from stomach wounds or poison gas as they did.... I have a home to which I may return, and nobody will be dependent upon me. And I have the best parents in the whole wide world who will always care for me and protect me.[160]

Perhaps because of his youth, Marks appears to have accepted the possibility of dependence more easily than other disabled men could. Rather unusually for a memoirist, however, in describing his feelings about his disability in terms of dependence rather than of mourning, Marks constructs his identity in wartime as domestic rather than martial.

Unlike Dennis, Marks at no point constructs his memoir in terms of mourning or commemoration. The memoir ends with the words, 'We live. The war is over.'[161] While there is a brief epilogue describing a meeting between Marks and a German in South Africa after the war, in which we learn that Marks has become a teacher, there is no mention of the men he fought with, none of the celebration of the comradeship or shared experience that Dennis uses to give meaning to his memories of the war. By ending his memoir at the moment of the Armistice, Marks appears to make no connection between his identity as a soldier in war time and his postwar identity as a teacher and husband. Indeed, throughout the book his identity as a soldier is viewed as separate: 'Some of us realise that it is not our real selves who laugh. Something other than our real selves has taken possession of us for the time being.'[162] Yet he is forced to acknowledge that this separate self existed and experienced the discomforts, horrors and fears of war. Those experiences changed him. 'How times have changed,' he writes. 'In civilian life we should never dream of laughing at such an incident. The incident itself would not be possible, to begin with, and we should ostracise anyone who dreamed of making fun out of tragedy. We have changed too.'[163] In revisiting that identity through a present-tense narrative, 15 years after the Armistice, Marks acknowledges, however privately, that his experiences as a soldier changed him and, in doing so, became part of his experiences as a man.

Read together, Dennis and Marks' memoirs demonstrate the ambivalence towards war experience that defined men's attitudes throughout the interwar period.[164] Where Marks describes in his present tense narrative an experience dominated by discomfort, danger and disillusion, Dennis retrospectively constructs a more positive interpretation of his experiences. Both, however, present warfare as a seminal moment in defining their identities as men, even if Marks ends with the Armistice. Both thus demonstrate through the very act of writing their memoirs the continuing importance of the masculine identity of the soldier to men who had fought in the First World War.

Conclusion

Where the letters of disabled ex-servicemen expose the ways in which war experience had undermined men's ability to construct appropriate identities in relation to ideals of heroic and domestic masculinity, postwar memoirs present a much more ambivalent picture. While drawing heavily on the themes and narrative structures seen in wartime letters and diaries, these postwar documents provide an alternative form of narrative through which masculine identities were constructed. Distanced, both in time and space, from the immediacy of life in the front line, postwar memoirs provided ex-servicemen with greater space for reflection on both war experience and their ability to integrate that experience into their postwar civilian lives.

What can be seen in memoirs is an intensification of many of the elements of masculine construction seen in other narrative forms. Grousing develops in memory into disillusionment, and the discomforts of warfare become increasingly prominent; conversely, comradeship increases in its recalled significance, while courage is fully redefined in the light of the recognition that all men felt fear. Memoirs, in their retrospection and distance from the experience of war, allowed men to develop coherent narratives of masculinity that encompassed many of the contradictions of immediate lived experience.

This is not to say that memoirs presented a single narrative of the war as either disillusioning or ennobling.[165] The multiple perceptions of warfare simply demonstrates the diversity of individual experiences of warfare. Yet, in reading these diverse experiences alongside each other, we can begin to see how retrospective narratives, whatever their tone, constructed the war as something that had changed the men who served as men, physically, emotionally and, above all, permanently. The war alone did not change them. Postwar experiences continued to shape men. But the experience of serving in the First World War remained a seminal moment and, indeed, the seminal moment in memoirists' lives as men.

Conclusion

Men's identities are never set in stone and nowhere is this more evident than in the microcosm of war with its power to disrupt the gender order. Viewed over the course of the First World War, British service-men's perceptions of their own identity as soldiers can be seen to have been contingent upon a number of factors, including the imminence of danger, the weather, the location and nature of military service, the ability to remain in contact with the home front and access to sources of bodily comfort. Postwar domestic identities were equally contingent on the specific social and cultural situation in which men found them-selves, being informed by factors such as age, the availability of work and housing, a man's health and that of his family.

How these identities were expressed was also affected by the narrative form used and the audience being addressed. The need to reassure a domestic audience informed the choice of examples used to illustrate masculine behaviours, both military and domestic, in letters home, while the need to comfort the bereaved shaped the meanings ascribed to the men's deaths in letters of condolence. Audience also dictated which form of masculine identity men chose to present in their narratives. The expectations of the Ministry of Pensions clearly influenced the ways in which pensioners constructed their requests for assistance in terms of domestic self-reliance and family support, compared with the almost exclusive focus on martial identities that were the source of so many of the memories reconstructed in postwar memoirs.

The importance of audience in influencing men's narrative construc-tions of personal masculine identities indicates the extent to which such identities were structured as much by cultural discourses of appropri-ate masculinity as by direct experiences. The cultural stereotypes of the soldier hero, the breadwinner and the good husband and father were the benchmarks by which men evaluated their own and others' behaviour, whether in terms of ability to endure, to be a good comrade or to support dependants. But while masculinities may have been constructed within a framework of cultural ideals and social expectations concerning what made the appropriate martial and domestic male, within that framework men's subjective identities were fluid and potentially contradictory. The stoicism of letters was belied by the grousing of contemporaneous diaries and the construction of the disabled as valiant servants of the state who were made heroic through their sacrifice for her was undermined by their ongoing reliance on state support.

Despite these complexities, commonalities among the narratives do emerge. The focus on experiences of shellfire, the need to express the danger, uncanniness and horrors of war, however inarticulately, the emphasis on service and sacrifice as defining qualities of martial courage, all form common threads uniting the ways in which men constructed wartime masculinities as both unique and potentially heroic. Similarly, the need to communicate with and about the home front, the numerous discussions of domestic responsibilities and the creation of bonds of fictive kinship with the bereaved indicate the extent to which British servicemen were, and remained throughout the war, civilians in uniform, defined as much by their domestic as their military identities.

*   *   *

Above all, however, all men's narratives present one very simple message: war changed men. Such change could involve death, the destruction of a man's body or mind, the loss of a future or simply a more cynical outlook on life. It could also, however, mean improvements in physical health through exercise, growth into maturity through increased responsibility and the broadening of horizons through contact with men from other parts of the world and other walks of life. Indeed, in most soldiers' narratives the positive and negative effects of the war on the individual combined to form an ambivalent attitude towards war experience. What every narrative looked at here reflects is the ways in which the writer's experiences made him different both from those who did not fight and from the man he had been before the war.

This sense of difference caused men who served in the First World War to construct themselves as a separate generation. As R. G. Dixon noted,

I am certainly not superior to other men because of what war has helped to make me.... It is simply that I exist on a different plane from that on which they live, and from that plane I received a different view of life from that which they see. It is therefore a question of difference.[1]

But it was not only others, too young or too old or the wrong gender to have shared their experiences of warfare, who servicemen perceived themselves to be different from in the years after the war. War had also changed them from themselves, from the men they had been, or aspired to become had they not gone to war. Despite the dreams of domesticity that inspired and motivated them, the men who returned from war were not the same as those who had departed. Some were, as promised by Newman, more handy about the house, having learned to look after themselves in extreme conditions. Others were damaged physically and mentally in ways that forced them into positions of domestic dependence that were the antithesis of the independent men they had been or expected to become. Some never returned to their domestic identities at all, becoming, through death in battle, identified entirely as soldiers. Even those who did return successfully to a domestic identity continued to reflect the importance of war experience to their postwar identities through the continuing need to tell their story, constructing and reconstructing their memory of the war as the seminal moment of their lives.

The experience of war and its memory is thus shown by these narratives to be a persistent force in shaping the identities of all men who served. The long-term nature of its influence was certainly felt by pensioners whose bodies were permanently inscribed with physical reminders in the form of wounds, illness and amputations. For men with mental disabilities, such effects were less visible but, in many cases, no less permanent, with the possession of a pension serving as an acknowledgement on behalf of the state that the war had changed them in ways that they could not necessarily recover from. Even for men superficially uninjured by the war, their previous identities continued to exert an influence in the sense of dislocation felt by many when they attempted to put off their role of soldiers in favour of civil identities as domestic providers.

Although it has been argued that the persistent influence of the war on men's behaviour and identities was inherently disabling, through both physical damage or the emotional warping of men by exposure to the horror and uncanniness of war,[2] this was not necessarily the case. War could shape men's identities in positive ways as well. Skills learnt in warfare could be applied to postwar life, despite the fears which some men expressed that the contrary would be true. Horizons broadened by exposure to men of other classes, nationalities and perspectives could, as E. F. Chapman noted, never again be narrowed again.[3] Even the violence and horror that dominated men's narratives could be seen as effecting positive change in men in the form of improved endurance, adaptability and the capacity to be a good comrade *in extremis*, all qualities that continued to be associated with social and cultural ideals of heroic masculinity. These positive effects were as persistent in shaping men's postwar identities as more negative responses of disillusionment and fatalism, making them equally important in defining British First World War servicemen's memories and identities.

* * *

The persistence of the influence of martial identity had repercussions for postwar gender relations. Men may have returned from the war eager to resume the domesticity that they had dreamed of while away.[4] Yet the changes wrought on them by the war made a simple return impossible. Jobs were scarce, housing was limited and, for those suffering from disability, masculine independence could be impossible to achieve. Some men did react with anger towards women. For others, the support of women became a necessity, a situation which could be not only humiliating for the men but which could force wives into roles as carers and wage earners that they had neither expected nor desired.[5] Widows similarly found themselves faced with unanticipated challenges in supporting themselves and their children, while bereaved parents faced a grief that a generation of improved childhood healthcare had rendered far less familiar to British society.[6]

On a personal level, changes to gender relations took the form of domestic disruptions that altered the lives and expectations of men and women throughout British society. The restlessness described by memoirs cannot have been easy to live with for wives or parents. Difficulties in finding work and suitable housing put pressure on relationships between men and their dependants, leading to an increase in the divorce rates.[7] Personal relationships had to be renegotiated around a subject that became increasingly difficult for veterans and civilians to discuss with each other as celebrations of survival gave way to a spirit of national mourning.[8] This growing silence of veterans about their experiences indicates the failure of men to integrate their identities as soldiers into the domestic life that they returned to. For all its continuing importance in defining individuals as appropriate, even heroic, men, rather than emasculated victims, the soldier male was not a figure who fit comfortably into a postwar society exhausted by four years of total war.

*   *   *

Yet the dominance of martial identities has increased over the years, becoming ever more important to cultural perceptions of First World War servicemen in Britain.[9] Since the revival of interest in the First World War in the 1960s, the memories of former servicemen have been avidly collected and published.[10] Several veterans have become media figures, appearing regularly on radio and television programmes to recall and rehearse their wartime memories. Today, as these last remaining veterans are, one by one, dying, they are guaranteed obituaries in the British national press, whatever rank they achieved in the armed forces or status they attained in civil life.[11] These men are now all over 100 years old, yet these public commentaries on their lives, like the memoirs of other survivors, celebrate and commemorate only their few years of war experience. Like the dead of wartime, through their longevity, these veterans' identities have become almost entirely those of soldiers.

At the same time, the figure of the ordinary soldier has become increasingly mythic. In the poetry taught to school children, in fictional representations of the war and in popular histories of the war, he has come to be portrayed almost exclusively as a victim of the horrors of warfare, the mental distress these horrors caused and the jingoistic old men and the women who sent young men into futile battle.[12] Even for the veterans themselves, writing and rewriting, telling and retelling their stories, their identities, and those of the dead comrades they recalled, have increasingly to reflect this myth. Yet this is not the image of wartime masculinity that emerges from personal documents. Rather, in letters, diaries and even memoirs, men constructed themselves as purposeful, even heroic, in warfare. Disillusionment and fatalism are evident, but rarely as a consistent condemnation of the war. Instead, the war retains its cultural place as an arena in which men were defined both as martial heroes and domestic protectors. Even for those disabled by the war, war experience remained a defining sphere in which they had proved their masculinity through the sacrifice of personal health and postwar domestic felicity.

*   *   *

Close examination of servicemen's personal narratives thus forces us to reassess our assumptions about war experience, war disability, the memory of war and gender relations. While the physical experience of warfare is clearly central to these narratives, they also reveal the ways in which men linked such experiences to a range of abstract cultural images and ideals in their attempts form a coherent narrative. They located wartime masculinities in a lived reality that encompassed the home front as well as the fighting front, pre-war background as well as wartime experience. British men who served in the First World War were more than just soldiers, just as they were more than simply bodies. We must, therefore, look again at arguments about how the war distanced those who fought in it from civilian culture and society, asking instead how the descriptive language that men utilized served to construct their subjective identities within that culture.

The extent to which masculine identity transcends the physical is as evident in the letters of the war disabled as it is in the letters and diaries of servicemen. In these documents too men turned to abstract ideals, of masculine independence, service and sacrifice to construct identities that extended beyond the body. Their failure to adequately rationalize their social and economic positions through these ideals serves as further evidence for the problems that British society had in reintegrating such men.[13] Yet they demonstrate the extent to which such disability was a social issue, particularly in its effects on the family. These sources provide a window into the private realities of family breakdown in the wake of warfare that is only beginning to be explored. Further study is needed if we are to fully understand how war disability affected not only men and their identities but also those of their parents, wives and children.

The use of familiar imagery and tradition ideals in men's efforts to describe their experiences of both wartime and the postwar world emphasizes the cultural continuity that structured men's constructions of individual identity. War may have been viewed as a unique experience, but these narratives demonstrate the ways in which it was narrated as part of continuum that was, in the first instance, personal. This reflects the cultural continuity in memories of warfare that Jay Winter has identified, with the war marking a defining moment rather than a break in the cultural narrative.[14] The continuing centrality of the war to the shape of men's identities long after their war service was complete is equally reflective of the continuing importance of the history of the First World War to British culture and the way in which it is remembered. Dan Todman has suggested that the transmission of the memory of the war through family narrative and cultural creation as much as through formal history makes the war distinctive, even unique as a historical event. Men's written memoirs play an important role in this process, both in their construction of individual understandings of warfare and in their transmission of these understandings to following generations.

Men's personal narratives of warfare thus raise questions as to the extent to which the experience of war disrupted both personal identity and cultural continuity and the place of individual experience within cultural memory. In doing so, they bring into focus the question of the uniqueness of women's experiences of warfare as reflected in their writings. While men's narratives do not challenge the assertion that the war provided a unique space for women to form a literary voice, they do force us to consider the extent to which it was women's narratives alone that bridged the gap between home and fighting front, between past and future.[15] In acknowledging that men located their masculinity in ideals of domesticity during the war as much as women used the opportunities war offered to gain experience beyond the home, and that their perceptions of war experience as purposeful, even heroic, continued to shape their identities as husbands and fathers in the years after the war, the question arises as to how the perspectives of men and women interact. Far from the parallel strands of the double helix,[16] constructions of gender in these narratives suggests multiple points of contact. The symbolic spaces where men and women meet between the home and fighting fronts that they both explore in personal narratives is a subject that requires further investigation.

Ultimately, the complexity and ambivalence expressed by all the narratives examined here allows for a deeper understanding of the masculine experience of warfare, one in which neither the victim nor the hero dominates, but in which the war retains its central role in defining men. These understandings of what it was to be a man, with their roots in 19th-century definitions of manliness but shaped by individual experiences of the war and its aftermath, served to define the identities of a generation of men. Through written narratives of all genres, they would continue to influence the understandings of both warfare and masculinity for the men of the generations that succeeded them.

Notes

Introduction

1. George Orwell (1970) 'My Country, Right or Left' in Sonia Orwell and Ian Angus (eds), *Collected Essays, Journalism and Letters*, vol. I (London: Penguin Books), p. 589.
2. Samuel Hynes (1976) *The Auden Generation* (London: The Bodley Head), pp. 17–21.
3. Stefan Dudink et al. (2004) 'Editors' Preface' in Stefan Dudink et al. (eds), *Masculinities in Politics and War: Gendering Modern History* (Manchester: Manchester University Press), p. xii.
4. Leo Braudy (2003) *From Chivalry to Terrorism: War and the Changing Nature of Masculinity* (New York: Alfred A. Knopf), p. xvi.
5. Samuel Hynes (1997) *The Soldiers' Tale: Bearing Witness to Modern War* (New York: Penguin Books), p. 5.
6. Nicoletta F. Gullace (2002) *'The Blood of Our Sons': Men, Women, and the Renegotiation of British Citizenship During the Great War* (New York: Palgrave Macmillan), pp. 101–115.
7. For a discussion of tensions between heroic and domestic masculinities at the turn of the century, see John Tosh (1999) *A Man's Place: Masculinity and the Middle-class Home in Victorian England* (New Haven: Yale University Press), Chapter 8.
8. Hynes, *The Soldiers' Tale*, pp. 1–2; Paul Fussell (1975) *The Great War and Modern Memory* (Oxford: Oxford University Press), p. ix.
9. Sandra M. Gilbert (1987) 'Soldiers' Heart: Literary men, literary women, and the Great War' in Margaret Randolph Higonnet et al. (eds), *Behind the Lines: Gender and the Two World Wars* (New Haven: Yale University Press), p. 207.
10. Siegfried Sassoon (1979) 'The Glory of Women' in Jon Silken (ed.) *The Penguin Book of First World War Poetry* (London: Penguin Books), p. 132; Richard Aldington (1929) *Death of a Hero* (London: Chatto and Windus).
11. J. M. Winter (1985) *The Great War and the British People* (London: Macmillan Education Ltd.), pp. 10–18; Samuel Hynes (1991) *A War Imagined: The First World War and English Culture* (New York: Atheneum), pp. 11–17. See also Tracey Hill (ed.) (1997), *Decadence and Danger: Writing, History and the Fin de Siécle* (Bath: Sulis Press); Frank Mort (1987) *Dangerous Sexualities: Medico-moral Politics in England Since 1830* (London: Routledge & Kegan Paul) and Daniel Pick (1989) *Faces of Degeneration: A European Disorder, c.1848–1918* (Cambridge: Cambridge University Press).
12. Gullace, *'The Blood of Our Sons'*, pp. 37–46.
13. Janet S. K. Watson (2004) *Fighting Different Wars: Experience, Memory, and the First World War in Britain* (Cambridge: Cambridge University Press), pp. 29–41; Susan Kingsley Kent (1993) *Making Peace: The Reconstruction of*

Gender in Interwar Britain (Princeton: Princeton University Press), pp. 72–73; 'Introduction' in Higonnet et al., *Behind the Lines*, pp. 4–6.

14. Joan W. Scott, 'Rewriting History' in Higonnet et al., *Behind the Lines*, p. 25.
15. Scott, 'Rewriting History', p. 27.
16. Kingsley Kent, *Making Peace*; Gail Braybon (1981) *Women Workers and the First World War* (London: Routledge); Deborah Thom (1998) *Nice Girls and Rude Girls: Women Workers in World War I* (London: I.B. Tauris Publishers).
17. Susan R. Grayzel (1999) *Women's Identities at War: Gender, Motherhood, and Politics in Britain and France During the First World War* (Chapel Hill: The University of North Carolina Press); Janis Lomas (2000) ' "Delicate Duties": Issues of class and respectability in government policy towards wives and widows of British soldiers in the era of the Great War', *Women's History Review*, 9:1, 123–147; Susan Pedersen (1993) *Family, Dependence and the Origins of the Welfare State: Britain and France, 1914–1945* (Cambridge: Cambridge University Press), pp.79–137.
18. For comparative approaches to the question of gender roles and relations, looking at how the lives of both men and women were changed, see Gullace, *'Blood of Our Sons'* and Watson, *Fighting Different Wars*.
19. Gilbert, 'Soldier's Heart' in Higonnet et al., *Behind the Lines*, p. 203.
20. Ibid., p. 225.
21. Kingsley Kent, *Making Peace*, p. 115.
22. Claire M. Tylee (1988) ' "Maleness run riot": The great war and women's resistance to militarism', *Women's Studies International Forum*, 11:3, 199–210.
23. Eric J. Leed, (1979) *No Man's Land: Combat and Identity in World War I* (Cambridge: Cambridge University Press), p. 4.
24. Deborah Cohen (2001) *The War Come Home: Disabled Veterans in Britain and Germany 1914–1939* (Berkeley: University of California Press), p. 127; Seth Koven (1994) 'Remembering and Dismemberment: crippled children, wounded soldiers and the Great War in Great Britain', *American Historical Review*, 99:4, 1167–1202.
25. Helen B. McCartney (2005) *Citizen Soldiers: The Liverpool Territorials in the First World War*, (Cambridge: Cambridge University Press), pp. 90–103; David Englander (1994) 'Soldiering and Identity: reflections on the Great War', *War in History*, 1:3, 304.
26. Cohen, *The War Come Home*, p. 189.
27. Ibid., p. 144.
28. Michael Roper 'Maternal Relations: moral manliness and emotional survival in letters home during the First World War' in Dudink et al., *Masculinities in Politics and War*, p. 297.
29. Leed, *No Man's Land*, pp. 163–186; Elaine Showalter (1987) *The Female Malady: Women, Madness, and English Culture, 1830–1980* (London: Virago), pp. 176–178; Alison Light (1991) *Forever England: Femininity, Literature and Conservatism Between the Wars* (London: Routledge), p. 7. The symbolism is perhaps most evident in the portrayal of shell-shocked soldiers in contemporary novels such as Pat Barker's *Regeneration* trilogy (1991–1995).
30. Gullace, *'The Blood of Our Sons'*, p. 93.
31. Hynes, *A War Imagined*, p. 215.

32. Martin Green (1980) *Deeds of Adventure, Dreams of Empire* (London: Routledge and Kegan Paul), pp. 31–35; Michael Paris (2000) *Warrior Nation: Images of War in British Popular Culture, 1850–2000* (London: Reaktion Books), pp. 54–58; John MacKenzie (1992) 'Introduction: popular imperialism and the military' in John MacKenzie (ed.) *Popular Imperialism and the Military, 1850–1950* (Manchester: Manchester University Press), p. 1; Jeffrey Richards, 'Poplar Imperialism and the Image of the Army in Juvenile Literature' in MacKenzie (ed.), *Popular Imperialism and the Military*, pp. 81–87; Graham Dawson (1994) *Soldier Heroes: British Adventure, Empire and the Imagining of Masculinities* (London: Routledge), pp. 120–128, 167–168; Max Jones (2003) *The Last Great Quest: Captain Scott's Antarctic Sacrifice* (Oxford: Oxford University Press), pp. 245–251.

33. Gullace, *'Blood of Our Sons'*, p. 49; Keith Surridge (2001) 'More than a great poster: Lord Kitchener and the image of the military hero', *Historical Research*, 74:185, 308–309.

34. Michael Paris (2000) 'Boys' Books and the Great War', *History Today*, 50:11, 49.

35. Rosa Maria Bracco (1993) *Merchants of Hope: Middlebrow Writers and the First World War, 1919–1939* (Oxford: Berg), pp. 196–199.

36. Dawson, *Soldier Heroes*, p. 1. The durability of the figure of the soldier hero in other European cultures has been discussed by George Mosse (1996) *The Image of Man: The Creation of Modern Masculinity* (Oxford: Oxford University Press), pp. 181–183.

37. Michael Adams (1990) *The Great Adventure: Male Desire and the Coming of World War I* (Bloomington: Indiana University Press), p. 29; Keith McClelland (1991) 'Masculinity and the "Representative Artisan" in Britain, 1850–80' in Michael Roper and John Tosh (eds), *Manful Assertions: Masculinities in Britain since 1800* (London: Routledge), pp. 82–85.

38. John Tosh (1994) 'What Should Historians Do With Masculinity? Reflections on nineteenth-century Britain', *History Workshop Journal*, 38, 185.

39. Wally Seccombe (1986) 'Patriarchy Stabilized: the construction of the male breadwinner norm in nineteenth-century Britain', *Social History* 2:1 (January 1986), 54.

40. Tosh, *A Man's Place*, pp. 1–2.

41. Ibid., pp. 193–194.

42. Gullace, *'Blood of Our Sons,'* Chapter 2.

43. Joanna Bourke (1996) *Dismembering the Male: Men's Bodies, Britain and the Great War* (London: Reaktion Books), pp. 167–170; Tosh, *A Man's Place*, p. 196; Winter, *The Great War and the British People*, pp. 250–253; Light, *Forever England*, p. 8.

44. Dennis Winter (1979) *Death's Men: Soldiers of the Great War* (London: Penguin Books), p. 16.

45. Dan Todman (2005) *The Great War: Myth and Memory* (London: Hambledon), p. xiv; Michael Roper (2005) 'Between manliness and masculinity: the "war generation" and the psychology of fear in Britain, 1914–1970', *Journal of British Studies*, 44:2, 345.

46. Todman, *The Great War*, p. 187.

47. Examples of this sort of history include the numerous volumes culled from interviews and sources at the Imperial War Museum by Lyn MacDonald

and Max Arthur, as well as more analytical works such Dennis Winter's *Death's Men*.

48. Sharon Ouditt (1994) *Fighting Forces, Writing Women: Identity and Ideology in the First World War* (London: Routledge), p. 3.
49. Jane Potter (2005) *Boys in Khaki, Girls in Print: Women's Literary Responses to the Great War 1914–1918* (Oxford: Clarendon Press); Light, *Forever England*.
50. Angela K. Smith (2000) *The Second Battlefield: Women, Modernism and the First World War* (Manchester: Manchester University Press), p. 19.
51. Ibid., p. 5.
52. Ibid., p. 40.
53. Margaret Millman (2003) 'In the Shadows of War: continuities and discontinuities in the construction of masculine identities in British soldiers, 1914–1924', PhD. diss., University of Greenwich, p. 20.
54. Dawson, *Soldier Heroes*, pp. 22–26; Paris, *Warrior Nation*, pp. 49–71.
55. Millman, 'In the Shadows of War', p. 13.
56. Horne, 'Masculinities in politics and war' in Dudink et al., *Masculinities in Politics and War*, p. 28; Millman, 'In the Shadows of War', p. 3; Mosse, *The Image of Man*, pp. 17–24.
57. Bourke, *Dismembering the Male*.
58. Santanu Das (2005) *Touch and Intimacy in First World War Literature* (Cambridge: Cambridge University Press), p. 5.
59. Rachel Duffett (2008) 'A War Unimagined: Food, Memory and the Rank and File Soldier' in Jessica Meyer (ed.), *British Popular Culture and the First World War* (Leiden: Brill), pp. 47–70.
60. Bourke, *Dismembering the Male*, Chapter 1.
61. Hynes, *The Soldiers' Tale*, pp. xii–xiii.
62. Claire M. Tylee (1990) *The Great War and Women's Consciousness: Images of Militarism and Womanhood in Women's Writings, 1914–1964* (Basingstoke: Macmillan), pp. 15–16.
63. Watson, *Fighting Different Wars*, pp. 4–9 and *passim*.
64. McCartney, *Citizen Soldiers*; Keith Grieves (ed.) (2004) *Sussex and the First World War* (Lewes: Sussex Record Society).
65. Winter, *Death's Men*, p. 20.
66. The concept of 'sites of memory' was initially defined by Pierre Nora (ed.), *Les lieux de mémoire*, 7 vols. (Paris: Gallimard, 1984–1992), although it has been expanded on considerably by First World War historians. See, for example, Jay Winter (1995) *Sites of Memory, Sites of Mourning: The Great War in European Cultural History* (Cambridge: Cambridge University Press), p. 10.
67. Todman, *The Great War*, p. 187.
68. Hynes, *The Soldiers' Tale*, pp. 3–4.
69. Millman, 'In the Shadows of War'; Martin Middlebrook (1971) *The First Day of the Somme* (London: Allen Lane); Martin Middlebrook (1978) *The Kaiser's Battle* (London: Allen Lane).
70. Michael Roper (2000) 'Re-remembering the Soldier Hero: the psychic and social construction of memory in personal narratives of the Great War', *History Workshop Journal*, 50, 183–184.
71. Todman, *The Great War*, pp. 201–208.
72. In the case of the First World War, this problem is compounded by the large number of semi-autobiographical novels, such as Siegfried Sassoon's

(1937) *The Complete Memoirs of George Sherston* (London: Faber and Faber) and Frederick Manning's (1929) *Her Privates We* (London: Hogarth), and autobiographical fictions, such as Robert Graves's (1929) *Good-bye to All That* (London: Jonathan Cape). See Fussell, *The Great War and Modern Memory*, pp. 205–206.
73. Roper, 'Re-remembering the Soldier Hero', 183.

1   Writing home: Men's letters from the front

1. Imperial War Museum, London (hereafter IWM), 03/5/01, Papers of C. T. Newman, C. T. Newman, letter to Winnie, 8 September 1917.
2. Peter B. Boyden (1990) *Tommy Atkins' Letters: The History of the British Army Postal Service from 1795* (London: National Army Museum), pp. 5, 28.
3. Ibid., p. 28. 8,150,000 of those letters were sent from the Western Front.
4. Englander 'Soldiering and Identity', 304.
5. Ibid., 305.
6. McCartney *Citizen Soldiers*, p. 96.
7. Roper, 'Maternal relations' in Dudink et al., *Masculinities in Politics and War*, p. 297.
8. Englander, 'Soldiering and Identity', 316–317; Bourke, *Dismembering the Male*, p. 152; McCartney, *Citizen Soldiers*, pp. 7–8, 89–95; Gary Sheffield (2000) *Leadership in the Trenches: Officer-Man Relations, Morale and Discipline in the British Army in the Era of the First World War* (Basingstoke: Macmillan Press), pp. 72, 151.
9. The War Office (1922) *Statistics of the British Military Effort of the British Empire During the Great War 1914–1920* (London: HMSO), p. 363.
10. Paris, *Warrior Nation*, pp. 43–45; Dawson *Soldier Heroes*, p. 1.
11. Tosh *A Man's Place*, p. 195; Bourke, *Dismembering the Male*, pp. 22–23.
12. McCartney, *Citizen Soldiers*, p. 90.
13. Letters could also be censored in transit, with men occasionally noting that their letters appear to have been opened en route. See Englander, 'Soldiering and Identity', 309.
14. IWM, 05/39/1, Papers of R. Macgregor, R. Macgregor, letter to Father, 22 October 1915. For other examples of letters intended for publication, see the IWM, 77/167/1, Papers of J. F. B. O'Sullivan.
15. IWM, 80/1/1, Papers of D. Manning, D. Manning, letter to his wife, 28 May 1916.
16. Newman, letter to Winnie, 11 June 1916.
17. IWM, 92/3/1, Papers of E. F. Chapman, E. F. Chapman, letter to Mother, 5 February 1917.
18. IWM, 86/40/1, Papers of G. R. Barlow, G. R. Barlow, letter to Alice, 6 April 1918.
19. IWM, 67/260/1, Papers of J. H. and R. Watkins, T. Watkins, letter to Mother and Father, 17 April 1917. Tom was killed by a shell four months later. His brother Richard, who served in the infantry, appears to have survived the war.
20. Newman, letter to Winnie, 15 July 1916.
21. Chapman, letter to Mother, 20 September 1916.

22. IWM, 83/3/1, Papers of B. A. Reader, B. A. Reader, letter to Mother, 14 March 1916.
23. IWM, 88/57/1, Papers of B. Britland, B. Britland, letter to Mother, 6 July 1915.
24. IWM, 87/56/1, Papers of W. B. P. Spencer, letter to Mother, 22 December 1914.
25. IWM, 85/15/1, Papers of C. E. Foster, C. E. Foster, letter to unnamed recipient, 9 July 1915.
26. Reader, letter to Mother, 26 July 1916.
27. IWM, 85/32/1, Papers of O. Lyle, O. Lyle, letter to Captain Philip Lyle, January 1916.
28. Reader, letter to Arthur, 8 April 1916.
29. Spencer, letter to Mother, 2 February 1915.
30. Spencer, letter to Mother, 3 January 1915.
31. Chapman, letter to Mother, 27 September 1916.
32. Macgregor, letter to Father, July 1916.
33. Newman, letter to Winnie, 20 September 1915.
34. Joanna Bourke (1999) *An Intimate History of Killing: Face-to-Face Killing in Twentieth-Century Warfare* (London: Granta Books), p. 371.
35. Newman, letter to Winnie, 18 August 1917.
36. The sense of isolation that this induced is one element of the 'soldiers' tale' identified by Hynes as a quality shared by all personal narratives of war. Hynes *The Soldier's Tale*, p. 5.
37. IWM, 84/34/1, Papers of J. E. Hind, J. E. Hind, letter to unnamed recipient, n.d.
38. IWM, 85/1/1, Papers of C. M. Tames, C. M. Tames, letter to Milly, n.d.
39. IWM, Con Shelf, Letters of R. P. Harker, R. P. Harker, letter to Ethel, 16 December 1914.
40. IWM, 97/37/1, Papers of S. G. Wright, S. G. Wright, letter to Father, excerpted in the *Daily Telegraph*, 'Worst Day of the War: Bombardment Makes Sky Like a Sheet of Ruled Paper', 1915.
41. Macgregor, letter to Father, 19 December 1915.
42. IWM, 80/25/1, Papers of J. W. McPherson, J. W. McPherson, letter to Ja, 29 August 1915.
43. McPherson, letter to Dougal, n.d.
44. Tames, letter to Milly, n.d.
45. Leed, *No Man's Land*, p. 20.
46. Reader, letter to Mother, 28 April 1916.
47. Reader, letter to Mother, 8 July 1916.
48. Sheffield, *Leadership in the Trenches*, p. 146; Joanna Bourke (2001) 'The Emotions in War: Fear and the British and American military, 1914–1945', *Historical Research Journal*, 74, 324.
49. Newman, letter to Winnie, 24 March 1918.
50. IWM, 69/25/1, Papers of G. Donaldson, G. Donaldson, letter to Mother, 16 July 1916.
51. Donaldson, letter to Mother, 2 July 1916.
52. Lyle, letter to Phillip, n.d.
53. Jessica Meyer (2004) '"Gladder to be Going Out Than Afraid": Shellshock and heroic masculinity in Britain, 1914–1919' in Jenny Macleod and Pierre

Purseigle (eds), *Uncovered Fields: Perspectives in First World War Studies* (Leiden: Brill), pp. 202–208.

54. Barlow, letter to Auntie Alice, 29 May 1916.
55. Barlow, letter to Alice, 21 September 1918.
56. Reader, letter to Mother, 4 May 1916.
57. Reader, letter to Mother, 14 July 1916.
58. Stefan Collini argues that the concept of 'character', as central to public and political thought from the mid-19th century onwards, embraced qualities of self-restraint, perseverance, strenuous effort, courage in the face of adversity and duty. He also notes that this evaluative definition of the term was based on tests of the individual's will power in various forms. Stefan Collini (1991) *Public Moralists: Political Thought and Intellectual Life in Britain, 1850–1930* (Oxford: Clarendon Press), pp. 100–113. For the relevance of this concept to the military sphere, see David Englander (1997) 'Discipline and morale in the British army, 1917–1918' in John Horne (ed.), *State, Society and Mobilization in Europe during the First World War* (Cambridge: Cambridge University Press), pp. 125–126.
59. Barlow, letter to Auntie Alice, 11 June 1916.
60. Winter *The Great War and the British People*, p. 2.
61. Peter Clarke (1996) *Hope and Glory: Britain 1900–1990* (London: Penguin Books), pp. 40–41. Jay Winter notes that the same was true for the civilian population in wartime. Winter, *The Great War and the British People*, pp. 216–218.
62. Foster, letter to unnamed recipient, 13 July 1915.
63. Britland, letter to Mother, 10 July 1915.
64. IWM, Con Shelf, Letters of M. Holroyd, M. Holroyd, letter to unnamed recipient, 15 March 1915.
65. Barlow, letter to Auntie Alice, 3 April 1916.
66. Newman, letter to Winnie, 13 May 1917.
67. Newman, letter to Winnie, 13 May 1916.
68. Hind, letter, addressee unknown, n.d.
69. Barlow, letter to Alice, 26 January 1917.
70. Barlow, letter to Alice, 3 November 1918.
71. Macgregor, letter to Father, 19 December 1915.
72. Holroyd, Letter to unnamed recipient, 28 April 1915.
73. Chapman, letter to Mother, 14 February 1917.
74. Paris, *Warrior Nation*, p. 62.
75. IWM, Con Shelf, Letters of F. E. Packe, F. E. Packe, letter to Mother, 12 May 1916.
76. Chapman, letter to Mother, 17 May 1917.
77. Newman, letter to Winnie, 27 March 1918.
78. Foster, letter to an unnamed recipient, 10 November 1915.
79. Reader, letter to Mother, 8 July 1916.
80. Reader, letter to Father, 14 July 1916.
81. Newman, letter to Winnie, 10 October 1917.
82. McPherson, letter to Ja, 12 September 1915.
83. Hind, letter to unknown recipient, n.d.
84. Donaldson, letter to Mother, 26 June 1916.
85. Chapman, letter to Mother, 12 October 1916.

86. Enthusiasm fluctuated for individuals over the course of the war, depending on a variety of factors, including the weather, unit losses, the success of actions and the regular supply of supplies and mail. McCartney, *Citizen Soldiers*, p. 240.
87. Donaldson, letter to Mother, 9 July 1916.
88. Newman, letter to Winnie, 28 March 1918.
89. Adrian Gregory (2004) 'British "War Enthusiasm" in 1914: a reassessment' in Gail Braybon (ed.), *Evidence, History and the Great War: Historians and the Impact of 1914–1918* (Oxford: Berghan Books), pp. 67–85.
90. Spencer, letter to Aunt Mary, 29 January 1915.
91. Reader, letter to Mother, 22 July 1916.
92. Holroyd, letter to unnamed recipient, 6 May 1915.
93. Barlow, letter to Auntie Alice, 22 February 1916.
94. IWM, Con Shelf, Letters of C. W. Dawson, C. W. Dawson, letter to Mother, 4 February 1917.
95. Packe, letter to Mother, 5 March 1915.
96. Watkins, letter to Mother and Father, 17 March 1915.
97. Roper, 'Maternal Relations' in Dudink et al., *Masculinities in Politics and War*, p. 302.
98. Newman, letter to Miss Blackburn, 7 January 1915.
99. Newman, letter to Winnie, 25 August 1915.
100. Macgregor, letter to Father, 19 December 1915.
101. Macgregor, letter to Edie in a section addressed to Mother, 14 October 1917.
102. Newman, letter to Winnie, 25 August 1915.
103. Barlow, letter to Alice, 5 January 1917.
104. Harker, letter to Ethel, 16 December 1914.
105. IWM, Con Shelf, Letters of G. and E. Butling, A. Butling, letter to Eric, n.d.
106. Newman, Letter to Winnie, 26 September 1916.
107. Ibid.
108. Tames, letter to Milly, 22 March 1915.
109. Barlow, letter to Auntie Alice, 12 April 1916.
110. Donaldson, letter to Mother, 5 June 1916.
111. Holroyd, letter to parents, 24 December 1914.
112. Holroyd, letter to unnamed recipient, 28 January 1915.
113. IWM, 83/17/1, Papers of A. T. Pile, A. T. Pile, letter to Father, Mother and Lizzie, 14 June 1918.
114. McPherson, letter to Ja, 12 September 1915.
115. IWM, Con Shelf, Letters of E. E. F. Baker, E. E. F. Baker, letter to Parents, 1/2 January 1918.
116. Britland, letter to Mother, 28 June 1915.
117. Newman, letter to Winnie, 8 September 1917.
118. Barlow, letter to Alice, 28 August 1917.
119. Barlow, letter to Auntie Alice, 28 September 1915.
120. IWM, 80/19/1, Papers of J. G. Taylor, J. G. Taylor, letter to Mother, 2 July 1917.
121. Duffett 'A War Unimagined' in Meyer (ed.) *British Popular Culture and the First World War*, p. 63.

122. Lyle, letter to Philip Lyle, 1915.
123. Harker, letter to Ethel, 24 February 1914.
124. Barlow, letter to Alice, 14 August 1917.
125. Hind, unnamed recipient, n.d.
126. Hind, letter to unnamed recipient, February, year unknown.
127. Newman, letter to Winnie, 23 June 1916. The use of the maternal metaphor re-emphasizes the femininity of the occupation he is engaged in.
128. Newman, letter to Winnie, 9 February 1917.
129. Newman, letter to Winnie, 16/17 June 1916.
130. Macgregor, letter to Mother, 13 September 1914.
131. Britland, letter to Mother, 10 July 1915.
132. Jessica Meyer (2005) 'The First World War and Narratives of Heroic and Domestic Masculinity in Britain, 1915–1937', PhD. dissertation (University of Cambridge), pp. 92–94.
133. Newman, letter to Winnie, 4 October 1915.
134. Gullace *'The Blood of Our Sons'*, p. 39; Todman *The Great War Myth and Memory,* p. 125.
135. Newman, letter to Winnie, 21 April 1915.
136. Hynes *A War Imagined,* p. 12–19.
137. McPherson, letter to Ja, 13 September, 1915. Such ideas also influenced the author 'Sapper' who used them in short stories such as 'A Word to the Malingerers'. 'Sapper' (1915) *Sergeant Michael Cassidy* (London: Hodder & Stoughton).
138. Barlow, letter to Alice, 6 January 1918.
139. Newman, letter to Winnie, 8 May 1915.
140. Papers of C. T. Newman, W. Blackburn, to Cyril, 1/3 July 1915.
141. Hind, letter to Dad, n.d.
142. Barlow, letter to Alice, 6 April 1918.
143. Macgregor, letter to Mother, 16 November 1915.
144. Taylor, letter to Father, 18 May 1918.
145. Dawson, letter to Mother, 23 June 1918.
146. Newman, letter to Winnie, 20 December 1915.
147. Dawson, letter to Mother, 12 November 1918
148. Macgregor, letter to Father, 10 October 1917.
149. Barlow, letter to Alice, 22 July 1918.
150. Macgregor, letter to Father, 25 January 1916.
151. Manning, letter to his wife, 7 April 1917.
152. On the importance of paternalism in the British Army during the war, see Sheffield, *Leadership in the Trenches,* pp. 72–81.
153. Papers of R. C. Trench, privately held, letter to Clare, 8 April 1917.
154. Sheffield, *Leadership in the Trenches,* p. 84.
155. Macgregor, letter to Father, 28 September 1917.
156. Macgregor, letter to Father, 24 November 1914
157. Manning, letter to his wife, 3 March 1916.
158. T. Watkins, letter to Mother and Father, 30 May 1917.
159. Trench, letter to Clare, 2 April 1917.
160. Trench, letter to Clare, 20 March 1917.
161. Macgregor, letter to Father, 16 December 1916.

162. Newman, letter to Winnie, 10 February 1916.
163. Tosh 'What Should Historians Do With Masculinity?', 185.
164. Pedersen *Family, Dependence, and the Origins of the Welfare State*, pp. 107–119.
165. Newman, letter to Winnie, 11 November 1917.
166. Dawson, letter to Mother, 30 September 1918.
167. Taylor, letter to Father, 18 May 1918.
168. Taylor, letter to Mother, 8 December 1918.
169. Barlow, letter to Alice, 21 December 1916.
170. Barlow, letter to Alice, 31 August 1916.
171. Barlow, letter to Alice, 13 October 1918.
172. Chapman, letter to Mother 1917.
173. IWM, Con Shelf, Papers of C. S. Rawlins, opening note.
174. Rawlins, letter to Mother, 31 May 1915.
175. Rawlins, letter to Family, 19 July 1915.
176. Rawlins, letter to Family, 7 June 1915.
177. Rawlins, letter to Mother, 25 June 1916.
178. Rawlins, letter to Family, 12 June 1915.
179. Rawlins, letter to Goss, 15 June 1915.
180. Rawlins, letter to Mother, 11 July 1915.
181. Rawlins, letter to Mother, 3 September 1915.
182. Rawlins, letter to Muv, 7 August 1915.
183. Rawlins, letter to Mother, 5 October 1915.
184. Rawlins, letter to Mother, 12 October 1915.
185. Rawlins, letter to Goss, 15th August 1915.
186. Rawlins, letter to Goss, 15 June 1915.
187. Rawlins, letter to Mother, 4 July 1915.
188. Rawlins, letter to Mother, 26 July 1915.
189. Rawlins, letter to Mu, 26 June 1915.
190. Rawlins, letter to Mother, 3 September 1915.
191. Rawlins, letter to Father, 10 July 1915.
192. Rawlins, letter to Goss, 13 August 1915.
193. Rawlins, letter to Father, 2 July 1915.
194. Rawlins, letter to Mother, 13 July 1915.
195. Rawlins, letter to Mother, 12 October 1915.
196. Ibid.
197. Rawlins, letter to Mother, 1 July 1915.
198. Rawlins, letter to Mother, 12 October 1915.

2 Wartime diaries

1. J. G. Fuller (1990) *Troop Morale and Popular Culture in the British and Dominion Armies 1914–1918* (Oxford: Clarendon Press), pp. 7–15; Englander 'Soldiering and Identity', 302–304. For the role of trench journalism in the French forces, see Stéphane Audoin-Rouzeau (1992) *Men at War 1914–1918: National Sentiment and Trench Journalism in France during the First World War,* Helen McPhail (trans.), (Oxford: Berg).

2. Hugh Cecil (1996) 'British War Novelists' in Hugh Cecil and Peter H. Liddle (eds), *Facing Armageddon: The First World War Experienced* (London: Leo Cooper), pp. 801–802.
3. Englander, 'Discipline and Morale in the British Army, 1917–1918' in Horne, *State, Society and Mobilization in Europe During the First World War*, pp. 142–143.
4. See, for example, IWM, P.399, A. M. McGrigor, Ts. diaries.
5. The War Office (1971) *Field Service Pocket Book: 1914* (Newton Abbot: David & Charles Publishers; original edition London: HMSO, 1914), pp. 215–216.
6. IWM, 85/32/1, G. W. Broadhead, Ms. diary, 15 June 1916; 8 November 1916.
7. IWM, 77/155/1, H. J. Hayward, Ms. diaries, 30 January 1918.
8. IWM, 92/3/1, O. P. Taylor, Ts. diary, 11 January 1918.
9. IWM, 77/124/1, F. S. Collings, Ms. diary, 25 August 1915.
10. Todman, *The Great War*, p. 1.
11. IWM, 67/264/1, A. Beevers, Ms. diary, 22 July 1915.
12. Broadhead, 10 June 1916.
13. IWM, P.315, J. C. Tait, Diary, 18 April 1916.
14. Broadhead, 7 June, 1916.
15. IWM, 78/10/1, F. P. J. Glover, Ms. diary, 29 December 1916.
16. IWM, 91/23/1, C. C. May, Diaries, 18 February 1916.
17. IWM, 78/22/1, J. H. Mahon, Ms. diary, p. 81.
18. Mahon, pp. 20–21.
19. May, 28 February 1916; 31 January 1916.
20. Collings, 8 September, 1915.
21. IWM, 80/28/1, K. H. Young, Ms. diary, 15 July 1916.
22. Young, 12 August 1916.
23. IWM, 85/22/1, H. Wilson, Ts. diary, 28 November 1915.
24. IWM, 85/23/1, A. Anderson, Ms. diary, p. 48.
25. IWM, 77/74/1, R. W. Wilson, Ts. diary, 26 July 1917.
26. IWM, 86/76/1, H. T. Clements, Ms. diaries, 27 February 1916.
27. Glover, 14 July 1917.
28. R. W. Wilson, 3–6 January 1918.
29. H. Wilson, 13 January 1916.
30. May, 2 January 1916.
31. Bourke *Dismembering the Male*, pp. 15–16.
32. IWM, 88/5/1, K. C. Leslie, Ms. diary, 17 February 1915.
33. Tait, 2 December 1915.
34. Ibid., 14 January 1916.
35. Young, 27 July, 1916.
36. IWM, 67/221/1, R. B. Wilkinson, Ts. diaries, 1 July 1916.
37. Sheffield *Leadership in the Trenches*, p. 151.
38. McCartney *Citizen Soldiers*, pp. 129–130; Englander, 'Soldiering and Identity', p. 307.
39. IWM, 90/37/1, J. W. Barnett, Ts. diary, 29 April 1915; 28 April 1915.
40. IWM, 05/53/1, J. H. Fordham, Ms. diary, 6 May 1915; 14 May 1915.
41. Broadhead, 31 May 1916.
42. Hayward, 8 June 1918.
43. IWM, 98/33/1, M. W. Littlewood, Ts. diary, 16 July 1918.
44. Littlewood, 9 April 1917.

45. IWM, 93/20/1, C. K. McKerrow, Ts. diary, 23 May 1916.
46. Wilkinson, 27 June 1915.
47. Tait, 23 May 1916.
48. Glover, 9 October 1916.
49. May, 16 March 1916.
50. McKerrow, 29 March 1916.
51. Tait, 1 June 1916.
52. Ibid., 23 May 1916.
53. Barnett, 23 October 1914.
54. Ibid., 1 May 1915.
55. Clements, 4 November 1915.
56. Littlewood, 9 April 1917.
57. Collings, 21 September 1915.
58. Anderson, p. 47.
59. Ibid., p. 44.
60. Littlewood, 18 April 1917.
61. Fordham, 28 August 1915.
62. IWM, 88/11/1, J. Colinsky, Ts. diary, 28 October 1917.
63. Colinsky, 3 November 1917; 8 November 1917; 1 November 1917; 7 April 1917.
64. Ibid., 7 June 1917.
65. Clements, 30 June 1916.
66. McKerrow, 3 August 1916.
67. Barnett, 24 September 1914.
68. R. W. Wilson, 1 July 1917.
69. Bourke, 'The Emotions in War', 324.
70. Fordham, 7 July 1915.
71. Barnett, 25 October, 1914.
72. McKerrow, 23 May 1916. He did not write of this incident in his letters to his wife.
73. Ibid., 25 September 1916.
74. Anderson, p. 50.
75. Littlewood, 26 November 1917.
76. Tait, 1 June 1916.
77. Barnett, 24 April 1914.
78. Mahon, p. 28.
79. Tait, 30 March 1916.
80. McKerrow, 10 March 1916; 18 July 1916; 4 August 1916.
81. Collings, 11–14 February 1915.
82. Mahon, p. 29.
83. McKerrow, 20 March 1916.
84. Barnett, 17 October 1914.
85. Ibid., 27 October 1914.
86. McKerrow, 1 April 1916.
87. Wilkinson, 3 July 1915.
88. Mark Connelly (2002) *The Great War, Memory and Ritual: Commemoration in the City and East London, 1916–1939* (Suffolk: The Royal Historical Society, Boydell Press), pp. 54–55.

89. Collings, 30 September 1915.
90. Ibid, 1917.
91. May, 6 April 1916.
92. Barnett, 25 October 1914.
93. May, 24 June 1916.
94. Tait, 5 June 1916.
95. May, 8 November 1915.
96. Clements, 29 August 1914.
97. IWM, P.371, A. E. Bundy, Ts. diary, 2 January–1 March 1918.
98. Clements, 21 February 1915.
99. Fordham, 23 April 1915.
100. McKerrow, 1 September 1915.
101. Young, 30 August 1916.
102. Hayward, 23 May 1918.
103. May, 28 June 1916.
104. R. W. Wilson, 3 July 1917.
105. Anderson, p. 78.
106. McKerrow, 4 April 1916.
107. May, 29 February 1916.
108. Colinsky, 7 August 1917.
109. Diary of F. J. P. Glover, C. O. 5th Division East Surrey Regiment, copy of letter, 13 October 1917.
110. McKerrow, 12 July 1916.
111. Sheffield, *Leadership in the Trenches*, pp. 80–85.
112. McKerrow, 31 July 1916.
113. Littlewood, 9 April 1917.
114. H. Wilson, 22–23 November 1915.
115. May, 15 April 1916.
116. McKerrow, 11 July 1916.
117. R. W. Wilson, 3 October 1917.
118. May, 25 March 1916.
119. Ibid., 23–25 December 1915.
120. McKerrow, 9 October 1916.
121. May, 27 February 1916.
122. Tait, 1 March 1916.
123. Hayward, 8 March 1916.
124. Littlewood, 19 June 1918.
125. May, 11 November 1915.
126. Ibid., 4 February 1916; 12 May 1916.
127. Ibid., 19 November 1915.
128. Leslie, 19 February 1915.
129. Clements, 24 March 1916.
130. Glover, 5 May 1917.
131. Clements, 31 March 1916.
132. Anderson, p. 4.
133. The connection between cleanliness and civilian masculinity derives in part from the association that Victorian reformers made between cleanliness, 'character' and respectability. Tom Crook (2006) ' "Schools for the moral training of the people": public baths, liberalism and the promotion of

cleanliness in Victorian Britain,' *European Review of History/Revue européenne d'Histoire* 13:1, 27–30.
134. Duffett, 'A War Unimagined' in Meyer (ed.), *British Popular Culture and the First World War*, pp. 47–70.
135. Broadhead, 25 June 1916.
136. Littlewood, 4 August 1917.
137. Clements, 6 November 1915.
138. R. W. Wilson, 12 November 1917.
139. Anderson, 7 October 1914, p. 2.
140. Ibid., pp. 60–61.
141. Clements, 27 February 1916.
142. Anderson, p. 49.
143. R. W. Wilson, 15 July 1917.
144. Littlewood, 6 May 1917.
145. McKerrow, 27 August 1915.
146. Ibid., 12 April 1916.
147. Fordham, 11 June 1915.
148. McKerrow, 11 July 1916.
149. May, 29 January 1916.
150. McKerrow, 10 November 1916.
151. At least three of the original diaries were lost in transit.
152. McGrigor, 8 October 1915. Hamilton's headquarters were located on the island of Imbros.
153. Ibid., 1 January 1916.
154. Ibid., 22 March 1916.
155. Ibid., 2 April 1916.
156. Ibid., 9 April 1916.
157. Ibid., 17 April 1916.
158. Ibid., 23 April 1916.
159. Ibid., 28 April 1916.
160. Ibid., 16 November 1915.
161. Ibid., 18 July 1916.
162. Ibid., 9 January 1917.
163. Ibid., 5 October 1917.
164. Ibid., 7 April 1918; 29 April 1918.
165. Ibid., 9 July 1918.
166. Ibid., 28 November 1915.
167. Ibid., 31 August 1917.
168. Ibid., 5 October 1917.
169. Ibid., 4 November 1915.
170. Ibid., 9 March 1916.
171. Ibid., 6 April 1916.
172. Ibid., 6 January 1917; 27 March 1917.
173. Ibid., 22 April 1917.
174. Ibid., 9 December 1915.
175. Ibid., 19 November 1915.
176. Ibid., 9 February 1917; 12 February 1918.
177. Ibid., 30 May 1916; 10 December 1915.
178. Ibid., 14 January 1919.

3   Remembering the heroic dead: Letters of condolence

1. Mark Connelly (2002) *The Great War, Memory and Ritual: Commemoration in the City and East London, 1916–1939* (Woodbridge: The Boydell Press), pp. 36–42; Alex King (1998) *Memorials of the Great War in Britain: The Symbolism and Politics of Remembrance* (Oxford: Berg), pp. 20–35.
2. Winter *Sites of Memory, Sites of Mourning*, pp. 29–53.
3. IWM, 82/26/1, Papers of A. R. Williams; IWM, 01/52/1, Papers of W. J. C. Sangster.
4. Acton, *Grief in Wartime*, p. 5 and *passim*.
5. Ibid., p. 10.
6. IWM, 05/40/1, Papers of J. H. MacGregor, Mary Simpson, letter to Miss MacGregor, 4 February 1917.
7. IWM, PP/MCR/62, Papers of G. B. Buxton, Rachel Barclay, letter to un-named recipient, n.d.
8. IWM, P.434, Papers of F. Henley, H. Powell, letter to Mr Henley, 2 November 1916.
9. IWM, 02/5/1, Papers of E. Nicholson, Frederick Brindley, letter to Mrs Nicholson, 5 October 1917.
10. Todman *The Great War*, p. 46.
11. Papers of F. Henley, Will Stagg, letter to Mrs Henley, 5 November 1916.
12. IWM, 96/24/1, Papers of W. M. Anderson, J. M. Greer, letter to Mrs Anderson, 18 May 1917.
13. Papers of W. M. Anderson, Dorothy Cartwright, letter to Mrs Anderson, 22 May 1917.
14. IWM, Con Shelf, Letters of G. & W. Stewart, C. D. Linnell, letter to Mrs Stewart, 23 April 1917.
15. IWM, 02/16/1, Papers of W. H. J. St. L. Atkinson, J. R. Wolkley, letter to unnamed recipient, n.d.
16. Papers of J. H. MacGregor, Jean Thompson, letter to Mrs MacGregor, 1 March 1917.
17. David French (2005) *Military Identities: The Regimental System, the British Army, and the British People, c.1870–2000* (Oxford: Oxford University Press), pp. 76–98.
18. Papers of W. J. C. Sangster, Thomas Scott, letter to Baillie Sangster, 3 October 1915.
19. IWM, Con Shelf, Letters of E. K. Smith, G. Mould, letter to Mrs. E. Smith, 24 January 1916.
20. Papers of G. and W. Stewart, Pt. H. Adams, letter to Mr and Mrs Stewart, 24 April 1917.
21. Hynes *The Soldiers' Tale*, pp. 9–10.
22. Letters of R. P. Harker, Horace Waterall, letter to Ethel Harker, 20 March 1915.
23. IWM, 95/31/1, Papers of N. L. Woodroffe, William Cavish, letter to Miss Woodroffe, 11 January 1915.
24. Papers of W. B. P. Spencer, Sidney J. Belsham, letter to Frederic Spencer, 19 March 1915; Papers of N. L. Woodroffe, William Cavish, letter to Miss Woodroffe, 11 January 1915. This last correspondence continued until 1917.

25. Winter, *The Great War and the British People*, pp. 88–92.
26. Letters of R. P. Harker, Lt.-Col. V. Falbe, letter to Ethel Harker, 20 March 1915.
27. Papers of F. Henley, E. Mannering, letter to Mr Henley, 29 October 1916.
28. Leonore Davidoff (1973) *The Best Circles: Society, Etiquette and the Season* (London: The Cresset Library), pp. 54–56.
29. Papers of F. Henley, Leonard Stokes, letter to Mr Henley, n.d.
30. Papers of W. B. P. Spencer, A.L.T., 'The Wee Rector: A Story for the Junior School,' *Glasgow High School Magazine*, n.d. This epitaph had been adapted as the epitaph for the dead of Waggon Hill from the Boer War: 'Tell England, you who pass this monument/We died for her and rest here well content.'
31. Papers of W. J. C. Sangster, Brigadier-General D. G. Prendergast, speech reported in 'Christ's College, Blackheath' paper, n.d.
32. Mosse, *The Image of Man*, p. 51.
33. David Cannadine (1981) 'War and Death, Grief and Mourning in Modern Britain' in Joachim Whaley (ed.), *Mirrors of Mortality: Studies in the Social History of Death*, The Europe Social History of the Human Experience (London: Europa Publications Limited), p. 195. Far from being undermined by the mass deaths of the war, as Cannadine argues, traditional rhetorics persisted in both public and private mournings. See Hynes *A War Imagined*, pp. 269–282; King, *Memorials of the Great War*, pp. 129–132; Connelly, *The Great War, Memory and Ritual*, p. 63, as well as F.I. Rae's comment that R. Smylie 'went to…danger like a bridegroom to his wedding' (IWM, 86/9/1, Papers of R. S. Smylie, F. I. Rae, letter to Mrs. Smylie, 1916), which echoes Sir Ian Hamilton's 1905 celebration of Boer War soldiers who met death 'as a bridegroom…goes to meet his bride.' Quoted in Cannadine, 'War and Death, Grief and Mourning', p. 196.
34. See, for example, A. E. Housman (1916) 'To an Athlete Dying Young', *A Shropshire Lad* (London: Grant Richards Ltd.), pp. 26–28.
35. Jones, *The Last Great Quest*, p. 228.
36. For the on-going importance of religious practice and the reformulation of the Christian message to comprehend the experiences of the war, see Winter, *Sites of Memory, Sites of Mourning*, pp. 64–71; Patrick Porter (2005) 'New Jerusalems: Sacrifice and Redemption in the War Experiences of English and German Military Chaplains' in Pierre Purseigle (ed.), *Warfare and Belligerence: Perspectives in First World War studies* (Leiden: Brill), pp. 101–132.
37. Papers of G. B. Buxton, Godfrey Buxton, letter to unnamed recipients, n.d.
38. Papers of W. J. C. Sangster, Lady Adam Smith, letter to Mrs Sangster, 18 March 1916.
39. Papers of J. H. MacGregor, Arthur G. Evans, letter to Mrs MacGregor, 2 February 1917.
40. IWM, 94/23/1, Papers of G. A. Potts, Memorial card in memory of David Ewart Potts, n.d.
41. Winter, *Sites of Memory, Sites of Mourning*, p. 27.
42. Paris *Warrior Nation*, pp. 71–78.
43. Papers of R. S. Smylie, Corporal Frank Spunwood, letter to Mrs Smylie, n.d.
44. Papers of F. Henley, Major F. Stewart Modera, letter to Mr Henley, 29 October 1916.

45. IWM, 99/23/1, Papers of W. Nicholson, Martin, letter to Florrie, 14 August 1916.

46. Papers of G. & W. Stewart, T. Bacon, letter to Mr Stewart, 2 May 1917.

47. Papers of J. H. MacGregor, C. H. Greene, letter to Mr MacGregor, n.d.

48. Papers of J. H. MacGregor, Grace Bowie, letter to Mrs MacGregor, 3 February 1917.

49. Papers of W. J. C. Sangster, James Carle, letter to Mr and Mrs Sangster, 3 March 1916.

50. Papers of N. L. Woodroffe, Garth Wolford, letter to Aunt Bee [Mrs Woodroffe], 4 December 1914.

51. IWM, 01/51/1, Papers of H. Henfrey, George Greenwood, letter to H. Henfrey, 24 July 1915.

52. Papers of N. L. Woodroffe, Mary Woodroffe, letter addressed to 'My dearest Godchild', 2 February 1917.

53. Papers of F. Henley, E. Mannering, letter to Mr. Henley, 29 October 1916.

54. Gullace *'The Blood of Our Sons'*, pp. 37–46.

55. Papers of W. B. P. Spencer, A.L.T., 'The Wee Rector'.

56. Papers of J. H. MacGregor, J. MacGregor, letter to 'My dear Uncle', 18 March 1917.

57. Papers of J. H. MacGregor, Fanny C. Beames, letter to Edith, 2 February 1917.

58. Papers of W. M. Anderson, Jas. G. Davidson, letter to Mrs Anderson, 25 May 1917.

59. Papers of W. J. C. Sangster, S. McCall, letter to Mrs Sangster, March 1916.

60. IWM, 87/3/1, Papers of T. M. Field, illegible correspondent, letter to Lady Field, 6 June 1916.

61. Papers of G. & W. Stewart, Robert Wright, letter to Mrs Stewart, 19 April 1915.

62. Papers of W. B. P. Spencer, Harold Dehry, letter to Mr Spencer, 21 March 1915.

63. Papers of W. J. C. Sangster, Sir George Adam Smith, letter to Mr Sangster, 4 March 1916.

64. Papers of W. Nicholson, David, letter to Florrie, 13 August 1916.

65. John Tosh (2005) 'Authority and Nurture in Fatherhood' in John Tosh (ed.), *Manliness and Masculinities in Nineteenth Century Britain: Essays on Gender, Family and Empire* (Harlow: Pearson Education Ltd.), pp. 132–135.

66. Winter, *Sites of Memory, Sites of Mourning*, pp. 35–36. Winter also discusses correspondence with voluntary organizations such as the Red Cross which carried out a great deal of research into the place and nature of men's deaths on behalf of the bereaved.

67. Todman, *The Great War*, p. 48; Winter, *Sites of Memory, Sites of Mourning*, pp. 39–42.

68. Papers of W. M. Anderson, Captain J. M. Greer, letter to Mrs Anderson, 18 May 1917.

69. Papers of G. & W. Stewart, Lt.-Col. S. MacDonald, letter to Mr Stewart, 14 April 1917.

70. Papers of N. L. Woodroffe, Frank Witts, letter to Mrs Woodroffe, 13 November 1914.

71. Papers of J. H. MacGregor, Alan Wilson, letter to Mrs MacGregor, 18 February 1917.
72. How accurate any of these accounts were remains open for question. As Winter points out of the stock messages conveyed by superior officers' letters, 'Whatever balm these words provided, most people knew that they were not wholly true and always incomplete.' Winter, *Sites of Memory, Sites of Mourning*, p. 35.
73. IWM, 01/60/1, Memorial booklet in memory of W. Lindsay, (York: 2001), 2nd Lt. W. Gillam, letter to Mr Lindsay, 4 August 1917.
74. IWM, 78/15/1, Papers of J. Matthews, C. D. R. Greenway, letter to Mrs Matthews, 15 August 1915.
75. Papers of A. R. Williams, Lt. Collinson, letter to Mr Williams, n.d.
76. Papers of C. K. McKerrow, Fred Williamson, letter to Mrs M'Kerrow, 21 December 1916.
77. Papers of W. J. C. Sangster, David. A. Waddell, letter to Mr Sangster, 6 April, 1916.
78. Papers of F. Henley, Lt.-Col. W. B. Garnett, letter to Mr Henley, 28 October, 1916.
79. Papers of W. B. P. Spencer, C. H. Rowe, letter to Mr Spencer, 18 March, 1915.
80. Papers of R. S. Smylie, Quartermaster, 1st Royal Scottish Fusiliers, letter to Mrs Smylie, 21 July 1916; Papers of E. Nicholson, Captain H. W. M. Kewick, letter to Mrs Nicholson, 15 September 1917; Papers of H. Henfrey, Sergeant W. Sutcliffe, letter to Mr and Mrs Henfrey, 3 July 1915.
81. Meyer, 'Narratives of Heroic and Domestic Masculinity', pp. 73–75.
82. Papers of A.R. Williams, A. W. Thorpe, letter to the parents of A. R. Williams, n.d.
83. IWM, 81/1/1, Papers of R. Farley, Captain A. MacDougall, 31 July 1916.
84. Papers of W. J. C. Sangster, Pt. William Troup, letter to Mr Sangster, 12 January 1916.
85. Papers of A. R. Williams, 2nd Lt. G. S. Halliwell, letter to the parents of A.R. Williams, n.d.
86. Papers of C. K. McKerrow, Captain James Oag, letter to Mrs M'Kerrow, 25 February 1917.
87. Papers of C. K. McKerrow, Robert Manners, letter to Mrs M'Kerrow, 27 December 1916.
88. Papers of C. K. McKerrow, Major George F. Ashton, letter to Mrs M'Kerrow, 22 December 1916.
89. IWM, 97/37/1, Papers of E. H. Owen, J. W. F. McNaught Davis, letter to Mrs Owen, 3 January 1915.
90. Papers of G. & W. Stewart, Captain C. E. Fysh, letter to Mrs Stewart, 16 April 1917.
91. Papers of R. S. Smylie, F. I. Rae, letter to Mrs Smylie, n.d.
92. Papers of G. & W. Stewart, S. MacDonald, letter to Mrs Stewart, 18 November 1918.
93. IWM, 77/177/1, Papers of G. W. Colebrook, Hugh Blyde, letter to Mr Colebrook, 19 October 1915.
94. Papers of H. Henfrey, Pt. George Greenwood, letter to Mrs Henfrey, 24 July 1915.

95. Papers of H. Henfrey, Lt. J. Harold Smith, letter to Mr and Mrs Henfrey, 3 July 1915.
96. Papers of W. J. C. Sangster, David A. Waddell, letter to Mr Sangster, 6 April 1916.
97. Papers of R. Farley, A. MacDougall, letter to Mr Farley, 31 July 1916; Papers of A. R. Williams, 2nd Lt. S. Iredale, letter to the parents of A. R. Williams, n.d.
98. Papers of E. K. Smith, Sergeant G. Mould, letter to Mrs E. Smith, 24 January 1916.
99. Papers of W. B. P. Spencer, 2nd Lt. Sydney J. Belsham, letter to Frederic Spencer, 19 March 1915. André Loez notes in relation to French soldiers during the war that there were moments when tears were viewed as appropriate, including as part of rituals of mourning. André Loez, 'Tears in the Trenches: A History of Emotions and the Experience of War' in Macleod and Purseigle (eds), *Uncovered Fields*, pp. 220–222.
100. Papers of F. Henley, Captain Douglas S. Hodgson-Jones, letter to Mr Leete Henley, 28 October 1916.
101. Siegfried Sassoon (1918) *The Old Huntsman and Other Poems* (New York: E. P. Dutton and Company), p. 28.
102. Connelly, *The Great War, Memory and Ritual*, pp. 83–87; Todman, *The Great War*, pp. 53–72.
103. For more details of Trench's extensive correspondence, see Anthony Fletcher (2004) 'An Officer on the Western Front', *History Today*, 54:8, 31–37 and Anthony Fletcher (2005) 'Patriotism, Identity and Commemoration: new light on the Great War from the papers of Major Reggie Chenevix Trench', *History*, 60, 532–549.
104. Papers of R. C. Trench, Robert W. Lloyd to Mrs Trench, 28 April 1930. Many letters followed the appearance of Trench's obituary in *The Times* (*London*) on 15 April 1918.
105. Fletcher, 'Patriotism, Identity and Commemoration', 547.
106. Papers of R. C. Trench, William Swan, letter to Mrs Trench, 3 May 1918.
107. Ibid.
108. Papers of R. C. Trench, Isabelle Davis, letter to 'Madame' [Clare Trench], 3 May 1918.
109. Papers of R. C. Trench, G. Maud Alibon to Mrs Trench, 4 April 1918.
110. The family had strong connections to the Church of England. Richard Chenevix Trench, Dean of Westminster and later Archbishop of Dublin, was Reggie's grandfather.
111. Papers of R. C. Trench, Isabelle Davis, letter to Clare Trench, 3 May 1918.
112. Papers of R. C. Trench, Muriel Steel, letter to Clare, 27 April 1918.
113. Papers of R. C. Trench, Guy Beech, letter to Mrs (Isabelle) Trench, 16 May 1918.
114. Papers of R. C. Trench, Geo. Fern, letter to Mrs (Clare) Trench, 8 April 1918.
115. Papers of R. C. Trench, Charles Ovenden, letter to Mrs (Isabelle) Trench, 10 April 1918.
116. Papers of R. C. Trench, Walter Wood, letter to Mrs (Isabelle) Trench, 12 January 1919.
117. Papers of R. C. Trench, Edward Burney, letter to Clare, 30 January 1919.
118. Papers of R. C. Trench, Walter Howard, letter to Clare, 8 April 1918.

119. Papers of R. C. Trench, Muriel Steel, letter to Clare, 27 April 1918.
120. Papers of R. C. Trench, Ethel Gore Booth, letter to Clare, 12 April 1918.
121. Papers of R. C. Trench, Edward Burney, letter to Clare, 23 April 1918.
122. Papers of R. C. Trench, Edward Burney, letter to Mrs (Clare) Trench, 10 April 1918.
123. Ibid.
124. Papers of R. C. Trench, illegible correspondent, letter to Mrs (Clare) Trench, 15 April 1918.
125. Papers of R. C. Trench, E. W. S. Maconachy, letter to Mrs (Clare) Trench, 13 April 1918.
126. Papers of R. C. Trench, William Swan, letter to Mrs (Clare) Trench, 3 May 1918.
127. Papers of R. C. Trench, Joyce Shipley, letter to Clare, 15 April 1918.
128. Papers of R. C. Trench, Ethel Gore Booth, letter to Clare, 12 April 1918.
129. Papers of R. C. Trench, Dorothy G. Horsford, letter to Mrs (Clare) Trench, n.d.
130. Papers of R. C. Trench, Aunt Ida, letter to Clare, 24 April 1918.
131. Papers of R. C. Trench, R. A. Copleson, letter to Clare, n.d.
132. Fletcher, 'An Officer on the Western Front', 31.
133. Papers of R. C. Trench, Drummer T. Field, copy of letter to unknown recipient, 28 January 1919; Pt. L.A. Barnard, letter to Mrs (Clare) Trench, 10 May, 1918; Pt. Baichat, letter to Mrs (Clare) Trench, 1 February 1919; Corporal F. Bradley, letter to unknown recipient, 10 April 1918; Sergeant Lawrence, letter to 'Madame' [Clare Trench], 24 April 1918; CQMS S. A. Wild, letter to Mrs (Clare) Trench, 3 May, 1918; F. W. Horsfield, letters to Mrs (Clare) Trench, 27 March 1918 and 11 April, 1918; Major R. A. Pratt, letter to Mrs (Clare) Trench, 9 April 1918; Captain M. W. Barrows, letter to Mrs (Clare) Trench, 27 April 1918.
134. Papers of R. C. Trench, Walter Howard, letter to Clare, 8 April 1918.
135. Papers of R. C. Trench, Ethel Gore Booth, letter to Clare, 12 April 1918.
136. Papers of R. C. Trench, A. J. Lane, letter to Mrs (Clare) Trench, written from 16 Hill St., Croft, Leics., n.d.; A. J. Lane, letter to Mrs (Clare) Trench, 17 December 1918; A. J. Lane, letter to Mrs (Clare) Trench, 27 January 1961.
137. Papers of R. C. Trench, Robert W. Lloyd, letter to 'Madam' [Clare Trench], 28 April 1930.
138. Papers of R. C. Trench, Captain Stebbings, letter to Mrs (Clare) Trench, 20 April 1918.
139. See Chapter 2 above and Fletcher, 'Patriotism, Identity and Commemoration', 548.

4 'Fit only for light work': Disabled ex-servicemen and the struggle for a domestic masculinity

1. Official statistics put the number of deaths in the British Expeditionary Force, including both British and Dominion troops, at 715,038. Major T. J. Mitchell and G. M. Smith (1931) *Medical Services: Casualties and Medical Statistics of the Great War: History of the Great War based on Official Documents*

(Nashville, Tennessee: The Imperial War Museum, London, Department of Printed Books and The Battery Press, Inc.), p. 12.

2. Ibid., p. 316. This represents some 27% of those who served in the British armed forces.
3. Ibid., pp. 335–349.
4. Clarke (1996) *Hope and Glory*, pp. 102–108.
5. Helen Bolderson (1991) *Social Security, Disability and Rehabilitation: Conflicts in the Development of Social Policy 1914–1946* (London: Jessica Kingsley Publishers), pp. 35–47.
6. Todman *The Great War*, p. 53–56.
7. Adrian Gregory (1994) *The Silence of Memory: Armistice Day, 1919–1946* (Oxford: Berg), p. 83. For a discussion of disabled men's political isolation see Cohen *The War Come Home*, pp. 46–59 and Douglas Higbee (2007) 'The British Veterans Movement, 1917–1921' in Meyer (ed.) *British Popular Culture and the First World War*, pp. 197–216.
8. Jay Winter (1999) 'Remembrance and Redemption: A Social Interpretation of War Memorials', *Harvard Design Magazine* 9, pp. 71–77.
9. Cohen, *The War Come Home*, pp. 32–46.
10. Koven 'Remembering and Dismemberment', 1172; Wendy Jane Gagen (2004) 'Disabling Masculinity: Ex-servicemen, Disability and Gender Identity, 1914–1930,' PhD. diss., (University of Essex), pp. 200, 290.
11. Cohen, *The War Come Home*, pp. 119–124, 130–131; Bourke, *Dismembering the Male*, pp. 73–75.
12. Gullace *The 'Blood of Our Sons'*, p. 94.
13. Ben Shephard (2002) *A War of Nerves: Soldiers and Psychiatry 1914–1994* (London: Pimlico), p. 150.
14. Shephard, *A War of Nerves*, p. 111; Peter Barham (2004) *Forgotten Lunatics of the Great War* (New Haven: Yale University Press), pp. 64–66.
15. Helen Bettinson (2002) ' "Lost Souls in the House of Restoration"?: British Ex-servicemen and War Disability Pensions, 1914–1930', PhD. diss., (University of East Anglia), p. 9.
16. The National Archives, London (hereafter NA), PIN 15/38, Letter to the General Secretary, the British Legion (Scotland) from the Ministry of Pensions, 12 January 1934.
17. Ministry of Pensions leaflet, c.1920, cited in Bourke, *Dismembering the Male*, p. 66.
18. Gagen, 'Disabling Masculinity', pp. 49–52; Gullace, *'The Blood of Our Sons'*, p. 38.
19. Bettinson, ' "Lost Souls in the House of Restoration?" ', p. 43.
20. Jay M. Winter, *The Great War and the British People* (London: Macmillan Education Ltd.), pp. 50–53.
21. Bettinson, ' "Lost Souls in the House of Restoration?" ', p. 66.
22. Cohen, *The War Come Home*, pp. 29–35.
23. The pensions bill was also reduced during this time by natural means including the death of pensioners, the remarriage of war widows and the attainment of majority by minor dependants.
24. Bourke, *Dismembering the Male*, p. 60.
25. Ibid., p. 59.
26. Cohen, *The War Come Home*, pp. 103–104.

27. Bettinson, ' "Lost Souls in the House of Restoration?" ', p. 335.
28. Ibid., pp. 294–295.
29. Koven, 'Remembering and Dismemberment', pp. 1193–1200.
30. Journals such as *Recalled to Life* (June 1917–April 1918) and its successor *Reveille* (August 1918 – February 1919) were dedicated to encouraging disabled men to participate in the re-education and training schemes offered through the Ministry of Pension and the Ministry of Labour, to which responsibility for training was passed in 1919.
31. Sir Alfred Keogh (1917) 'The Treatment of the Disabled: A Memorandum', *Recalled to Life* 1, 20, 35.
32. Bettinson, ' "Lost Souls in the House of Restoration?" ', pp.74–79.
33. NA, PIN 26/21580, Charles Evans, letter to Ministry of Pensions, 6 January 1925.
34. NA, PIN 26/19950, Dr A. W. Davidson, Letter to Dr. F. Murchie, Officers' Treatment Branch, Ministry of Pensions, 27 November, 1928.
35. NA, PIN 26/21089, O. P. Allcock, Letter to the Secretary, Officers' Branch, Ministry of Pensions, 2 July 1925.
36. NA, PIN 26/19934, G. V. Corbet, Letter to Ministry of Pension, 8 June 1927.
37. NA, PIN 26/21239, Illegible correspondent, Letter to Ministry of Pensions, 5 March 1924.
38. On the importance of self-control to definitions of heroic masculinity, see Meyer, 'Gladder to be going out that afraid' in Macleod and Purseigle (eds), *Uncovered Fields*, p. 208 and Chapter 5 below.
39. NA, PIN 26/21188, C. S. Bellamy, Letter to the Imperial Pensions Board, Ottawa, 9 March 1923.
40. NA, PIN 26/21764, Mrs G. M. Hetherington, Letter to the Director General of Awards, Ministry of Pensions, 6 June 1920.
41. 41 NA, PIN 26/6, Application in Respect of Disablement Made for the First Time More Than Seven Years from Termination of Great War Service, 9 November 1931.
42. NA, PIN 26/21593, Dr E. Weaver Adams, Letter to Ministry of Pensions, 5 April 1923.
43. Tosh *A Man's Place*, pp. 2–3. Self-help was also a tenet of Victorian heroic masculinity. See Green *Dreams of Adventure, Deeds of Empire* pp. 205–212.
44. NA, PIN 26/21791, J. J. Holland, Letter to Director General of Awards, Ministry of Pensions, 2 July 1921.
45. NA, PIN 26/21205, G. H. Birch, Letter to Ministry of Pensions, 11 March 1922.
46. NA, PIN 26/19930, J. L. Campbell-White, Letters to Ministry of Pensions, 25 October 1920 and 2 November 1920. The 'Ministry of Appts.' refers to the Ministry of Labour which controlled the Labour Exchanges where unemployed ex-servicemen deemed fit enough to work were directed to find employment.
47. NA, PIN 26/21230, Application for Alternative Retired Pay, 25 August 1921.
48. NA, PIN 26/21697, W. C. Greene, Letter to the Ministry of Pensions, 8 February 1922.
49. NA, PIN 26/21655, F. C. Gerrard, Letter to Deputy Commissioner of Medical Services, Officers' Treatment Branch, Ministry of Pensions, 26 June 1923.

50. NA, PIN 26/19942, J. J. R. Larkin, Letter to the Secretary, Ministry of Pensions, 12 May 1920.
51. NA, PIN 26/21142, J. W. B. Balfour, Letter to Director General of Medical Services, Officers' Treatment Branch, Ministry of Pensions, n.d.
52. NA, PIN 26/21162, Proceedings of Medical Board, 20 February 1920.
53. Sonya O. Rose (1992) *Limited Livelihoods: Gender and Class in Nineteenth-Century England* (London: Routledge), pp. 138–152.
54. L. C. B. Seaman (1970) *Life in Britain Between the Wars*, English Life Series (London: B. T. Batsford Ltd.), p. 35. See also Clarke, *Hope and Glory*, pp. 133–134, 151–158.
55. NA, PIN 26/19942, J. J. R. Larkin, Letter to the Secretary, Ministry of Pensions, 16 July 1924.
56. Cohen, *The War Come Home*, pp. 5, 39.
57. NA, PIN 26/35, Report of Work of Sub-Committee Since Formation, Employment Sub-Committee for Disabled Sailors and Soldiers, Bedford and District Employment Committee, 9 July 1920.
58. Norman Fenton (1926) *Shell Shock and Its Aftermath* (London: Henry Kimpton), p. 87.
59. NA, PIN 26/21651, A. Gear, Letter to the Secretary, Officers' Branch, Ministry of Pensions, 1929.
60. NA, PIN 26/21097, C. F. Ambler, Letter to Ministry of Pensions, 13 May 1932.
61. NA, PIN 26/21580, Notes of the Ministry Representative at an Entitlement Appeal Tribunal, 21 August 1925.
62. NA, PIN 26/21555, P. G. Eckersall, Letter to the Secretary, Ministry of Pensions, 22 August 1919.
63. NA, PIN 26/21764, Mrs G. M. Hetherington, Letter to the Director General of Awards, Ministry of Pensions, 6 June 1920.
64. NA, PIN 26/19884, Surgeon-in-Charge, Limb Section, Limb Fitting Centre, Nottingham, Letter to Director General of Medical Services, 4 June 1924.
65. NA, PIN 26/19954, R. F. Williams, Letter to Ministry of Pensions, 3 November, 1933.
66. Bourke, *Dismembering the Male*, p. 45.
67. NA, PIN 26/19894, Memorandum from the Commandant, Queen Mary's Convalescent Auxiliary Hospital, Roehampton, to the Director of Artificial Limb Supplies, 18 August 1919.
68. NA, PIN 26/19875, Surgeon-in-Charge, Limb Fitting Centre, Norwich, Letter to Director General of Medical Services, Ministry of Pensions, 20 July 1925.
69. Bourke, *Dismembering the Male*, pp. 43–56.
70. NA, PIN 26/21506, Proceedings of Resurvey Board, 26 October 1921.
71. NA, PIN 26/21142, Pensions Appeal Tribunal (Assessment), Neurological Report, 31 January 1929.
72. NA, PIN 26/21089, O. P. Allcock, Letter to the Ministry of Pensions, 21 April 1921.
73. NA, PIN 26/19972, Report of Special Enquiry Officer, 1 May 1937.
74. NA, PIN 26/21506, Proceedings of Resurvey Board, 17 October 1922.
75. NA, PIN 26/19949, R. K. Pillers, Letter to Director General of Awards, Ministry of Pensions, 20 October 1920.

76. NA, PIN 26/21570, Medical Report, 3 June 1935.
77. NA, PIN 26/21505, Minute from Director General of Medical Services to District Commissioner of Medical Services, Metropolitan Area, 8 March 1928.
78. NA, PIN 26/21593, Review of Entitlement, Pensions Appeal Tribunal, 4 May 1923. This judgement was later overturned.
79. NA, PIN 26/21215, Dr. Paget, Clinic Case Paper, 29 March 1922.
80. NA, PIN 26/21282, Medical Board, 25 July 1919.
81. NA, PIN 26/21173, Doctor's attestation, 17 September 1923.
82. NA, PIN 26/21565, Proceedings of Medical Board, 18 September 1919.
83. NA, PIN 26/21230, E. C. Booker, Letter to Director General of Awards, Ministry of Pensions, n.d.
84. NA, PIN 26/21672, Doctor's report, 1 July 1919.
85. NA, PIN 26/21097, C. F. Ambler, Letter to the Secretary, Officers' Branch, Ministry of Pensions, 29 April 1932.
86. NA, PIN 26/19972, Report of Special Enquiry Officer, 16 April 1930.
87. NA, PIN 26/21314, Medical Report Form, 27 June 1929.
88. NA, PIN 26/21282, Application for Appeal Tribunal, 16 April 1924.
89. NA, PIN 26/21555, P. G. Eckersall, Letter to the Secretary, Ministry of Pensions, 27 May 1919.
90. NA, PIN 26/21727, J. S. Hardy, Letter to the Ministry of Pensions, 14 June 1921.
91. Ibid.
92. NA, PIN 26/21580, C. E. Evans, Letter to Ministry of Pensions, 5 February 1919.
93. NA, PIN 26/21116, P. Ashe, Letter to the Secretary, Ministry of Pensions, 18 January 1919.
94. This eagerness can be seen in articles written for journals aimed at the war-disabled such as *Recalled to Life* and *Reveille*. *Recalled to Life* had as its subtitle 'A Journal devoted to the Care, Re-education, and Return to Civil Life of Disabled Sailors and Soldiers.' It includes articles such as 'The Treatment of the Disabled: A Memorandum' by Sir Alfred Keogh, 1, (June 1917), pp. 5–49 and 'A Talk with the Disabled', 1, (June 1917), 60–68, in which the benefits of training were emphasized. For a full analysis of the various training programmes run by the Ministry, see Andrew Latcham (1997) 'Journey's End: Ex-Servicemen and the State During and After the Great War', PhD. diss. (University of Oxford), pp. 72–79.
95. NA, PIN 26/21655, Minute from Officers' Friend Branch, 2 June 1920.
96. Gagen, 'Disabling Masculinities', pp. 234–241; Latcham, 'Journey's End', pp. 78–79, 442.
97. Green, *Dreams of Adventure*, 206.
98. NA, PIN 26/21727, Pension Appeals Tribunal, Reasons for Appeal, 14 April 1924.
99. NA, PIN 26/21791, J. J. Holland, Letter to the Secretary, Officers' Branch, Ministry of Pensions, 7 March 1919.
100. NA, PIN 26/21593, R. J. R. Farrow, Letter to Commissioner of Medical Services, Ministry of Pensions, 22 November 1924.
101. NA, PIN 26/19943, G. M. Lawless, Letter to Ministry of Pensions, 3 March 1919.

102. NA, PIN 26/21766, W. B. Hetherington, Letter to Ministry of Pensions, 24 March 1924.

103. NA, PIN 26/21314, J. Burdekin, Letter to Ministry of Pensions, n.d.

104. NA, PIN 26/21728, Report of Medical Examination, 17 March 1932.

105. NA, PIN 26/21285, H. O. Bristow, Letter to Ministry of Pensions, 25 November, 1920.

106. 106 NA, PIN 26/21460, M. J. L. Daly, Letter to Director General of Awards, Officers' Branch, 6 April 1920.

107. NA, PIN 26/21593, R. J. R. Farrow, Letter to the Secretary, Ministry of Pensions, 22 July 1921.

108. For analysis of British disabled ex-servicemen's relationships with charities, see Cohen, *The War Come Home*, Chapter 2 and Gagen, 'Disabling Masculinities', Chapters 6 and 7.

109. NA, PIN 26/21230, E. C. Booker, Letter to the Secretary, Ministry of Pensions, 30 May 1927. Booker was resident in Canada at this time, receiving his pension in Canadian dollars.

110. NA, PIN 26/21460, M. L. J. Daly, Letter to Director General of Medical Services, Ministry of Pensions, 28 December 1919.

111. NA, PIN 26/21580, C. E. Evans, Letter to Ministry of Pensions, 9 April 1920.

112. NA, PIN 26/19930, J. L. Campbell-Wright, Letter to Ministry of Pensions, 28 July 1920.

113. Ibid., 7 April 1920. Wives and children were not the only dependants that men cited in their correspondence to the Ministry. C. J. Stanfield had a mother and sister to support, while G. M. Graham was 'the one consolation' of a mother recovering from a stroke. NA, PIN 26/21684, Humbert Wolf, Letter to Admiral Bett, 28 September 1921.

114. NA, PIN 26/19930, J. L. Campbell-Wright, Letter to Ministry of Pensions, 28 July 1920.

115. NA, PIN 26/21580, C. E. Evans, Letter to Ministry of Pensions, 3 March 1919.

116. NA, PIN 26/21271, F. V. Branford, Letter to Ministry of Pensions, 26 October 1923.

117. NA, PIN 26/21636, C. W. N. Fuller, Letter to Officers' Branch, Ministry of Pensions, 19 August 1924.

118. NA, PIN 26/21593, R. J. R. Farrow, Letter to Director General of Awards, Ministry of Pensions, 18 January 1923.

119. NA, PIN 26/21777, J. R. Hill, Letter to the Secretary of State, War Office, 28 June 1917.

120. NA, PIN 26/21098, F. H. Ball, Letter to the Secretary, Officers' Branch, Ministry of Pensions, 26 May 1926.

121. NA, PIN 26/21230, E. C. Booker, Letter to the Secretary, Officers' Branch, Ministry of Pensions, 25 August 1930.

122. Ibid., Letter to Director General of Awards, Ministry of Pensions, 21 November 1920.

123. NA, PIN 26/21636, Medical Case Sheet, Latchmere Hospital, 15 January 1925.

124. NA, PIN 26/19930, J. L. Campbell-White, Letter to Ministry of Pensions, 15 February 1921.

125. A. J. Brock (1918) 'The War Neurasthenic: A Note on Methods of Reinte-grating him with his Environment', *The Lancet*, p. 436. The Weir-Mitchell treatment was pioneered by the American physician, Silas Weir Mitchell. It involved complete rest and isolation for the patient whose every action was prescribed and monitored by the doctor.
126. NA, PIN 15/54, Sir John Collie, Report on the Special Medical Board, p. 6.
127. For discussion of the medical theories concerning the treatment of shell shock, see Meyer, '"Gladder to be Going Out Than Afraid"' in Macleod and Purseigle (eds), *Uncovered Fields*, pp. 198–202.
128. NA, PIN 26/19938, C. E. G. Harrison, Letter to Ministry of Pensions, 28 October 1930; NA, PIN 26/19926, C. S. Baines, Letter to the Secretary, Ministry of Pensions, 22 March 1931; NA, PIN 26/19930, J. L. Campbell-White, Letter to Ministry of Pensions, 20 February 1921.
129. NA, PIN 26/21666, A. C. Gilmer, Letter to the Secretary, Ministry, 6 March 1919.
130. NA, PIN 26/21230, E. C. Booker, Letter to the Secretary, Officers' Branch, Ministry of Pensions, 25 August 1930.
131. NA, PIN 26/21596, Report of Dr. W. A. MacWilliam, 18 January 1930.
132. NA, PIN 26/19950, C. J. Stanfield, Letter to Director General of Medical Services, 13 December 1934.
133. NA, PIN 26/21506, Proceedings of Resurvey Board, 17 October 1922.
134. NA, PIN 26/19972, Report of Special Enquiry Officer, 16 April 1930.
135. NA, PIN 26/21239, Mrs W. H. Botterill, Application for Treatment Assistance, 5 March 1924.
136. Ibid., W. H. Botterill, Letter to his wife, 9 April 1924.
137. NA, PIN 26/21205, G. H. Birch, Letter to Ministry of Pensions, 11 March 1922.
138. NA, PIN 26/21230, Neurological Report, Shaughnessy Hospital, 17 April 1924.
139. NA, PIN 26/21705, A. C. H. Groom, Letter to Officers' Branch, Ministry of Pensions, 13 September 1922.
140. NA, PIN 26/21555, P. G. Eckersall, Letter to the Secretary, War Office, 1 March 1917.
141. Koven, 'Remembering and Dismemberment', 1170–1171; Bourke, *Dismembering the Male*, pp. 74–75.
142. NA, PIN 26/21239, Ella C. Flint, M. B., Report, 23 April 1924.
143. NA, PIN 26/19947, J. F. Marshall, Letter to Director General of Medical Services, Appliances Branch, Ministry of Pensions, 25 October 1924.
144. NA, PIN 26/19945, Cannon Nisbet C. Marris, Letter to Regional Director, Ministry of Pensions, Nottingham Region, 6 January 1921.
145. NA, PIN 26/19935, Area Deputy Commissioner of Medical Services, Newcastle, Letter to Director General of Medical Services, Ministry of Pensions, 5 August 1936; Area Deputy Commissioner of Medical Services, Newcastle, Minute to Director General of Medical Services, Ministry of Pensions, 10 August 1936.

146. NA, PIN 26/21672, Doctor's Report, 1 July 1919.
147. NA, PIN 26/19934, Area Deputy Commissioner of Medical Services, Newcastle Area, Letter to Director General of Medical Services, Ministry of Pensions, 8 June 1927.
148. NA, PIN 26/21580, Charles Evans, Letter to Ministry of Pensions, 6 January 1925. Evans was married and had one child. His wife and child were apparently living with relatives of his wife at this time.
149. NA, PIN 26/21230, Neurological Report, Shaughnessy Hospital, 17 April 1924; Medical Re-examination Form, 21 May 1924.
150. NA, PIN 26/21156, Report of Medical Examination, 10 May 1935.
151. NA, PIN 26/19943, Report of Director of Medical Services II, n.d.; Report to Director General of Medical Services, 26 May 1936.
152. NA, PIN 26/21580, C. E. Evans, Letter to the Secretary, Ministry of Pensions, 27 April 1925.
153. NA, PIN 26/19930, J. L. Campbell-White, Letter to Ministry of Pensions, 17 September 1920.
154. NA, PIN 26/21675, Notes of the Ministry Representative at Entitlement Appeal Tribunal, 10 July 1924.
155. Ibid., Memorandum, n.d.
156. NA, PIN 26/21718, W. J. Halifax, Letter to Officers' Branch, Ministry of Pensions, 25 August 1922.
157. NA, PIN 26/21728, A. Harman, Letter to the Ministry of Pensions, n.d.
158. Ibid., Transcript Report of Appeal Tribunal, 26 January 1922.
159. Ibid., Memo 92, 10 January 1922.
160. Ibid., Report of Special Enquiry Officer, Awards, September 1933.
161. Ibid., L. Baget, Memorandum 157, 28 November 1929.
162. Ibid., Anonymous letter to the Ministry of Pensions, September 1933.
163. Ibid., A. Harman, Letter to the Ministry of Pensions, 8 November 1933.
164. Ibid., Report of Special Enquiry Officer, 21 October 1933.
165. Bettinson, ' "Lost Souls in the House of Restoration?" ', p. 113. War widows were similarly policed by the authorities, see Lomas ' "Delicate Duties" ', 130–132.
166. NA, PIN 26/21728, Reasons for Appeal, Appeal Tribunal, n.d.; A. Harman, Letter to Ministry of Pensions, n.d.
167. Ibid., A. Harman, Letter to the Ministry of Pensions, n.d.
168. Ibid., Report of Medical Board, 8 October 1929.
169. Ibid., A. Harman, Letter to the Ministry of Pensions, 4 September 1933.
170. Ibid., Area Deputy Commissioner of Medical Services, Acton, Minute to the Secretary, Ministry of Pensions, 8 November 1933.
171. Ibid., Report of Medical Board, 27 March 1934.
172. Ibid., A. Harman, Letter to Ministry of Pensions, n.d.
173. Ibid.
174. NA, PIN 26/21728, Report of Special Enquiry Officer, 26 September, 1933.
175. Ibid., A. Harman, Letter to the Ministry of Pensions, n.d.
176. Ibid.
177. Ibid., A. Harman, Letter to the Ministry of Pensions, 4 September 1933.
178. Ibid., A. Harman, Letter to the Ministry of Pensions, 8 November 1933.
179. Ibid., A. Harman, Letter to Ministry of Pension, n.d.

5 'The very basic test of manhood': War memoirs and the remembering of martial masculinities

1. Robert Graves and Alan Hodge (1944) *The Long Week-End: A Social History of Great Britain 1918–1939* (New York: W.W. Norton and Company, first published 1940), p. 16.
2. Thomas Hope Floyd (1920) *At Ypres with Best-Dunkley*, On Active Service Series (London: John Lane) was based on Floyd's letters written during the war. See also Winter (1979) *Death's Men*, pp. 16–17; Esther MacCallum-Stewart (2005) 'The First World War and Popular Literature', PhD. Diss., (University of Sussex), p. 20. Winter lists 14 memoirs published between 1919 and 1927.
3. Winter, *Death's Men*, p. 15; Todman *The Great War*, p. 29.
4. An example of this type of memoir is C. C. Miller's 'A Letter from India to my Daughters in England', IWM, 83/3/1, Ts. memoir, 1938.
5. The *Mudhook Machine Gunner*, for instance, based on a manuscript entitled 'Such a Quest' by D. J. Polley, was edited for publication in 1998 by A. C. Mott (Bromley, Kent: Galago).
6. Todman, *The Great War*, pp. 192–193.
7. Ibid., p. 193.
8. Roper 'Re-remembering the Soldier Hero, 191.
9. Ibid., 183.
10. Indeed, many published books acknowledge their heavy reliance on contemporaneous letters and diaries.
11. Dominic Harman (2001) ' "The Truth About Men in the Front Line": Imagining the Experience of War in Memoirs of the Western Front', *University of Sussex Journal of Comparative History*, 2, 3.
12. Miller, 'A Letter from India to my Daughters in England', p. 21.
13. W. Griffith (1981) *Up To Mametz*, (London: Severn House Publishers Ltd., first published London: Faber and Faber, 1931), p. 66.
14. IWM, 90/1/1, S. H. Raggett, 'Reminiscences of War (1914–1918)', Ts., 1920, p. 6.
15. IWM, 81/21/1, A. J. Turner, 'Zero Hour: Hazy Recollections of Laughter and Tears in One Man's Mini-war', Ts., 1978, pp. 32–33.
16. IWM 87/18/1, W. Clarke, 'Random Recollections of '14/'18,' Ts., n.d., p. 5.
17. IWM, Con Shelf, E. B. Lord, untitled memoir, Ts., n.d., p. 43.
18. Griffith, *Up to Mametz*, pp. 59–60.
19. Lord, p. 21.
20. IWM, 78/58/1, G. V. Dennis, 'A Kitchener Man's Bit (1916–1918)', Ts., 1928, p. 80.
21. Dennis, 'A Kitchener Man's Bit', p. 96.
22. Turner, 'Zero Hour', p. 38.
23. Polley, *The Mudhook Machine Gunner*, p. 64.
24. Raggett, 'Reminiscences of War,' p. 18.
25. IWM, 85/28/1, S. T. Kemp, 'Remembrance,' Ts., n.d., p. 32.
26. Turner, 'Zero Hour,' p. 33.
27. Polley, *The Mudhook Machine Gunner*, p. 19.
28. Raggett, 'Reminiscences of War,' pp. 30–31.

29. Lord, pp. 20–21.
30. Griffith, *Up To Mametz*, p. 46.
31. Turner, 'Zero Hour,' p. 38.
32. Kemp, 'Remembrance,' p. 56–57.
33. Raggett, 'Reminiscences of War,' p. 30.
34. Miller, 'A Letter from India', p. 20.
35. IWM, 77/167/1, J. F. B. O'Sullivan, 'A Rest in Philosophe,' June 1916.
36. Thomas Penrose Marks (1977) *The Laughter Goes from Life: In the Trenches of the First World War* (London: William Kimber), p. 112.
37. Raggett, 'Reminiscences of War,' p. 30.
38. IWM, 87/8/1, R. M. Luther, 'The Poppies are Blood Red,' Ms., n.d., p. 19.
39. IWM, 84/16/1 and Con Shelf, H. Sturdy, untitled memoir, Ms., 1934, p. 27.
40. IWM, 81/23/1, A. J. Heraty, 'A Duration Man,' Ts., n.d., p. 20.
41. Sturdy, pp. 33–34.
42. IWM, 88/18/1, H. Clegg, untitled memoir, Ts., n.d., p. 50.
43. Evidence of Lt.-Col. J. S. Y. Rogers (1922) *Report of the War Office Committee of Enquiry into Shell-Shock* (London: HMSO), p. 62.
44. Sturdy, p. 40.
45. IWM, 92/36/1, R. G. Dixon, 'The Wheels of Darkness', Ts., circa 1970s, p. 72.
46. Griffith, *Up to Mametz*, p. 234.
47. IWM, 82/25/1, C. W. Hughes, 'The Forgotten Army', Ts., 1925, p. 35.
48. Hughes, 'The Forgotten Army', p. 38.
49. IWM, 87/55/1, P. R. Hall, 'Recollections 1915–1919', Ts., n.d., p. 1.
50. Lord, p. 18.
51. Raggett, 'Reminiscences of War', p. 1.
52. Miller, 'A Letter from India', pp. 18–19.
53. Bourke, *An Intimate History of Killing*, p. 61 and *passim*.
54. Dixon, 'The Wheels of Darkness', p. 133.
55. Raggett, 'Reminiscences of War', Ts. memoir, p. 1.
56. IWM, 86/53/1, W. Kerr, untitled memoir, Ts. n.d., p. 66.
57. Sassoon, *The Complete Memoirs of George Sherston*, pp. 343–345.
58. Dixon, 'The Wheels of Darkness,' p. 20.
59. See Chapter 3 above.
60. Polley, *The Mudhook Machine Gunner*, p. 20.
61. IWM, 82/22/1, F. de Margry, 'From Saddle-bag to Infantry Pack', Ts., n.d., pp. 12–13.
62. Green, *Dreams of Adventure, Deeds of Empire*, pp. 204–207.
63. Dixon, 'The Wheels of Darkness,' p. 35.
64. Ibid., pp. 28–29.
65. Miller, 'A Letter from India', p. 22.
66. Hall, 'Recollections', pp. 16–17.
67. Lord, p. 25.
68. Miller, 'A Letter from India', p. 19.
69. Griffith, *Up to Mametz*, pp. 81–82.
70. Clarke, 'Random Recollections', p. 6.
71. Polley, *The Mudhook Machine Gunner*, p. 61.
72. Bourke, *An Intimate History of Killing*, p. 238.
73. Leed, *No Man's Land*, p. 150.
74. Turner, 'Zero Hour', p. 54.

75. G. Fisher quoted in Lyn Macdonald (1993) *1915: The Death of Innocence* (London: Headline), p. 476.
76. Charles Moran (1945) *The Anatomy of Courage* (London: Constable), p. x.
77. Collini *Public Moralists*, p. 105.
78. Raggett, 'Reminiscences of War', p. 38.
79. Lord, p. 3.
80. Dixon, 'The Wheels of Darkness', p. 132.
81. Miller, 'A Letter from India', pp. 21–22.
82. Hughes, 'The Forgotten Army', p. 93.
83. Turner, 'Zero Hour', p. 31.
84. Dixon, 'The Wheels of Darkness', p. 134.
85. George Harbottle ([1981]) *Civilian Soldier 1914–1919: A period relived* (Newcastle: Carlis Print Limited), p. 51.
86. Miller, 'A Letter from India', p. 21.
87. Moran, *The Anatomy of Courage,* pp. 32–33.
88. G. Fisher in Macdonald, *1915: The Death of Innocence*, p. 476.
89. Kemp, 'Remembrance', p. 16.
90. Raggett, 'Reminiscences of War', p. 8.
91. J. F. B. O'Sullivan, untitled, 10–13 September, 1916.
92. Mark VII [Max Plowman] (1927) *A Subaltern on the Somme in 1916* (London: J. M. Dent & Sons Ltd.), p. 240.
93. Evidence of W. J. Adie, *Report of the War Office Committee of Enquiry into 'Shell-Shock'*, p. 17.
94. IWM, 83/43/1, Papers of R. L. Watson, 'U. P. S. Luncheon', *Epsom Herald*, 28 March, 1930.
95. IWM, PP/MRC/261, F. A. Shuffrey, untitled memoir, Ms., n.d., unpaginated.
96. IWM, 86/57/1, R. Foot, ' "Once a Gunner –": Reminiscences of 1914–1918 World War', Ts., 1964, p. 125.
97. Papers of R. L. Watson, 'The Speech I Will Not Make to My Old Battalion'.
98. Kemp, 'Remembrance', p. 27.
99. Papers of R. L. Watson, 'U. P. S. Luncheon'.
100. Ibid.
101. Mark VII, *A Subaltern on the Somme*, p. 101.
102. Ibid., pp. 100–101.
103. IWM, 97/10/1, J. McCauley, 'A Manx Soldier's War Diary', Ts., c.1920s, p. 45.
104. Raggett, 'Reminiscences of War', p. 7.
105. Dixon, 'The Wheels of Darkness', p. 88.
106. Bourke, *Dismembering the Male*, p. 170.
107. Higbee (2007) 'The British Veterans Movement' in Meyer (ed.) *British Popular Culture and the First World War*, pp. 211–215.
108. Mosse, *The Image of Man*, p. 19.
109. Polley, *The Mudhook Machine Gunner*, p. 2.
110. Ibid., pp. 41–42.
111. M. L. Walkington (1980) *Twice in a Lifetime* (London: Samson Books), p. 18.
112. Adams, *The Great Adventure*, p. 48; Green, *Dreams of Adventure*, p. 272.
113. Kemp, 'Remembrance', p. 36.
114. Winter, *The Great War and the British People*, p. 2.
115. Raggett, 'Reminiscences of War', p. 1.
116. Turner, 'Zero Hour', pp. 5–6.

117. Dennis, 'A Kitchener Man's Bit', p. 10.
118. Luther, 'The Poppies are Blood Red', p. 31.
119. Griffith, *Up to Mametz*, pp. 31–32.
120. H. J. Hadlow ([1985]) *The Experiences of a Volunteer in the First World War* (Eynsford: H. J. Hadlow), p. 132.
121. Hadlow, *The Experiences of a Volunteer*, pp. 126–127.
122. Polley, *The Mudhook Machine Gunner*, p. 42.
123. Griffith, *Up to Mametz*, p. 103.
124. Dixon, 'The Wheels of Darkness', p. 5.
125. Ibid., p. 5.
126. Dennis, 'A Kitchener Man's Bit', p. 6.
127. Ibid., p. 300.
128. Ibid., p. 294.
129. Ibid., p. 303
130. Ibid., p. 127.
131. Ibid., p. 189.
132. Ibid., p. 60.
133. Ibid., p. 96.
134. Ibid., p. 86.
135. Ibid., p. 83
136. Ibid., p. 65.
137. Ibid., p. 63.
138. Ibid., p. 163.
139. Ibid., p. 74. See also Chapter 1 above.
140. Ibid., p. 156.
141. Ibid., pp. 10–11.
142. Ibid., p. 61.
143. Ibid., preface.
144. Ibid., p. 304.
145. Ibid., p. 305.
146. Ibid., p. 300.
147. Ibid., p. 303.
148. Marks, *The Laughter Goes From Life,* p. 9.
149. Ibid., p. 70.
150. Ibid., p. 48. See also Bourke, *An Intimate History of Killing*, pp. 155–168.
151. Marks, *The Laughter Goes from Life*, pp. 116–117.
152. Ibid., p. 92.
153. Ibid., p. 45.
154. Ibid., p. 104.
155. Ibid., p. 40.
156. Ibid., p. 1.
157. Ibid., pp. 56–57.
158. Ibid., p. 58.
159. Ibid., p. 74.
160. Ibid., p. 171–172.
161. Ibid., p. 188.
162. Ibid., p. 97.
163. Ibid., p. 97.
164. Todman, *The Great War and Modern Memory,* p. 224.
165. Ibid., p. 193.

Conclusion

1. Dixon, 'The Wheels of Darkness', p. 5.
2. Leed *No Man's Land*, p. 20.
3. See Chapter 1, footnote 172, above.
4. Bourke *Dismembering the Male*, p. 162.
5. Jessica Meyer (2004) ' "Not Septimus Now": Wives of Disabled Veterans and Cultural Memory of the First World War in Britain', *Women's History Review* 13:1, pp. 117–138.
6. Lomas, ' "Delicate Duties"', 123–147; Cannadine, 'War, Death, Grief and Mourning', 193.
7. Winter *The Great War and the British People*, pp. 263–266.
8. Gregory *The Silence of Memory*, pp. 61–86; Todman, *The Great War*, pp. 51–56.
9. Roper 'Re-remembering the Soldier Hero', 186.
10. Well-known examples of this form of First World War history include the work of Martin Middlebrook, Lyn Macdonald and, most recently, Max Arthur.
11. See, for example, the obituary of William Young, http://www.timesonline. co.uk/tol/comment/obituaries/article2141036.ece, first published 26 July, 2007 and the obituary of William Roberts, http://www.timesonline.co.uk/ tol/comment/obituaries/article712802.ece, first published 4 May, 2006.
12. Todman, *The Great War*, pp. 169–177.
13. Bourke, *Dismembering the Male*, pp. 162–170.
14. Winter *Sites of Memory, Sites of Mourning*, pp. 223–224.
15. Smith *The Second Battlefield*, p. 40.
16. Margaret and Patrice Higonnet, 'The Double Helix' in Higonnet et al. (eds) *Behind the Lines*, pp. 31–47.

Bibliography

Primary sources

Archival collections

The National Archives, Kew:

PIN 15/38
PIN 26/6
PIN 26/35
PIN 26/19875
PIN 26/19884
PIN 26/19894
PIN 26/19926
PIN 26/19930
PIN 26/19934
PIN 26/19935
PIN 26/19938
PIN 26/19942
PIN 26/19943
PIN 26/19945
PIN 26/19947
PIN 26/19949
PIN 26/19950
PIN 26/19954
PIN 26/19972
PIN 26/21089
PIN 26/21097
PIN 26/21098
PIN 26/21116
PIN 26/21142
PIN 26/21156
PIN 26/21162
PIN 26/21173
PIN 26/21188
PIN 26/21205
PIN 26/21215
PIN 26/21230
PIN 26/21239
PIN 26/21271
PIN 26/21282
PIN 26/21285
PIN 26/21314
PIN 26/21460
PIN 26/21505

PIN 26/21506
PIN 26/21555
PIN 26/21565
PIN 26/21570
PIN 26/21580
PIN 26/21593
PIN 26/21596
PIN 26/21636
PIN 26/21651
PIN 26/21655
PIN 26/21666
PIN 26/21672
PIN 26/21675
PIN 26/21684
PIN 26/21697
PIN 26/21705
PIN 26/21718
PIN 26/21728
PIN 26/21764
PIN 26/21766
PIN 26/21777
PIN 26/21791

Imperial War Museum, London:

A. Anderson, 85/23/1
W. M. Anderson, 96/24/1
W. H. J. St. L. Atkinson, 02/16/1
E. E. F. Baker, 95/21/1 & Con Shelf
G. R. Barlow, 86/40/1
J. W. Barnett, 90/37/1
A. Beevers, 67/264/1
B. Britland, 88/57/1
G. W. Broadhead, 85/32/1
A. E. Bundy, P.371
G. and E. Butling, Con Shelf
G. B. Buxton, PP/MCR/62
E. F. Chapman, 92/3/1
W. Clarke, 87/18/1
H. Clegg, 88/18/1
H. T. Clements, 86/76/1
G. W. Colebrook, 77/177/1
J. Colinsky, 88/11/1
F. S. Collings, 77/124/1
W. J. Cotter, Con Shelf & 84/58/1
C. W. Dawson, Con Shelf
F. de Margry, 82/22/1
G. V. Dennis, 78/58/1
R. G. Dixon, 92/36/1

G. Donaldson, 69/25/1
R. Farley, 81/1/1
T. M. Field, 87/3/1
R. Foot, 86/57/1
J. H. Fordham, 05/53/1
C. E. Foster, 85/15/1
F. P. J. Glover, 78/10/1
P. R. Hall, 87/55/1
R. P. Harker, Con Shelf
H. J. Hayward, 77/155/1
H. Henfrey, 01/51/1
F. Henley, P.434
A. J. Heraty, 81/23/1
J. E. Hind, 84/34/1
M. Holroyd, 97/37/1
C. W. Hughes, 82/25/1
S. T. Kemp, 85/28/1
W. Kerr, 86/53/1
K. C. Leslie, 88/15/1
W. Lindsay, 01/60/1
M. W. Littlewood, 98/33/1
E. B. Lord, 79/12/1
R. M. Luther, 87/8/1
O. Lyle, 85/32/1
J. McCauley, 97/10/1
J. H. MacGregor, 05/40/1
R. Macgregor, 05/39/1
A. M. McGrigor, P399
C. K. McKerrow, 93/20/1
J. W. McPherson, 80/25/1
J. H. Mahon, 78/22/1
D. Manning, 80/1/1
J. Matthews, 78/15/1
C. C. May, 91/23/1
C. C. Miller, 83/3/1
C. T. Newman, 03/5/01
E. Nicholson, 02/5/1
W. Nicholson, 99/27/1
J. F. B. O'Sullivan, 77/167/1
E. H. Owen, 97/37/1
F. E. Packe, P.320
A. T. Pile, 83/17/1
G. A. Potts, Con Shelf & 94/23/1
S. H. Raggett, 90/1/1
C. S. Rawlins, 76/121/1 & Con Shelf
B. A. Reader, 83/3/1
W. J. C. Sangster, 01/52/1
F. A. Shuffrey, PP/MCR/261
E. K. Smith, Con Shelf & 93/25/1

R. S. Smylie, 86/9/1
W. B. P. Spencer, 87/56/1
G. & W. Stewart, Con Shelf
H. Sturdy, PP/MCR/C44 & 84/16/1 & Con Shelf
J. C. Tait, P315
C. M. Tames, 85/1/1
J. G. Taylor, 80/19/1
O. P. Taylor, 92/3/1
A. J. Turner, 81/21/1
J. H. & R. Watkins 67/260/1
R. L. Watson, 83/43/1
R. B. Wilkinson, 67/221/1
A. R. Williams, 82/26/1
H. Wilson, 85/22/1
R. W. Wilson, 77/74/1
N. L. Woodroffe, 95/31/1
S. G. Wright, 97/37/1
K. H. Young, 80/28/1

Privately held:

Papers of R.C. Trench

Printed sources

Periodicals:

The Lancet
Recalled to Life
Reveille
The Times (London)

Books and articles:

Aldington, Richard. *Death of a Hero*. London: Chatto and Windus, 1929.
Carrington, Charles. *Soldier from the Wars Returning*. London: Hutchinson, 1965.
Edmonds, Charles [Charles Carrington.] *A Subaltern's War*. 3rd ed. London: Peter Davies Ltd., 1929.
Fenton, Norman. *Shell Shock and Its Aftermath*. London: Henry Kimpton, 1926.
Floyd, Thomas Hope. *At Ypres with Best-Dunkley*. London: J. Lane, 1920.
Graves, Robert. *Goodbye to All That*. London: Jonathan Cape, 1929.
Graves, Robert and Alan Hodge. *The Long Week-End: A Social History of Great Britain 1918–1939*. New York: W. W. Norton and Company, 1994. First published 1940.
Griffiths, Wyn. *Up to Mametz*. London: Faber and Faber, 1931.
Hadlow, H. J. *The Experiences of a Volunteer in the First World War*. Privately printed, [1985].
Harbottle, George. *Civilian Soldier: A Period Relived*. Newcastle: Carlis Print Limited, [1981].
Housman, A. E. *A Shropshire Lad*. London: Grant Richards Ltd., 1916.
Manning, Frederick. *Her Privates We*. London: Hogarth, 1929.

Mark VII [Max Plowman]. *A Subaltern on the Somme in 1916.* London: J. M. Dent and Son, 1927.

Marks, Thomas Penrose. *The Laughter Goes from Life: In the Trenches of the Frist World War.* London: William Kimber, 1977.

Mitchell, T. J. and G. M. Smith. *Medical Services: Casualties and Medical Statistics of the Great War: History of the Great War Based on Official Documents.* Nashville, Tennessee: The Imperial War Museum, London, Department of Printed Books and The Battery Press, Inc., 1931.

Moran, Charles. *The Anatomy of Courage.* London: Constable, 1945.

Orwell, George. *Collected Essays, Journalism and Letters, Vol. I.* London: Penguin Books, 1970.

Polley, D. J. *The Mudhook Machine Gunner.* A. C. Mott (ed.). Bromley, Kent: Galago, 1998.

'Sapper' [Herman Cyril McNeile]. *Sergeant Michael Cassidy.* London: Hodder and Stoughton, 1915.

Sassoon, Siegfried. *The Complete Memoirs of George Sherston.* London: Faber and Faber, 1937.

———. *The Old Huntsman and Other Poems.* New York: E. P. Dutton and Company, 1918.

Walkington, M. L. *Twice in a Lifetime.* London: Samson Books, 1980.

War Office. *Field Service Pocket Book: 1914.* Newton Abbot: David & Charles Publishers, 1971. First published London: His Majesty's Stationary Office, 1914.

———. *Statistics of the British Military Effort of the British Empire During the Great War 1914–1920.* London: His Majesty's Stationary Office, 1922.

War Office Committee of Enquiry into 'Shell-Shock'. *Report of the War Office of Committee of Enquiry in to 'Shell-Shock'.* London: His Majesty's Stationary Office, 1922.

Secondary literature

Books:

Acton, Carol. *Grief in Wartime: Private Pain, Public Discourse.* Basingstoke: Palgrave Macmillan, 2007.

Adams, Michael. *The Great Adventure: Male Desire and the Coming of World War I.* Bloomington: Indiana University Press, 1990.

Audoin-Rouzeau, Stéphane. *Men at War 1914–1918: National Sentiment and Trench Journalism in France During the First World War.* Helen McPhail (trans.). Oxford: Berg, 1992.

Barham, Peter. *Forgotten Lunatics of the Great War.* New Haven: Yale University Press, 2004.

Bolderson, Helen. *Social Security, Disability and Rehabilitation: Conflicts in the Development of Social Policy 1914–1946.* London: Jessica Kingsley Publishers, 1991.

Bourke, Joanna. *An Intimate History of Killing: Face-to-Face Killing in Twentieth-Century Warfare.* London: Granta Books, 1999.

———. *Dismembering the Male: Men's Bodies, Britain and the Great War.* London: Reaktion Books, 1996.

Boyden, Peter B. *Tommy Atkins' Letters: The History of the British Army Postal Service from 1795.* London: National Army Museum, 1990.

Bracco, Rosa Maria. *Merchants of Hope: Middlebrow Writers and the First World War, 1919–1939*. Oxford: Berg, 1993.

Braudy, Leo. *From Chivalry to Terrorism: War and the Changing Nature of Masculinity*. New York: Alfred A. Knopf, 2003.

Braybon, Gail (ed.). *Evidence, History and the Great War: Historians and the Impact of 1914–1918*. Oxford: Berghan Books, 2004.

Cecil, Hugh and Peter H. Liddle (eds). *Facing Armageddon: The First World War Experienced*. London: Leo Cooper, 1996.

Clarke, Peter. *Hope and Glory: Britain 1900–1990*. London: Penguin Books, 1996.

Cohen, Deborah. *The War Come Home: Disabled Veterans in Britain and Germany, 1914–1939*. Berkeley: University of California Press, 2001.

Collini, Stefan. *Public Moralists: Political Thought and Intellectual Life in Britain, 1850–1930*. Oxford: Clarendon Press, 1991.

Connelly, Mark. *The Great War, Memory and Ritual: Commemoration in the City and East London, 1916–1939*. The Royal Historical Society. Woodbridge: The Boydell Press, 2002.

Das, Santanu. *Touch and Intimacy in First World War Literature*. Cambridge: Cambridge University Press, 2005.

Davidoff, Leonore. *The Best Circles: Society, Etiquette and the Season*. London: The Cresset Library, 1973.

Dawson, Graham. *Soldier Heroes: British Adventure, Empire and the Imagining of Masculinity*. London: Routledge, 1994.

Dudink, Stefan et al. *Masculinities in Politics and War: Gendering Modern History*. Manchester: Manchester University Press, 2004.

French, David. *Military Identities: The Regimental System, the British Army, and the British People, c.1870–2000*. Oxford: Oxford University Press, 2005.

Fuller, J. G. *Troop Morale and Popular Culture in British and Dominion Armies 1914–1918*. Oxford: Clarendon Press, 1990.

Fussell, Paul. *The Great War and Modern Memory*. Oxford: Oxford University Press, 1975.

Grayzel, Susan R. *Women's Idenities at War: Gender, Motherhood, and Politics in Britain and France During the First World War*. London: Routledge, 1981.

Green, Martin. *Dreams of Adventure, Deeds of Empire*. London: Routledge and Kegan Paul, 1980.

Gregory, Adrian. *The Silence of Memory: Armistice Day, 1919–1946*. Oxford: Berg, 1994.

Gullace, Nicoletta F. *'The Blood of Our Sons': Men, Women and the Renegotiation of British Citizenship During the Great War*. New York: Palgrave Macmillan, 2002.

Higonnet, Margaret Randolph et al. (eds). *Behind the Lines: Gender and the Two World Wars*. New Haven: Yale University Press, 1987.

Hill, Tracey (ed.). *Decadence and Danger: Writing, History and the Fin de Siècle*. Bath: Sulis Press, 1997.

Horne, John (ed.). *State, Society and Mobilization in Europe During the First World War*. Cambridge: Cambridge University Press, 1997.

Hynes, Samuel. *A War Imagined: The First World War and English Culture*. New York: Atheneum, 1991.

———. *The Auden Generation*. London: The Bodley Head, 1976.

———. *The Soldiers' Tale: Bearing Witness to Modern War*. New York: Penguin Books, 1997.

Jones, Max. *The Last Great Quest: Captain Scott's Antarctic Sacrifice.* Oxford: Oxford University Press, 2003.

King, Alex. *Memorials of the Great War in Britain: The Symbolism and Politics of Remembrance.* Oxford: Berg, 1998.

Kingsley Kent, Susan. *Making Peace: The Reconstruction of Gender in Interwar Britain.* Princeton: Princeton University Press, 1993.

Leed, Eric J. *No Man's Land: Combat and Identity in World War I.* Cambridge: Cambridge University Press, 1979.

Light, Alison. *Forever England: Femininity, Literature and Conservatism Between the Wars.* London: Routledge, 1991.

McCartney, Helen B. *Citizen Soldiers: The Liverpool Territorials in the First World War.* Cambridge: Cambridge University Press, 2005.

MacDonald, Lyn. *1915: The Death of Innocence.* London: Headline, 1993.

Macleod, Jenny and Pierre Purseigle (eds). *Uncovered Fields: Perspectives in First World War Studies.* Leiden: Brill, 2004.

MacKenzie, John (ed.). *Popular Imperialism and the Military, c.1850–1950.* Manchester: Manchester University Press, 1992.

Meyer, Jessica (ed.). *British Popular Culture and the First World War.* Leiden: Brill, 2008.

Middlebrook, Martin. *The First Day of the Somme.* London: Allen Lane, 1971.

———. *The Kaiser's Battle.* London: Allen Lane, 1978.

Mort, Frank. *Dangerous Sexualities: Medico-Moral Politics in England Since 1830.* London: Routledge & Kegan Paul, 1987.

Mosse, George. *The Image of Man: The Creation of Modern Masculinity.* Oxford: Oxford University Press.

Nora, Pierre. *Les lieux de memoire.* 7 vols. Paris: Gallimard, 1984–1992.

Ouditt, Sharon. *Fighting Forces, Writing Women: Identity and Ideology in the First World War.* London: Routledge, 2004.

Paris, Michael. *Warrior Nation: Images of War in British Popular Culture, c.1850–2000.* London: Reaktion Books, 2000.

Pedersen, Susan. *Family, Dependence and the Origins of the Welfare State: Britain and France 1914–1945.* Cambridge: Cambridge University Press, 1993.

Pick, Daniel. *Faces of Degeneration: A European Disorder, c.1848–1918.* Cambridge: Cambridge University Press, 1989.

Potter, Jane. *Boys in Khaki, Girls in Print: Women's Literary Responses to the Great War 1914–1918.* Oxford English Monographs. Oxford: Oxford University Press, 2005.

Purseigle, Pierre (ed.). *Warfare and Belligerence: Perspectives in First World War Studies.* Leiden: Brill, 2005.

Roper, Michael and John Tosh. *Manful Assertions: Masculinities in Britain Since 1800.* London: Routledge, 1991.

Rose, Sonya O. *Limited Livelihoods: Gender and Class in Nineteenth-Century England.* London: Routledge, 1992.

Seaman, L. C. B. *Life in Britain Between the Wars.* English Life Series. London: B. T. Batsford Ltd., 1970.

Sheffield, Gary. *Leadership in the Trenches: Officer-Man Relations, Morale and Discipline in the British Army in the Era of the First World War.* Basingstoke: Macmillan Press, 2000.

Shephard, Ben. *A War of Nerves: Soldiers and Psychiatry 1914–1994.* London: Pimlico, 2002.

Showalter, Elaine. *The Female Malady: Women, Madness and English Culture, c.1830–1980*. London: Virago, 1987.

Silken, Jon (ed.). *The Penguin Book of First World War Poetry*. 2nd ed. London: Penguin Books, 1979.

Smith, Angela K. *The Second Battlefield: Women, Modernism and the First World War*. Manchester: Manchester University Press, 2000.

Thom, Deborah. *Nice Girls and Rude Girls: Women Workers in World War I*. London: I. B. Tauris Publishers, 1988.

Todman, Dan. *The Great War: Myth and Memory*. London: Hambledon and London, 2005.

Tosh, John. *A Man's Place: Masculinity and the Middle-Class Home in Victorian England*. New Haven: Yale University Press, 1999.

———. *Manliness and Masculinities in Nineteenth Century Britain: Essays on Gender, Family and Empire*. Harlow: Pearson Education Ltd., 2005.

Tylee, Claire M. *The Great War and Women's Consciousness: Images of Militarism and Womanhood in Women's Writing, 1914–1964*. Basingstoke: Macmillan, 1990.

Watson, Janet S. K. *Fighting Different Wars: Experience, Memory and the First World War*. Cambridge: Cambridge University Press, 2004.

Whaley, Joachim (ed.). *Mirrors of Mortality: Studies in the Social History of Death*. The Europe Social History of the Human Experience. London: Europa Publications, 1981.

Winter, Dennis. *Death's Men: Soldiers of the Great War*. London: Penguin Books, 1979.

Winter, Jay M. *Sites of Memory, Sites of Mourning: The Great War in European Cultural History*. Cambridge: Cambridge University Press, 1995.

———. *The Great War and the British People*. London: Macmillan Education Ltd., 1985.

Articles:

Bourke, Joanna. 'The Emotions in War: Fear and the British and American military, 1914–1945', *Historical Research Journal*, 74 (2001), 314–330.

Crook, Tom. ' "Schools for the Moral Training of the People": Public Baths, Liberalism and the Promotion of Cleanliness in Victorian Britain', *European Review of History/Revue européenne d'Histoire*, 13:1 (March 2006), 21–47.

Englander, David. 'Soldiering and Identity: Reflections on the Great War', *War in History*, 1:3 (November 1994), 300–318.

Fletcher, Anthony. 'An Officer on the Western Front', *History Today*, 54:8 (August 2004), 31–37.

———. 'Patriotism, Identity and Commemoration: New Light on the Great War from the Papers of Major Reggie Chenevix Trench', *History*, 60 (2005), 532–549.

Koven, Seth. 'Remembering and Dismemberment: Crippled Children, Wounded Soldiers and the Great War in Great Britain', *American Historical Review*, 99:4 (October 1994), 1167–1202.

Lomas, Janis. ' "Delicate Duties": Issues of Class and Respectability in Government Policy Towards Wives and Widows of British Soldiers in the Era of the Great War', *Women's History Review*, 9:1 (April 2000), 123–147.

Meyer, Jessica. ' "Not Septimus Now": Wives of Disabled Veterans and Cultural Memory of the First World War in Britain', *Women's History Review*,13:1 (March 2004), 117–137.

Paris, Michael. 'Boys' Books and the Great War', *History Today*, 50:11 (November 2000), 44–49.

Roper, Michael. 'Between Manliness and Masculinity: The "War Generation" and the Psychology of Fear in Britain, 1914–1970', *Journal of British Studies*, 44:2 (April 2005), 343–362.

———. 'Re-remembering the Soldier Hero: The Psychic and Social Construction of Memory in Personal Narratives of the Great War', *History Workshop Journal*, 50 (Autumn 2000), 181–204.

Seccombe, Wally. 'Patriarchy Stabilized: The Construction of the Male Breadwinner Norm in Nineteenth-Century Britain', *Social History*, 2:1 (January 1986), 53–76.

Surridge, Keith. 'More than a Great Poster: Lord Kitchener and the Image of the Military Hero', *Historical Research*, 74:185 (August 2001), 298–313.

Tosh, John. 'What Should Historians Do With Masculinity? Reflections on Nineteenth-Century Britain', *History Workshop Journal*, 38 (Autumn 1994), 179–202.

Tylee, Claire M. ' "Maleness run riot" – The Great War and Women's Resistance to Militarism', *Women's Studies International Forum*, 11:3 (1988), 199–210.

Unpublished dissertations:

Bettison, Helen. ' "Lost Souls in the House of Restoration"?: British Ex-servicemen and War Disability Pensions, 1914–1930.' PhD. dissertation. University of East Anglia, 2002.

Gagen, Wendy Jane. 'Disabling Masculinity: Ex-servicemen, Disability and Gender Identity, 1914–1930.' PhD. dissertation. University of Essex, 2004.

Latcham, Andrew. 'Journey's End: Ex-servicemen and the State During and after the Great War.' PhD. dissertation. Oxford University, 1997.

MacCallum-Stewart, Esther. 'The First World War and Popular Literature.' PhD. dissertation. University of Sussex, 2005.

Meyer, Jessica. 'The First World War and Narratives of Heroic and Domestic Masculinity in Britain, 1915–1937.' PhD. dissertation. University of Cambridge, 2005.

Millman, Margaret. 'In the Shadows of War: Continuities and Discontinuities in the Construction of Masculine Identities in British Soldiers, 1914–1924.' PhD. dissertation. University of Greenwich, 2003.

Websites:

Harman, Dominic. ' "The Truth About Men in the Front Line": Imagining the Experience of War in Memoirs of the Western Front', *University of Sussex Journal of Contemporary History*, 2 (April 2001), www.sussex.ac.uk/history/1- 4-1-2.html

Obituary of William Roberts, http://www.timesonline.co.uk/tol/comment/obituaries/article712802.ece, first published 4 May, 2006.

Obituary of William Young, http://www.timesonline.co.uk/tol/comment/obituaries/article2141036.ece, first published 26 July, 2007.

Winter, Jay M. 'Remembrance & Redemption: a social interpretation of war memorials', *Harvard Design Magazine*, 9 (Fall 1999), www.gsd.harvard.edu/research/publications/hdm/back/9winter.html

Index

women, 2–4, 5, 8–9, 29, 118–19, 164,
   165, 167
  and citizenship, 3
  and mourning, 8
  employment of, 3, 4, 119–20
  recruitment of, 1
  writers, 4, 7–8, 167

Woodroffe, N. L., 78, 82, 85
Wright, S. G., 20

Young, K. H., 51, 52, 61
Ypres, 19, 25, 51, 52, 82, 151

Zeppelin raids, 28, 36

25540725R00129

Printed in Great Britain
by Amazon